Where You'll Long to Be Time & Again

In the heart of New Hope, an 18th century inn has experienced a rebirth, a rejuvenation, that is once again making history while moving softly through the ages.

Dine just the way you wish—elegant and posh, casual and relaxed, or watching the world go by on our open terrace. Our chef, concierge, and thoughtful staff takes pleasure in anticipating your every whim so that you'll long to visit time and again.

Meet friends at the fireside and dine with a view.

Dream in the comforts of Emily's Room.

Logan Inn
Circa 1722

Dine Splendidly ❧ Rest Luxuriously

Ten West Ferry Street
New Hope, Pennsylvania 18938
215.862.2300
www.loganinn.com

LACHMAN GALLERY
Fine Paintings & Persian Rugs

39 North Main Street, New Hope, PA 18938
215.862.6620
www.lachmanstudios.com

voted best art gallery 2000 in new hope

Hand-blown
glass by
Bernard Katz

Special Features

Welcome to Bucks & Hunterdon Counties.

Guest Writers

Doris Brandes has been a force in the Delaware Valley art scene for nearly three decades as a teacher, art center director, and from 1981 until 1993 as founder, editor, and publisher of *Art Matters*. An artist in her own right, she was listed in *Who's Who of American Women in 2000*, and is a founding director of Artsbridge and a trustee of the James A. Michener Art Museum.

Pat Tanner is a food and travel writer and radio talk show host based in Princeton, N.J. She is restaurant reviewer for Time Off, the magazine of the *Princeton Packet* newspapers, and writes for newspapers and magazines throughout New Jersey. She is the host of "Dining Today," a live, weekly radio show on food and dining in central New Jersey and Bucks County broadcast each Saturday from 9 a.m. to 10 a.m. on WHWH and WJHR.

Victoria Memminger is a freelance writer living in Bucks County, Pa. She began her career as a copy editor on *Good Housekeeping* magazine; after moving to Bucks County, she was the editor of the *Bucks County Gazette* and a feature writer for the *Hunterdon County Democrat*. She recently retired after 20 years as a public relations writer and editor for AT&T at the company's headquarters in Basking Ridge, N.J. Mrs. Memminger is a graduate of Middlebury College.

Catherine D. Kerr lives in New Hope with her husband, two children, and a dog who adores walking in the country. A former writer and editor for newspapers, she is the author of several books about this area. *Walking Bucks County, Pa.: Country & Town* and *The Back Roads Bike Book: A dozen scenic rides in and around Lambertville, N.J. and New Hope, Pa.*, are published by Freewheeling Press. They are available at bookstores and through the Freewheeling Press web site at www.freewheelingpress.com, where you can find information on cycling and walking in the area.

Table of Contents

Visit The Area Guide Book Web Site
www.areaguidebook.com

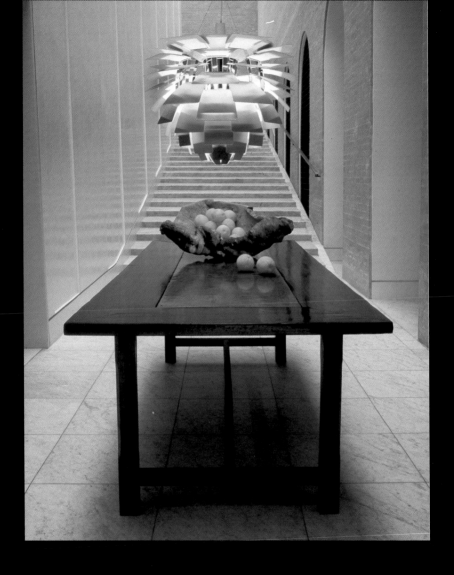

Adrienne Crombie
The artist behind the cover.

I arrived at the appointed hour, planned so Adrienne Crombie would have a break between her art class and our meeting. Her two students were still at work, absorbed in their exercise long after the class was to have ended, which gave me an opportunity to look around. Two tall windows overlooking Frenchtown, New Jersey, give the small studio good light and the street scene offers diversion when it is needed.

My eyes fixed on the painting hanging between the windows. *Portrait of Bob and Putput*, shown on the following page, raises intense curiosity: What are the man and the cat looking at? When I asked later who had influenced her work she answered, Vermeer and Caravaggio. Vermeer, of course! In *Bob and Put-*

Sidesaddle Portrait, Water-based oil on canvas, H. 48 x W. 32 inches.

put, as in so many of Vermeer's paintings, the emotionally charged eyes beg the viewer to see what they see. We can surmise, but can never see beyond the canvas.

Sitting down after the students left we talked about the area and her childhood. Adrienne calls Hunterdon County home and has always loved Frenchtown. She began drawing as a child and says there was never any question about becoming an artist, that it was art that always won her approval. She describes her training as empirical but quickly adds that she is not self-taught. A teacher herself, and judging from the enthusiasm of the students I met, a good one, she admits with some irony to having always had a prejudice about art teachers, the "those who can do. . ." syndrome.

In high school she took classes in Flemington from Leo Russell, who she remembers as teaching figure drawing in an extraordinary way and instilling in her his dictum that mastering the human form is the foundation for good draftsmanship. Later studies at New York's School of Visual Arts and the San Francisco Art Institute brought her to the juncture of art and commerce. She had worked hard, learned to apply old master techniques to her painting, and honed her draftsmanship. She was living in New York and it was time to use her skills to make money. When attempts to break into illustration failed she turned to animal portraits and succeeded. She was

Consummate Oysters, oil on linen, H. 30 x W. 34 inches.

finally making money but continued to broaden her bases learning to execute faux finishes and trompe l'oeil in acrylic.When she began to get commissions for murals Adrienne knew she had found her niche.

Suddenly, just as her career was taking off, Adrienne found herself in Columbia Presbyterian Hospital totally paralyzed by Guilliame Barre Syndrome. Miraculously, she walked out of hospital in two months and returned to Hunterdon to be nursed to full recovery by her parents.

Today Adrienne is a successful self-employed muralist, faux finish designer, trompe l'oeil decorative painter, and portrait artist, and still finds time for her own personal vision, small canvases she calls "erotic still lifes."

Two recent murals are close to her heart. *The Secret Garden*, painted in July

Portrait of Bob and Putput, oil and silver leaf on panel, H. 30 x W. 22 inches.

1998, fulfilled a desire to do something public for Frenchtown, a place she had always loved and which became her home when, in her words, "she had her life back." In 2000, *Milford Mural*, below, gave Adrienne an opportunity to interact with a whole community. Working with the Milford Guild, she raised the funds for the mural from the entire community and from the sale of prints of the artwork. In the end, there was enough to pay for both the mural and its lighting. The success of the Milford print prompted Adrienne to do others. The cover painting, *Sidesaddle Portrait*, will be available this summer.

You can see her work on the web at www.muralsbyadrienne.com., at Riverbank Arts in Stockton, New Jersey, and the murals by visiting Milford and Frenchtown, New Jersey.

Milford Mural, acrylic on cement, H. 10 x W. 20 feet.

9

top **10** reasons customers rate us
Superior

1. Buy Direct from the Cabinet Maker
2. Excellent Customer Service
3. Impeccable Craftsmanship
4. Total Design Flexibility - if you can design it, we can build it
5. Custom Glazed and Hand-Rubbed Finishes
6. Competitive Prices
7. Handmade - Locally in Bucks County, PA
8. Limited Lifetime Warranty
9. Over 1,000 Door Styles to choose from
10. We use the Finest Furniture Grade Wood

Superior Woodcraft, Inc.
Fine Handcrafted Cabinetry

160 N. Hamilton St., Doylestown, PA
215-348-9942
www.superiorwoodcraft.com

The Man Behind the Camera

This year's *Area Guide Book* is dedicated, with all my love and deep gratitude, to the memory of Martin E. Kennedy, the book's photographer, co-publisher, and my partner in life for the last twenty-four years.

Photography was a private passion and his public persona in the book. The photographs on these pages are among his favorites and, as Martin preferred, they speak for themselves without titles or captions. Shadows, reflections, textures, and geometric shapes—recurring themes throughout his work—are the under painting of landscapes that declare his reverence for our environment.

On the following page are four cover photographs from the past. Originally printed in black and white, they are seen here in color as he photographed them.

Nancy M. Wolfe-Kennedy

992

1993

Area Guide Book Covers—A Retrospective

994

1987

The Toughest Clean Out Jobs in the World
Done *Faster* than a Speeding Bullet

With responsible manpower and ready-to-roll equipment,
we clean out homes and commercial buildings fast, and
with more power than a locomotive. We haul away debris
from basements, attics, garages, barns or entire buildings,
and in most instances, at a single bound.

Although some customers like to refer to us as heroes, we much
prefer being thought of as the right men for your
toughest jobs. Call now for a free estimate.

*Providing special services to realtors and home owners
since 1986, including demolition, flat bed hauling,
and other specific tasks.*

Licensed & Insured

HUGHMAN POWER
Division of Hugh A. Marshall Contractors, Inc.
P.O. Box 182 • New Hope, PA 18938 • **215-862-2291**

Walking and Cycling the Countryside

by Catherine D. Kerr

A few days after moving to this area, I took a break from unpacking, pumped up my bicycle tires, and pedaled off to explore my new neighborhood. Within minutes I was rolling along Lower Creek Road near Stockton, riding beside the Wickecheoke Creek beneath a bright autumn canopy of leaves. Scarcely believing my good fortune in living so close to this scenic treasure, I made it the first entry on a mental list of great places for a local walk or a bike ride. I've been keeping that list for more than twenty years now, and I'm still adding to it.

An old red barn.

When it comes to scenery, Bucks and Hunterdon counties have been richly endowed. From the blue curves of the Delaware River to rolling farms and country roads inland, from Lakes Nockamixon and Galena in Bucks to the Spruce Run Reservoir and the Red Mill of nearby Clinton in Hunterdon, there is much to see and enjoy.

I am convinced that walking and bicycling are the best ways to experience these delights. Stone farmhouses and old red barns, fertile cornfields and crystal-clear creeks, patches of bold orange daylilies and breezes heavy with the scent of multiflora rose growing wild by the side of the road—these are some of the sensory impressions you'll carry away from a day or even a few hours of cycling or walking here. It may be true that you can cover more territory in a car, but I think you miss too much when you go whizzing by in a cocoon of glass and steel. Even a good whiff of a working dairy farm serves to confirm that you are really there, and when the sights and smells are more agreeable, it's easy

The Delaware Canal at Washington Crossing Park.

Delaware and Raritan Canal towpath.

short distance away from shops and restaurants. Away from the towns, where there is not as much development, the paths feel more like country byways. Some sections of the canals run right beside the Delaware—near Lumberville or just south of Lambertville, for example—and the towpaths provide broad views of the river.

It's easy to plan a walk or ride by the canal that suits your mood. You can go just far enough to work up an appetite, for example, before arriving in town for lunch or a coffee break. If you're looking for a longer outing, you can use the bridges across the river to create a loop route following the canals on both sides. The circuit along the towpaths through New Hope, Lambertville, Stockton, and Center Bridge totals about seven miles, for example, which may be a little long for a casual walk but could be covered in a leisurely bike trip of about an hour if you ride straight through.

continued on page 22

to linger and enjoy them a little longer because you can simply step to the side of the road without worrying about where to turn around or park.

If you're new to cycling and walking in Bucks and Hunterdon, the canals are an excellent place to begin. Pennsylvania's Delaware Canal and New Jersey's Delaware and Raritan Canal both run parallel to the Delaware River and are accessible at many points along the way. Both have towpaths covered in fine crushed stone to create an even surface that is good for walking or cycling. (Best of all, some would say, is the fact that they are completely flat.)

In places like New Hope and Lambertville, a canal walk is basically a town walk. The towpaths lead past the back yards of houses and are only a

Wickechoeke Creek below Green Sergeant covered bridge.

Objects of history, design, imagination and surprise with an emphasis on painted furniture, primitives, folk art and pottery.

Established 2001

Cycling

continued from page 18

The canal paths are multi-use trails, meaning that pedestrians, cyclists, and (in Pennsylvania) horses and mules share the way. To preserve harmony among all, cyclists should always give way to those on foot, and both groups should yield to horses and mules. (If you're uncertain about how to go past these four-legged towpath users, ask the mule drovers or equestrians for advice on how to proceed.)

Many local parks have trails that are good for walking or cycling. The Bowman's Hill Wildflower Preserve near New Hope has gravel-covered trails leading through a wooded area that is a showcase for a collection of nearly a thousand species of plants native to Pennsylvania. The main part of the preserve is surrounded by a tall fence to keep out hungry deer. Inside, you'll find a variety of trails including some that follow the course of Pidcock Creek. If you're

Ridge Road farm. Photo: Martin E. Kennedy

feeling very energetic, you can walk all the way up to Bowman's Hill Tower, which (for a small admission fee) offers a sweeping view of the surrounding countryside.

At Peace Valley Park in New Britain Township, a paved bike/hike trail goes most of the way around scenic Lake Galena, a six-mile route. This is one of the most popular places for off-road walking or cycling in Bucks County. The park also has fourteen miles of unpaved nature trails, some near the lake and others through woods and fields nearby.

In Hunterdon County, there are natural trails at the undeveloped Sourland Mountain Nature

continued on page 26

Lumberville from Bull's Island. Photo: Martin E. Kennedy

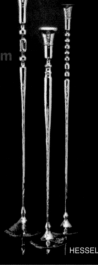

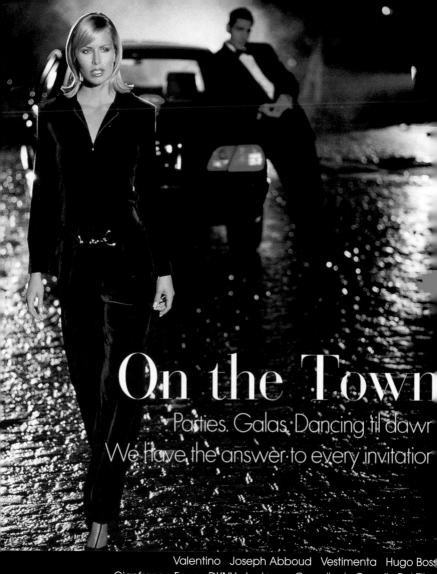

On the Town

Parties. Galas. Dancing til dawn
We have the answer to every invitation

Valentino Joseph Abboud Vestimenta Hugo Boss
Gianfranco Ferre DKNY Iceberg Corneliani Canali Pal Ziler
Fendi Gucci Ermenegildo Zegna Giorgio Armani Versace

SAVIONI

DESIGNER CLOTHING
FOR MEN & WOMEN

10 & 14 South Main Street New Hope PA 18938 • 215 862 5010

Remembrance

Charms
from the Past
Importers of French Antiques

129 West Bridge Street
New Hope, PA 18938
215-862-9890

Martin E. Kennedy, the Area Guide Book's photographer, counselor and publisher, and humorist and critic for nearly twenty-five years.

The book's watch-cat, P.

The Area Guide Book

The Original and Only Guide to Historic Bucks and Hunterdon Counties is published by EnandEm Graphics, Inc., Post Office Box 43, Lambertville, NJ 08530. Phone & Fax: 215-862-5094. Volume XXXII, 2001-2002 edition. www.areaguidebook.com

Publisher & Editor:
Nancy M. Wolfe-Kennedy

Photography:
Martin E. Kennedy
Nancy M. Wolfe-Kennedy

Exclusive Representative:
Strenk Sandor Advertising

Cover Painting Courtesy of:
Adrienne Crombie

Cover Designs:
Kevin Griffin, studio 58

Calendar Editor:
Birgitta H. Bond

Directories Editor:
Suzanne Halbherr

Composition & Prepress:
Bucks County Digital Imaging

Publishers Note: While every effort is made to assure the accuracy of the information in this book, things do change in the course of a year. A call to specific sites is suggested.

Additional copies are available from The Area Guide Book, P.O. Box 43, Lambertville, NJ 08530. 215-862-5094. For mail orders, please send $4.75 plus $1.50 postage. Orders in Pennsylvania and New Jersey add 29¢ (6%) state sales tax.

Editorial

Talking with Joe Maxian at Sand Castle Winery about how very special this area is reminded him of a conversation with a familiar-looking English visitor. Joe asked the man if he had been here before. "Yes," the visitor replied, "I come here twice each year." Joe asked why so often. "The people, history, nature, environment, and animals," he said. His words struck a chord for me. I offer them as pictures taken by another Englishman, Martin E. Kennedy, who came here, just once, and stayed.

Nancy M. Wolfe-Kennedy

Supportive Reflections

Community support runs deep at Univest. As we continue to build more financial products, we also invest in an important part of our culture - the arts.

Theater, dance, sculpture, painting, music, quilting, even poetry and storytelling: all are alive in our communities. Univest is proud to help keep the arts going strong and to continue encouraging and supporting the arts right here in our communities.

Support the arts... it's a strong reflection of all of us.

PROLOGUE

The fertile Delaware River Valley was visited by its first tourists when the "Wolf Tribe" of the Lenni-Lenape chose this area as their summer home. They planted crops, fished, and enjoyed the ease of the months when nature is its most generous. They were the first to discover the beauty of the area, something residents and visitors today rediscover with each changing season.

The first colonial population centers grew up around the eastern ports. As these became crowded, colonists moved by foot or horseback following paths cut through the heavily wooded countryside by resident Native American's. The first rough roads, and later the York Road, connected farms and villages and provided access to trading centers. When the York Road became the main highway between New York and Philadelphia residents of Bucks and Hunterdon Counties found themselves hosts to weary travelers and inns and taverns sprang up along the road offering food and lodging for man and beast.

As the stagecoach stops grew into communities which served travelers, the river towns were developing into industrial centers because the river provided easy access to raw materials and the ability to ship finished goods. With the advent of the railroad the early industrial towns lost their natural advantage and returned to the quieter lifestyle of the surrounding farm communities.

It was this quiet river valley that attracted the landscape painters at the turn of the century. In the 20s and 30s, prominent people in the theatre and business made this their country home. With them came the Bucks County Playhouse and then the restaurants and shops for which the area is renowned.

Today the two counties offer a multitude of choices for as many tastes. While New York and Philadelphia seem to have grown closer because of the interstate highways and the pressure of development has taken its toll, this area still remains a cultural and natural oasis in the midst of the northeast metropolitan corridor. On a summer evening you might hear the sound of a farmer's tractor slowly plowing the land, or a "gentleman" farmer's helicopter coming in to land.

Look in the art galleries and you'll find modern steel sculpture beside landscape paintings. It is this admixture of rural and sophisticated, old and new, that makes the area so interesting.

A Restaurant with More Color than the Average Rainbow

Now that you've arrived in New Hope,
you'll probably want to know where you
can find the greatest place to dine.
If an award winning restaurant serving
fine Continental cuisine in a room with a view
is what you're looking for . . .
And, dining with the locals is your cup of tea,
you'll find it all here. A colorful place
with a *very* colorful crowd.

The Raven

385 W. Bridge St., New Hope, PA
215-862-2081

Serving Lunch, Sunday Brunch & Dinner

John Wells's Ferry Tavern, c 1727, is hidden inside today's Logan Inn.

WELCOME TO NEW HOPE

When England claimed ownership of the 1,000 acres that make up the Borough of New Hope they were the peaceful, fertile riverside home of the Lenni-Lenape tribe. They passed into the hands of English colonists as part of King Charles II's land grant to William Penn. On March 22, 1681, William Penn granted this tract to Thomas Woolrich. It is believed that Woolrich never left England and that the land grant was sold to members of his family who did make the harrowing journey to the new world. The first of these we believe to be Robert Heath, Thomas Woolrich's brother-in-law, who arrived in 1700 and took possession of the 1,000 acre grant. Heath lived a short nine years after his arrival, but it was

long enough to build a grist mill in 1707 on Aquetong Creek and set the wheels in motion for industrial development based on the area's plentiful water supply. At his death the lands began to be divided by his family. In 1716 an interest in the property was sold to Charles Brockdon of Philadelphia, and, in 1717, 500 acres of the original tract were sold to John Wells of Lower Dublin Township.

Although Robert Heath built the mill and a home where Stony Hill and Sugan Roads meet, it is John Wells who is considered by many as the community's founder. While Wells may have operated a ferry earlier, he was formally licensed to erect and keep a ferry by act of the General Assembly of

Pennsylvania in 1722, and further licensed to keep a tavern in 1727.

The original Ferry Tavern is at the core of the building which stands at the corner of South Main and Ferry Streets as the Logan Inn. The inn is a fine example of the colonial habit of wrapping additions around existing structures. Extensive renovations completed in April 2001 by new owners, Carl and Pam Asplunch, again wrapped the old building and integrated historic preservation with modern amenities. Two cisterns which collected water for the town were found and preserved, as was the ice house at the rear of the inn.

The name Logan came to the inn about 100 years after it was first licensed and after the ferry

Chief Logan, town guardian.

had ceased operation. Reportedly, on February 22, 1828, as a part of a celebration, probably of Washington's birthday, the Ferry Tavern was renamed the Logan Inn (or House) and a metal cut-out of an Indian was installed towering above the roof of the inn.

There are differing accounts of this event: one that the Indian was Chief Logan and that the sign was paid for by a subscription of the townspeople in his honor; another that the identity of the Indian was never mentioned and that the sign was commissioned by the owners of the inn. We prefer the former legend which reports that a Lenni-Lenape chief, noted for his hospitality and kindness to the white settlers, developed a close friendship with William Penn's secretary, James Logan, and, as a sign of admiration, took Logan's name. Later, moving west to Ohio, Chief Logan gained fame as a mediator for the United States in its territorial wars with the Indians. When all of his relatives were killed in a massacre he withdrew his support. His final legacy is an eloquent speech which explained his refusal to continue to act as a peacemaker for the army. The cut-out, which remained above the inn for 50 years and is shown in woodcuts from that period, has been visible only sporadically since then. Today it is admired for its aesthetic design and is again a town landmark, rising, for the moment, from the lawn of the historical society's Parry Mansion Museum facing the inn.

Across from the inn, the house

The Parry family meals were prepared with iron utensils at the fireplace in this colonial kitchen.

The Parry Mansion Museum's front lawn with roses in bloom and a view of the back porch with restored antique Chief Logan weathervane.

Tours, Membership & Cultural Satisfaction

The Parry Mansion Museum, owned by The New Hope Historical Society, invites you to become a member for as little as $35. Whether you're a resident or visitor, you'll have the satisfaction of knowing your contribution is directly funding this 18th century building, its period furnishings, and art.

Call today to request our information packet. We'll reward you with special invitations to members-only affairs.

A peek inside the children's room where a life-size doll greets visitors.

THE NEW HOPE HISTORICAL SOCIETY
Main & Ferry Sts., P.O. Box 41, New Hope, PA 18938
215.862.5652 ❦ www.newhopehistoricalsociety.org

of Beaumont the hatter is of interest as an unusual local example of Georgian architecture and because of the history of its surroundings. When John Beaumont built the house in the 1780s his front door was at street level and his side yard extended across the canal and beyond. The construction of the canal took away the yard, splitting the property almost up to the side of the house. As if that weren't enough, when a bridge was built across the canal it raised the street level, surrounding the main entry to the house with a walled courtyard.

Going back to the town's beginnings, as ferry owners changed the town's name changed from Wells's Ferry to Canby's and then to Coryell's Ferry. It was as Coryell's Ferry, a name then shared with today's Lambertville, New Jersey, that the riverside communities played an important role in the events of the American Revolution.

Through the fall of 1776 the Americans were driven west by the British in defeat after defeat. When Washington and his men crossed the Delaware River into Pennsylvania they saw the first relief in months as the river gave them a natural line of defense. After safely making the crossing, Washington had all of the boats on the Jersey side of the river removed. This skillful maneuver stopped Cornwallis from following and gave Washington the time he so desperately needed to develop an offensive plan and to allow his bedraggled army to

regroup. His headquarters were set up around Coryell's Ferry and the starving Continental troops rested. Confronted with a "wide choice of difficulties," as he wrote to his brother, Washington determined to play a long shot and planned his first offensive action of the war.

With the cooperation of local patriots, the army commandeered every boat on the river and hid them just below Coryell's Ferry on Malta Island, which no longer exists today. Six hours before Washington and his men crossed at McKonkey's Ferry, Lieutenant James Monroe stole across the river into New Jersey with a small contingent of men, the vanguard sent ahead to disrupt British communications. At the appointed hour the makeshift armada proceeded down the river to McKonkey's Ferry, now Washington Crossing, where 2400 men waited to cross the freezing Delaware and begin the march on Trenton. The Hessians, still groggy

Benjamin Parry's barn, across the street from the Parry Mansion. Photo: Martin E. Kennedy

from Christmas celebrations were easily defeated in the dawn of December 26, 1776.

Industry

Growth in the early colonies was dependent on accessibility and New Hope fared well in this department. It was blessed first with the river by nature, and second by the Native American, whose trails became the route followed by the York Road. The York Road was the first major connecting link between New York and Philadelphia, and the towns along the road were guaranteed prosperity. Its strategic location, valley geography, and already burgeoning industry driven by the enormous power supply provided by the Aquetong Spring (later known as Ingham Spring), brought first

the Delaware Canal and later the railroad.

By 1707, Robert Heath had kept his promise to William Penn to "build and keep in repair a water corn mill [grist mill] for the use of the neighborhood." On a bend in South Sugan Road just over the railroad tracks are ruins of this first mill, and across the road are more substantial ruins of a cotton mill, circa 1820, built by William Maris.

Around the bend at the juncture of Stoney Hill and Sugan Roads near the ruins of the grist mill, stands the house variously known over the years as The Huffnagle Mansion, The Hood Mansion, and Springdale. The original section of the house, circa 1705, was built by Robert Heath and his son, Richard.

In the early 1700s industry in

and around the town included a fulling mill which shrunk cloth, a rolling and splitting mill which cut strips of metal to make nails, Heath's grist mill, woolen and flaxen mills, and an iron foundry.

Significant as these early mills were, true industrial prosperity for the village really began in 1781 with the arrival of Benjamin Parry, the grandson of Thomas Parry who came to America from Wales in 1715 as a Penn grantee, settling at Moorland Manor, a 1000 acre tract near present-day Hatboro.

Benjamin Parry came to the village of Coryell's Ferry at age twenty-four, bringing with him a substantial inheritance and plenty of business acumen. He purchased sixteen and a half acres from the widow of Dr. John Todd, property which included a grist and saw mill, circa 1745, at the mouth of Ingham Creek. These important mills had been advertised in the August 20, 1764 issue of The New York Mercury as "A new gristmill and sawmill at Coryell's Ferry on the Delaware River—sawmill can cut 1000 feet per day."

In the ten years that followed, Parry built a home, married Jane Paxson, acquired the water rights to Ingham Creek, increased his land holdings to include almost all of what is today New Hope, and owned and operated linseed oil, flaxseed oil, lumber and flour mills on both sides of the river.

He called his mill in Titusville, New Jersey, the Prime Hope Mill, and his Hopewell, New Jersey, mill, The Hope Mill. In 1790, when the mill in Coryell's Ferry

Old arch, new doors. Photo: Martin E. Kennedy

burned to the ground, he rebuilt only the grist and saw mills and called them The New Hope Mill. Shortly after the new mill opened, the town's name changed from Coryell's Ferry to New Hope.

In 1810, Parry developed the machinery, which he later patented and sold, to kiln dry corn and malt, two very important commodities in the young country. Parry's invention, perhaps inspired by the burning of his mills, revolutionized the milling industry. It reduced the risk of fire in the mills and at the same time allowed grain to be shipped to the Caribbean islands without fear of spoilage.

The Parry Family

In 1784, Parry built himself a home, a fieldstone mansion in the center of the village adjoining his mill complex. The larger original section of the house was built of natural blue and red fieldstone laid alternately in a pleasing pattern. In the later smaller addition, built as servant's quarters, only the

red fieldstone was used. Parry lived in the house for fifty-five years until his death in 1839 at the age of eighty-two. The Parry Mansion was home to his descendants for the next four generations.

Benjamin's son, Oliver, who was born in the Parry Mansion, spent most of his life in Philadelphia running the family-owned lumber yards. His son, Richard Randolph Parry, was born in Philadelphia in 1835 and returned to live in the mansion in 1861. He commuted from New Hope to his wholesale dry goods business in Philadelphia but was active in the community serving as senior warden at St. Andrew's Episcopal Church in Lambertville and as President of the New Hope Delaware Bridge Company for thirty-eight years. Richard's three children, Captain Oliver Randolph Parry and his sisters, Gertrude R. Parry and Adelaide R. Parry, all lived in the mansion. Although he considered the Parry Mansion his home, Oliver was an architect whose business life was divided between Philadel-

The Old Stone Church doors.

49

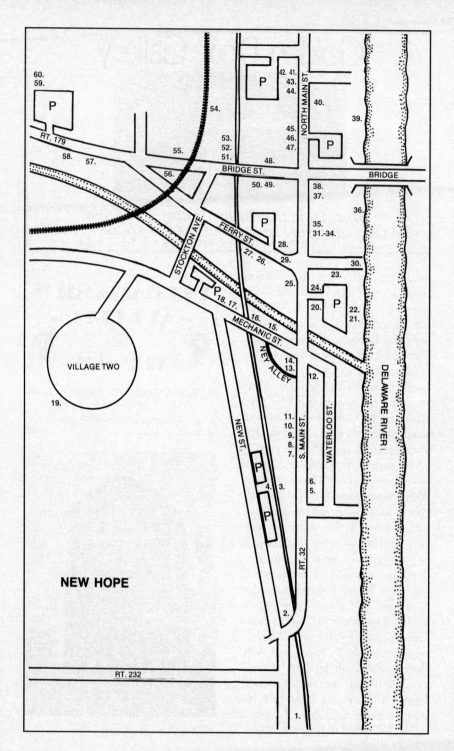

NEW HOPE

New Hope Map Key

1. Odette's
2. *Delaware Canal State Park
3. *Locktender's House Museum
4. *Barge Rides
5. Harvey Galleries
6. A Mano
7. New Hope Miniatures
8. The Picture Gallery
9. Zephyr Gallery
10. Havana
11. Sterling Leather
12. Medieval Gallery
13. Rebel Hearts
14. *New Hope Information Center
15. Tin Man Alley
16. Worldwinds
17. Moonlight
18. New Hope Inn
19. La Bonne Auberge
20. Golden Door Gallery
21. *Bucks County Playhouse
22. The River's Edge
23. Martine's
24. Farley's Bookshop
25. Parry Mansion Museum
26. Sally Goodman Antiques
27. La Bella Vita
28. Logan Inn
29. *Carriage Rides
30. *Riverfront Pocket Park

31. Four Season's Mall
32. Art Legends
33. Schatzies Treasures
34. Strenk Sandor Advertising
35. Heart of the Home
36. C'est La Vie
37. Savioni
38. Meow, Meow
39. The Landing
40. Jennett's Jacaranda Tree
41. *New Hope Borough Hall
42. *New Hope Police Department
43. Lachman Gallery
44. Topeo
45. Topeo South
46. Gothic Creations
47. Ferry Hill
48. Nagy Gallery
49. Cockamamie's
50. Suzie Hot Sauce
51. Gratz Gallery
52. The Tea Shoppe
53. Possum's
54. *Train Rides
55. Great Jones World
56. Hobensack & Keller
57. The Wedgwood Inns
58. Charms from the Past
59. *Steven S. Buck Theater
60. *New Hope-Solebury High School

*Attractions/Points of Interest

51

The Parry Mansion Museum from Main Street.

Two views from Ferry Street. Photos: Martin E. Kennedy

Ferry Hill
Decorative Arts and Antiques
15 N. Main St., New Hope, PA 18938   215-862-5335   www.ferryhill.com

phia and New York. The "Parry Sisters", neither of whom married, lived their entire lives in the house. Gertrude, who lived in the mansion for seventy years, died in 1954. An accomplished pianist, she enjoyed holding musicales in the Victorian parlor. Oliver and Adelaide Parry both died at the mansion in 1958 within five days of each other. The house was left by her father to Margaret Parry Lang, great, great, granddaughter of Benjamin Parry.

The Parry Mansion Museum

When Parry's mill in the center of New Hope ceased operation in the late 1930s it seemed likely that it would be leveled and replaced by new development. To preserve the 250-year-old mill, a group of concerned citizens purchased the property and converted it into the Bucks County Playhouse, which opened in 1939. For the next two decades the Parry property was secure in the hands of the family, although the barn along the creek suffered from disuse and neglect.

Headed by Dr. Arthur J. Ricker, a group of local residents founded The New Hope Historical Society in 1958. With a resolute sense of purpose, the society's late founder spearheaded a drive to preserve the historical, architectural and cultural fabric of New Hope. As its first project, the Parry Barn was purchased and restored. In 1960 it was opened to the public as an art gallery with paintings from private collections and from many of the area's famous artists hang-

ing on freshly white-washed walls. Forty years later, the Parry Barn remains a gallery displaying works in the Bucks County tradition.

In June of 1965, the historical society announced completion of negotiations to purchase the Parry Mansion from Margaret Parry Lang and her husband, O. Paul Lang. A down payment of $6,500 had sealed the agreement, with the balance of $58,500 to be paid at settlement scheduled for May 18, 1966. Dr. Ricker, who worked with the family on the sale, said the society hoped to make the mansion a museum that will "pay proper honor to the Parry name and heritage and display not only the priceless Parry heirlooms but other memorabilia of the area."

The Parry Mansion opened to the public in 1973 as a museum of decorative arts encompassing the period from 1775 to 1900. The furnishings reflect the decorative changes experienced by the Parry family and give the visitor a glimpse of the day-to-day life of the times. Each room on the first and second floors is decorated to reflect a twenty-five year period within the 125 years, and each one contains some of the Parry's own furnishings and personal items.

The Parry Mansion Museum is open from late April through early December on Friday, Saturday and Sunday from 1 to 5 pm. Group tours can be arranged throughout the year for groups of ten or more. There is an admission

charge. For more information write to The New Hope Historical Society, P.O. Box 41, New Hope, PA 18938, call 215-862-5652, or visit www.newhopehistoricalsociety.org.

Historic Preservation

The last three decades have been important for New Hope and the preservation of its heritage. In 1977 Anne Niessen began the enormous task of researching and registering every structure over 100 years old. Working with the New Hope Historical Society and the Borough government, she completed the research and the application for inclusion on the National Register of Historic Places. There was cause for celebration in March of 1985 when word was received that 243 properties had been placed on the National Register of Historic Places.

The recognition by the National Register includes two multiple resource districts. A major portion of the downtown area comprising one, and the second made up of the grouping of houses around the intersection of Sugan and Stony Hill Roads where Robert Heath built the first mill. In addition to the two districts four individual sites, The Rhodes Homestead, The Joshua Ely House, The William Kitchen House and Cintra were included on the Register.

An interesting statistic surfaced during the research. 181 of the 210 structures that comprised New Hope in 1876 were standing and occupied at the time of the survey.

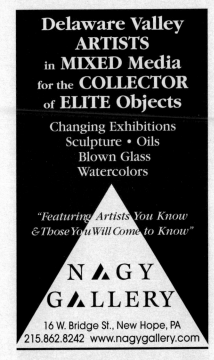

Historic houses, clockwise: circa 1795, Main Street, town's oldest frame house; circa 1740, East Mechanic Street; nineteenth century frame row houses on Ferry Street. Photo: Martin E. Kennedy

Historical Society Events

In addition to operating the Parry Mansion, the New Hope Historical Society plans a number of activities during the year, some of which are for members only, others for the public. This year's public events include the annual Garden Tour, held on June 9, Holidays at the Parry Mansion from November 16 through December 8, and a Christmas Candlelight Tour of the Mansion on November 25.

1990 brought the completion of New Hope's first park at the site of the old ferry landing at the foot of Ferry Street. It offers residents and visitors a quiet place to enjoy the beauty of the river and would not have come to fruition without the generous support of the Historical Society.

Membership in the New Hope Historical Society is open to everyone interested in history, cultural activities, and supporting the continuing preservation of New Hope. Annual membership is: $40 individual, $60 family, $100 business, $150 sponsor, $350 corporate, and $500 life. Inquiries about membership and members-only events should be sent to the New Hope Historical Society, P.O. Box 41, New Hope, PA 18938, or call 215-862-5652.

The Delaware Canal

The opening of the Delaware Division Canal in 1832 gave the manufacturers of New Hope a faster method of disbursing their products and easier access to raw materials from the northern forests

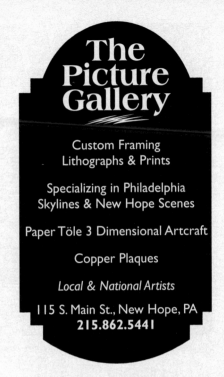

An antique carriage—a reminder of times past. Photo: Martin E. Kennedy

and coal fields. At its peak there were 3,000 boats traveling the route from Bristol to Easton moving over one million tons of coal a year. Until 1931, when the railroad finally put them out of business, mule drawn barges carried Bushkill Whiskey and coal to Bristol and returned to Easton with manufactured and imported goods.

New Hope held a special place in the canal system with four double locks spaced at intervals of 500 feet. At Lock 11, the northern most of the four, the original lock keeper's house is today a museum operated by the Friends of the Delaware Canal. This was the only point on the canal where four barges could pass at a time. Continuing south, at Lock 10 there was a lock keeper's house and at

Lock 9, the toll collector's office. Both of these structures are now private residences.

In 1854, the construction of an outlet lock at Lock 8 made it the shuttling point across the Delaware River to the Delaware & Raritan Canal in New Jersey. This allowed barges to make a continuous run to Princeton, New Brunswick, Newark Bay and New York City from Easton or Bristol.

Just north of Lock 8, the River House was an inn that had served river boatmen from its opening in 1794. Situated near the head of the dangerous Wells Falls, river pilots offered to guide boatmen through the rapids for $5.00 a trip. During the canal era, the inn catered to the canal boatmen offering overnight accommodations and necessary supplies. Big

Mag Featherstone, renowned for her ability to handle obstreperous guests, was one of the last proprietors during the canal days. As canal traffic waned the inn fell into disuse, only to be revitalized in the 1930s as New Hope's first tourist inn.

No longer offering overnight accommodations, in 1961 the inn became Chez Odette, under the ownership of Odette Myrtil, the Parisian stage and screen star best remembered as Bloody Mary in *South Pacific*. The current owners of Odette's, the Barbone family, have preserved the spirit of Chez Odette continuing its famous piano bar and offering cabaret shows that would please even Odette herself.

On the same day in 1931 that the last paying boat locked through, 40 miles of the canal were deeded to the state and made the Theodore Roosevelt State Park. In 1940 the state finally acquired the remaining 20 miles of the canal, and in 1989 it was renamed the Delaware Canal State Park. In 1978, through the long and persistent efforts of the Delaware Valley Protective Association and many others, the Delaware Canal was formally dedicated as a National Historic Landmark.

Founded in 1982, The Friends of the Delaware Canal is a nonprofit organization whose purpose is to educate the public about the historic value of the early canal system and its present significance as a scenic treasure and recreational facility. The Friends organization is

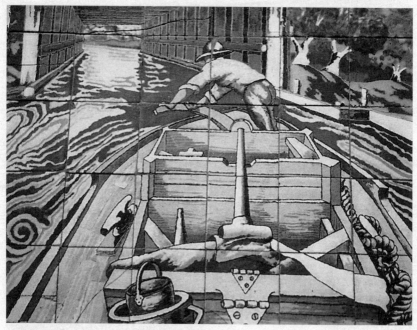
Painted tile canal scene graces a wall on Ney Alley.

a direct successor to the Delaware Valley Protective Association which worked from 1936 to 1982.

In 1987, the Friends completed and presented to the Commonwealth a Master Plan for the Delaware Canal. This plan calls for a 10-year, $32 million program for maintenance and restoration of the canal. Through the efforts of the Friends, the canal is a part of the Delaware and Lehigh Navigation Canal National Heritage Corridor, a federal preservation effort established by Congress in 1988. In 1989, the Friends spearheaded a drive to have the Delaware Canal recognized as a National Recreation Trail, and in April 1990 it became part of the National Trail System. In cooperation with the National Heritage Corridor, the group has placed narrative wayside signs and kiosks along the length of the canal.

The Friends have received local and national recognition for their preservation efforts. In both 1988 and 89 they received the "Take Pride in Pennsylvania" Award and were finalists, both years, in the "Take Pride in America" competition. The house serves as the first interpretive center within the park and is the Friends headquarters. Exhibits, artifacts, and restoration details are used to illustrate "Life at the Lock" and canal history. Guided walking tours of the canal are offered throughout the year and a "Traveling Canal Show" is available to schools and community groups.

For information on programs and membership in the Friends of the Delaware Canal stop by the

Lockhouse or write to them at 145 S. Main St., New Hope, PA 18938, or call 215-862-2021.

The Artists

While the presence of the river and the building of the canal were largely responsible for New Hope's being a hub of activity in the eighteenth and nineteenth centuries, the growth of the railroads diminished the use of waterways as the major lines of trade. By the end of the nineteenth century New Hope had faded into obscurity and it was, once again, a quiet country town. None-the-less, its surroundings were to be ranked with the most impressive landscape in the world. It is reported that William Penn, on a return to England, described the valley as the most beautiful of landscapes, far ahead of what could be found in England.

It was this perfect model that drew the first landscape painters at the end of the nineteenth century. Friends and students visited, were captivated, returned to stay, and before long New Hope began to be perceived as an art colony, despite the fact that none of these artists had any idea of forming a "colony". By the twenties, New voted among the first fifty icons of American Folk Art.

Born in New Hope in 1848, Picket worked in the family-owned boardyard which he inherited from his father in 1888 and sold a short time later. Following the sale of the boatyard he and his wife Emily moved a number of times and ran several stores in New Hope, one on Mechanic Street where he painted a mural which he called *The Tree of Life* on the outside of the building, and a second on Bridge Street, where it is believed he did most of his painting in a back room. He completed *Manchester Valley* in 1917 and gave it to the supervisor of the New Hope Schools. It stayed at the school on the hill above Mechanic

From Ferry Street—The Delaware Canal passes quietly through the center of New Hope.

The locktenders house at Lock II, home of the Friends of the Delaware Canal.

Street until 1931, and in 1939 was given to MOMA by Abigail Aldrich Rockefeller. An untrained artist who painted simply because he enjoyed it, only two other Picket paintings, *Coryell's Ferry* and *Washington Under the Council Tree*, are known to have survived, both in major museums. His wife said of his painting, she "didn't mind if Joe painted as long as he didn't get paint on the carpet."

The headline on an article written in 1940 by Chloe Doubble for the magazine, "Arts in Philadelphia" announces: "New Hope—Artistic Pasture of the mills and musicians, the acres and actors, the shad and the sculptors that are bright fragments of the composite called New Hope...A Survey." Nearly sixty years later, only the mills are no longer bright fragments. Her survey encompasses the entire area, which she describes as the "Doylestown-Lumberville-New Hope-Yardley stretch of Bucks County." Among the artists mentioned who were in fact residents of New Hope are John Folinsbee, Henry and Florence Snell, Harry Leith-Ross, Robert Spencer, R. Sloan Bredin and his wife Alice Price, Faye Swengel and Bernard Badura, Fern Coppedge, Jessie H. Drew-Baer, Harry Rosin, and the modernists C.F. Ramsey, Charles Evans and Lloyd Ney. The article lists close to 150 artists, writers, musicians, actors, editors, and educators, living in the area, including three-term Burgess, Dr. Roscoe C. Magill, a native of New Hope who was a noted eye specialist, prolific painter, and storyteller. She retells one of his favorite tales: "Dr. Magill liked the farmer's comments on looking over the shoulder of the man who stood painting in one of his fields. Willing to find some merit in the rather confusing composition the artist was perpetrating, the farmer felt the whole thing must be a lot harder to do than it looked. 'Painting two pictures at once, eh?' he congratulated, and went happily back to his cows."

Lloyd R. "Bill" Ney, whose abstract and non-objective paintings can be seen in the Museum of Modern Art in New York, is remembered as one of the town's finest artists and greatest characters. Ney supplemented his artist's income by working in a local brickyard and came home every day with part of his pay in bricks. When he had collected enough bricks he began building and rebuilding on Mechanic Street, which, with the adjacent Ney Alley, bore his particular stamp by the mid-40s. His most impressive structural legacy to the town is the "Ney Museum" which he built to house his work.

Called "the premier modernist of the Latin Quarter in New Hope," his affair with the town was artistic as well as architectural and he left behind an enormous body of work depicting the life and citizens of New Hope in the 40s and 50s.

Another local artist much loved by the community, and a one-time resident of the Ney Alley, was Harry Rosin. A compatriot of

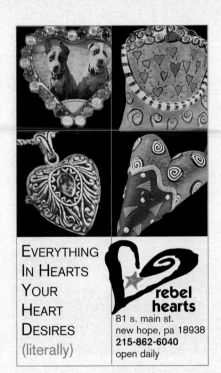

Robert Rosenwald's Sign of the Times *by the river bridge. Photo Martin E. Kennedy*

Robert E. Montgomery's untitled sculpture in the garden of the library. Photo: Martin E. Kennedy

William Selesnick's mural of a mule-drawn barge near Lock II. Photo Martin E. Kennedy

Bill Ney's from their student days, Harry came to New Hope as a young sculptor and instructor at the Pennsylvania Academy of Fine Arts in Philadelphia. Most famous for his sculpture of Tahitian women and children, his commissions included *Connie Mack*, *John B. Kelly*, *The Quaker* and *The Puritan*, all in Philadelphia. Rosin was a builder too and the unique one story structure on Ney Alley across from the Ney Museum attests to his skill.

The Ney Museum, which in recent years had been turned into residential apartments, was purchased in the spring of 1997 by artist and designer Milt Sigel. A Fulbright Scholar and Professor of Graphic Design at Bucks County Community College, his Studio 1 artist-in-residence studio and gallery opened in Ney's museum in fall 1998. The public is welcome whenever the open sign is out. Studio 1 will hold periodic shows of the work of Mr. Sigel and friends, once again filling the space with contemporary art.

The 2000 opening of the Lachman Gallery on North Main Street marked the arrival of Al Lachman as a new member of the New Hope art community and added another artist-owned gallery to the local art scene. Lachman was first captivated by the area some twenty years ago. In the years that followed his career took him across the country exhibiting nationally and selling his work at outdoor art shows. Last year he and his wife revisited the area, found that a

stone mill they remembered from their earlier visit was for sale, and made the commitment to settle here and open a gallery. With the gallery came a web site, less travel, and more time to paint.

Trained at the Art Students League and School of Visual Arts in New York, Lachman is well represented internationally in private and public collections. He is a past director of the Pastel Society of America (PSA) and was a founder and instructor at the PSA's School for Pastels Only at the National Arts Club in New York City.

In early 2001 the Canadian Government was searching for art to use in a campaign to increase public awareness of homelessness and to encourage the homeless to be enumerated in the national census. They found Lachman's series of twelve paintings of the homeless on his web site and chose four to reproduce as posters that were distributed throughout Canada in March, April, and May 2001 while the census was being taken.

The Theatre

Following the artists came the writers and actors seeking the same peaceful haven from the pressures of city life. By the 20s and 30s the area was called home by an impressive list of theatrical and literary personalities, among them Moss Hart, Oscar Hammerstein, Budd Schulberg, Pearl S. Buck, Don Walker, George Kaufman, Dorothy Parker, Nathanael West, S.J. Perlman, and native son, James A. Michener.

It was in this environment in

1939 that the idea for the Bucks County Playhouse emerged, the brainchild of playwright/resident Kenyon Nicholson and actor/producer St. John Terrell. A group of dedicated townspeople had formed the Hope Mill Association to save Benjamin Parry's 250-year-old gristmill from potential demolition for riverside development. The preservationists and thespians joined forces to save the mill by transforming it into a summer theatre.

The Bucks County Playhouse opened on July 1, 1939, with Edward Everett Horton starring in *Springtime for Henry*. At the opening, Producer Terrell announced to the audience: "after cooperative combat between cast, stagehands, and assistants, we finished the building a few minutes ago."

In the sixty-two years since its opening there have been nine producers and each has added his own special touch to the operation. The theatre was first a resident company under St. John Terrell; the star system was added by Theron Bamburger; under Mike Ellis's direction the playhouse became the State Theatre of Pennsylvania and was noted for tryouts of new plays; Walter Perner, Jr. brought current Broadway shows to New Hope, and Lee Yopp instituted year-round operation and an educational program for high school students.

Two summer seasons were mounted by a New York production company and by 1974 the future of the old gristmill seemed threatened once again. With the

Playhouse reflected in Ingham Creek, power source for colonial mills all along its banks. Photo: Martin E. Kennedy

same devotion and some of the same people that opened the playhouse in 1939, a new non-profit company, BCP, Inc., purchased the theatre to guarantee its continuation and again to protect it from development.

Having kept the theatre afloat through a difficult time, but without the manpower or the expertise to actually run the theatre, BCP, Inc. sold it in January of 1977 to RAM, III. New producer, Ralph Miller, approached theatre in a different way and using non-Equity actors in popular musicals managed to change the economics of running a small theatre with limited seating. The current 62nd season opened in May and ends in December. For reservations and information call the box office at 215-862-2041, or visit their web site at www.bucks countyplayhouse.com.

In addition to theatre, New Hope has become a favorite spot for cabaret, comedy and music. Throughout the year local night spots and restaurants feature nationally and internationally acclaimed performers from the worlds of cabaret, comedy, and folk, jazz and rock music.

New Hope Performing Arts Festival

The first New Hope Performing Arts Festival was mounted in 1987. Among the success stories of the festival is the 1992 *All in the Timing*, an evening of one act plays by David Ives. Following its premiere

at the festival, it was cited as one of the top ten productions of the year by Philadelphia Inquirer critic Cliff Ridley. Then, in the fall of 1993, it moved to New York. A year later *All in the Timing* was published by Dramatist Play Service and David Ives received the Outer Critics Circle award as playwright of the year.

The 1999 13th Annual New Hope Performing Arts Festival was the first to use the new state-of-the-art 500 seat Stephen Buck Memorial Theatre at the New Hope-Solebury High School on Bridge Street. Under the direction of Paul Licitra, the festival included the world premiere of *Midnight Rainbows* by Emmy award-winning playwright, Patrick Nolan. It was the first year of a partner-

Engine No. 40 crossing Pauline's Trestle.   *New Hope Station. Photo: Martin E. Kennedy*

Just around the bend from Pauline's Trestle. Photo: Martin E. Kennedy

ship between the festival and The International School of Performing Arts (ISPA), which brought four exciting opera programs to the New Hope Performing Arts Festival including a master class with Metropolitan Opera star, Sherrill Milnes.

The next year's 14th New Hope Performing Arts Festival, had as its theme "Diversity in the Arts" and included a performance of *Der Fledermaus* by the ISPA and, for the second year, a master class with Sherrill Milnes. Also on the schedule was a new musical *Colors*, by Ashton Wall, and a return engagement, for the third year, of Jennie Bray's Original Children's Theatre. This unusual troupe of young children write, perform, and sing their own original productions.

This year's festival opens in mid-July and continues through mid-August. It will include return engagements by the International School of Performing Arts and Jenny Bray's Original Children's Theatre. New this year are appearances by The River Ballet Company, performing *Coppelia*, and the Bucks County Choral Society's presentation of *Carmina Burana*. As in the past, there will be a weekend of one act plays and readings of new works.

For a complete schedule, ticket information, and reservations, call the New Hope Arts Commission office at 215-862-1699.

New Hope Auto Show

The 45th annual New Hope Auto Show will be held this year

A reminder of New Hope's past as a stage stop on the Swift Sure Line. Photo: Martin E. Kennedy

on August 11 and 12 on the New Hope-Solebury High School grounds with entry from Route 202 in New Hope. Sponsored by the New Hope-Solebury Community Association, the show has been acclaimed as one of the finest in the country. With 40 divisions, it offers antique, collector, and racing car buffs a chance to reminisce over the cars of their childhoods, view sports cars from all over the world, and dream over the Rolls Royces and Bentleys built for royalty. A gala parade of champions ends each day, with the prized Governor's Cup of the Commonwealth of Pennsylvania being presented on Sunday afternoon. Entry forms and information are available from the New Hope Automobile Show, P.O. Box 62, New Hope, PA 18938, 215-862-5665, www.newhopeautoshow.com.

In conjunction with the Community Association, the New Hope Chamber of Commerce is sponsoring an outdoor art show on the grounds of the auto show. Families whose interests are divided will be able to enjoy both automobiles and art, all in one location.

New Hope Highlights

An unusual facility which makes New Hope its home is the Bucks County Academy of Fencing, opened in January 1981 by Maestro Mark Holbrow. A New Hope native, Holbrow trained and competed at Princeton University under Stan Sieja and for three years prior to opening the academy was assistant fencing coach at Princeton. With its rich

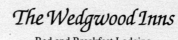

Chestnut Street: A quiet residential neighborhood in New Hope.

An early spring stroll along North Main Street.

Historic Ferry Street in a blanket of snow. Photo: Martin E. Kennedy

history, fencing is an appealing discipline looked upon as the chess game of the athletic arena.

The academy currently has approximately 200 students including beginners, recreational fencers, and nationally-ranked competition fencers in foil, epee, and sabre. Students range in age from 6 to 70. The academy employs two Fencing Masters, one Apprentice Master, and six Instructors, all certified by the United States Fencing Coaches Association, and is host for many divisional tournaments, which are held on Sunday afternoons.

Full information on classes and events is available from the Bucks County Academy of Fencing, 2 Stockton Avenue, New Hope, PA 18938, 215-862-5365, www.bcaf.com.

In 1991 a new page was added to the history of railroading in New Hope with the purchase of the New Hope and Ivyland Railroad by the Bucks County Railroad Preservation and Restoration Corporation. The train station and freight station were restored and brick work and charming landscaping were added to the entry approach. Watching the work proceed one felt the sense of anticipation that must have surrounded the arrival of the first passenger trains in New Hope on March 29, 1881.

The 9-mile, 50 minute round trip between New Hope and Lahaska is a scenic adventure through historic countryside. The relaxing excursion aboard restored 1920s railroad passenger cars takes one over Pauline's Trestle, where actress Pearl White was filmed for the 1914 movie, The Perils of Pauline. Traveling

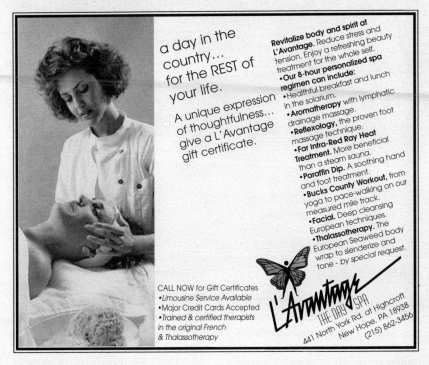
through the rolling hills and valleys of Bucks County you will experience first hand the sounds and romance of the "Golden Steam Era."

This year the railroad initiated new service between SEPTA's Warminster Station and Wycome Station. At the southern end of the railroad, this ride takes visitors through scenic countryside replete with flowing streams, rock cuts, and small towns.

The railroad schedules special trains during the season and on holidays, and welcomes groups and private parties year round. Events include: Song and Story Hour, Train Robbery, Fall Foliage Trains, and the North Pole Express.

For more information and reservations contact the New Hope and Ivyland Railroad at 215-862-2332, or visit www.newhoperailroad.com.

The New Hope Canal Boat Company offers a unique one-hour journey on the Delaware Canal. As a team of mules pulls the boat, one sees New Hope from a different vantage point and passengers experience life along the canal as it was in the 1800s and hear interesting tales of canal days related by an interpreter in period costume. For more information on barge rides call 215-862-0758.

Still other views of New Hope can be seen from the horse-drawn carriages which leave from in front of the Logan Inn near the cannon, or from boat rides avail-

New Hope & Ivyland's Engine No. 40 crossing the tressle used in "The Perils of Pauline."

able on the river at two locations on Main Street.

An unusual view of New Hope can be seen on foot as part of the Mystery and History Ghost Tours which were founded and designed by Adi-Kent Jeffrey, author of Ghosts in the Valley and More Ghosts in the Valley. On Saturday nights from June to November the inquisitive gather at the cannon at Main and Ferry Streets at 8 pm and commence a lantern-led walk where they learn about the doings of such places as the towpath; see the Phantom Hitchhiker who may appear in the moonlight; and pass the historic inn where Aaron Burr appears from time to time. In September, October, and November tours meet Fridays and Saturdays. Call 215-957-9988 for more information.

Now in its eighth year, The New Hope-Solebury Library's "Musical Fireworks" series has been an enormous success from its inception. An annual four-concert series from which all proceeds go to the library, the programs include a mix of musical styles: Broadway, classical, jazz, and opera, performed by top notch professionals, in a 90-minute no intermission format.

The series is produced by library president, John Walsh, and co-producer, Sylvia Walsh, who say it works "because the talent sparkles, the numbers are exciting and the audiences explode with applause." It's no wonder that professional performers are pleased to be asked to participate, even though no one is paid a penny, and there is a roster of 80 of them who are ready to contribute their time and talent. They like the fact that they are only asked to perform for 15 minutes, and, in the words of Fred Miller, whose Silver Dollar Singers have been part of "Musical Fireworks" since it began, "John and Sylvia have put together a professional organization that puts the talent first."

The 2001 season opened on May 25th with the mix of music that is the trademark of Musical Fireworks. The cast of fifteen professional performers included international concert pianist Clipper Erickson, international pianist Noriko Schneiderman with violinist Mia Wu, Fred Miller's Silver Dollar Singers, and cellists Seth Branum and Gary Li. The season continues with concerts on July 13, August 24, and October 12.

The concerts are held at the New Hope-Lambertville Rescue Squad's 350 seat concert hall across the river in Lambertville, New Jersey. The doors open at 6:30 for complimentary wine and cheese before the 7 pm performances, which have always been sold out. Tickets at a modest $17.50 are available, if you get there in time, at the library on Ferry Street in New Hope or by calling 215-862-2330.

Into The New Millennium

2000 was a year in which New Hope moved into the final stages of planning for a group of projects that will change the face of the town and saw new commitment to

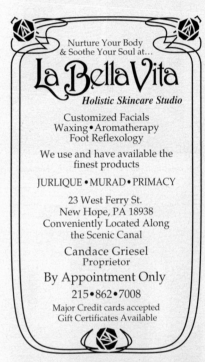

The church steeple. Photo: Martin E. Kennedy

A fine door on North Main Street.

the cultural life of the community.

The Union Camp paper bag mill on Bridge Street was the last industrial enterprise in New Hope and its closing several years ago left the large sprawling property empty. Whomever bought it would be taking on a major development, the largest project in New Hope's recent history, and one which would change the face of New Hope and would be unique to the site. After several failed attempts to design a project that worked both for the buyer and the borough, George E. Michael Inc., restorers of the Lambertville House across the river, purchased the property and began work on Union Square in spring 2000. Union Square will be a blend of new and restored buildings, in a park-like setting, which offers 130,000 square feet that will house offices, a restaurant, a 25-30 room hotel with a conference center and meeting rooms, retail stores, a satellite James A. Michener Art Museum, and a 5,000 square foot day spa. The complex will open in phases beginning with offices in summer 2001 and ending with the hotel and museum in 2002. For more information on Union Square call 215-862-1014.

Spring 2000 saw the opening of the first season by the Concordia Chamber Players, a group founded in 1997 by cellist, Michelle Djokic, as New Hope Chamber Players. Ms. Djokic, who was raised in the area and whose parents still live in New Hope, made her professional debut at the age of thirteen with the Philadelphia Orchestra,

and graduated from Julliard School of Music at twenty. A rising star, as a young cellist she won firsts in numerous international competitions, making her debut at Carnegie Hall in 1985 as a soloist with the New Jersey Symphony.

She has served as principal cellist of the Denver Symphony, The Aspen Festival Orchestra, The New York Virtuosi, The Rhode Island Philharmonic, and the McGill Chamber Orchestra. Her appearances as a soloist with orchestras throughout the United States, Canada, and Europe, have been to great critical acclaim.

Among the artists performing with her have been members of the Lincoln Center Chamber Music Society and David Kim,

Concertmaster of the Philadelphia Orchestra.

Ms. Djokic's love of chamber music, combined with a dream of bringing the highest caliber music to the community where she was raised, culminated in the group's first concerts, two in 1997 and three in 1998. She was unable to produce concerts in 1999 because of a family move to New Haven, Connecticut, where he husband is coach of the Yale Women's Squash Team.

2000 brought her back to the dream and a group of local people dedicated to making it work. The name change reflects a desire to build bridges between all of the towns in the area through the intimacy of chamber music. With non-

The "Parade of Champions" at the New Hope Auto Show. Photo: Martin E. Kennedy

profit status under the aegis of Partners in Progress, and a small, but determined board of directors, Concordia Chamber Players has become a permanent fixture in the cultural life of New Hope.

The 2001-2002 season includes three concerts scheduled for October, January, and April, all held at the Steven Buck Theater in New Hope on Sunday afternoons. Appearing in the new season will be Gail Niwa, William Purvis, Carmit Zori, Cynthia Phelps, Mi Hae Lee, and Donald Palma, among others.

In addition to the concerts, Concordia gives free informances in area schools in the week before each concert The informance offers young students an introduction to the music, the process, and the artist, which makes the concert experience more enriching, and the students are given free vouchers to attend the concerts.

For the full season schedule and ticket information call 215-297-5972, or visit their web site at www.concordiaplayers.com.

Plans to institute a New Hope Canal Walk are part of an initiative that brings together the Delaware and Lehigh National Heritage Corridor, HUD, the Pennsylvania Heritage Park Program, the Pennsylvania Department of Community Affairs Main Street Program, Heritage Conservancy, Friends of the Delaware Canal, the New Hope Historical Society, The New Hope Chamber of Commerce and the New Hope Borough Council.

As part of the corridor's 160-mile Delaware and Lehigh Trail from Wilkes-Barre to Bristol, the Canal Walk will showcase the corridor's outdoor exhibit signs, or waysides. Informational signs pertaining to local history, historic sites, natural history and canal structures will be placed along the towpath. Envisioned to feature the towpath and a series of connecting loops, the walk will not only provide a recreational opportunity but also will enable the story of the Delaware Canal, its importance to New Hope's development and its role in America's Industrial Revolution to unfold.

The scope of this project is vast, far-reaching, and very exciting for New Hope residents and visitors alike. While it would be expected to take time to complete, it will certainly be well worth the wait.

The New Hope Chamber and Partners in Progress

The Greater New Hope Chamber of Commerce, which is active planning events and working with local government to promote and preserve the special qualities of the community, was joined in 1995 by Partners in Progress, a non-profit community-wide organization whose volunteer members are committed to promoting pride in New Hope as a regional cultural and historic center to be enjoyed to the fullest by residents and visitors alike.

The Chamber-sponsored fall gala night for New Hope, conceived in 1994 by then chamber president Honey Scherlis, has been a great evening since its inception. 1995 brought new excitement to the event with the addition of the "Arty Awards,"

The River: A home.

New Hope's own version of the Oscars and the People's Choice Awards rolled into one. The evening is filled with anticipation as the Artys go to businesses and residents who have been voted the "best" that year by the community. Celebrity friends of New Hope always turn out for the occasion to make the evening's entertainment exceptional. This year's Artys will be presented on September 11th at the New Hope Fire Company's Eagle Hall on Sugan Road in New Hope. The evening will include cocktails, the award ceremony and a gala dinner, all held for the second year at one location. New Hope is a special community and this is always a very special evening. For ticket information call the New Hope Visitors Center at 215-862-5030.

The Chamber's eighth annu- nual New Hope Outdoor Arts & Crafts Festival will be held this year on Saturday and Sunday, October 6th and 7th. The festival runs from 11 am to 6 pm on Saturday and 11 am to 5 pm on Sunday, In the past this outstanding juried event has featured as many as 180 artists and craftsmen from 22 states. The show's high standards guarantee an exciting mix of art, crafts, painting, photography, sculpture, and art-to-wear. The exhibitors are located throughout the town with street performers to add to the festivities. The festival offers a wonderful opportunity to enjoy the arts, the town, and the outdoors on an early fall weekend.

The holiday season opens in New Hope on the weekend after Thanksgiving with the arrival of Santa and Mrs. Claus in a horse-

The River: A diversion.

drawn carriage setting the stage for the lighting of the town Christmas tree and Menorah. A celebration for the entire family, the evening is always filled with entertainment, refreshments, and plenty of time for the kids to visit with Santa. A full calendar of holiday events is available in November from the New Hope Visitors Center.

For more information on these and other Chamber activities call 215-862-5030, or write to the Greater New Hope Chamber of Commerce, P.O. Box 633, New Hope, PA 18938.

Partners in Progress (PiP), is a non-profit volunteer organization whose aim is to beautify and preserve the historical focus of the New Hope area. This non-political community spirit organization has accomplished much in its first seven years. Among their many projects have been the installation of period street lights on Mechanic Street, an annual spring clean up, planting flowers throughout the town, installing benches on the streets, and positioning welcome signs at the entrances to the village.

PiP is a strong and positive force that has worked with the whole community to achieve their goals. To fund its efforts, PiP stages events throughout the year. For information on membership and its events write to Partners in Progress, P.O. Box 506, New Hope, PA 18938, or call 215-862-5030.

New Hope Borough Information

The New Hope Visitors Center is in the old town hall at the corner of Main and Mechanic Streets and is open daily from 10 am to 6 pm and on Sundays from 10 am

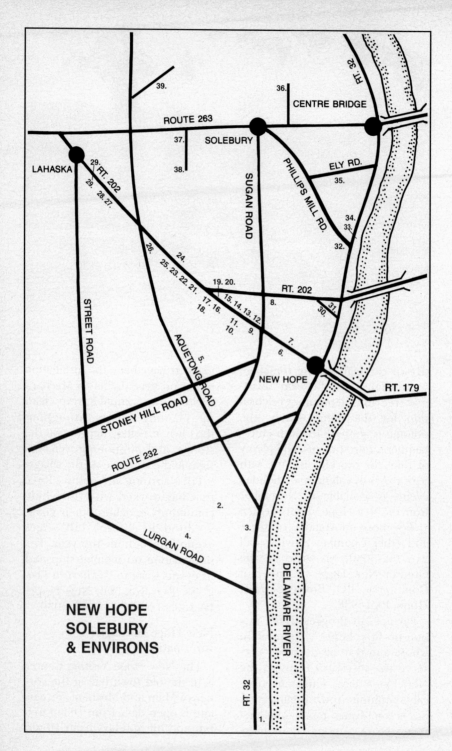

New Hope, Solebury & Environs Map Key

1. Pineapple Hill
2. *Bowman's Hill Wildflower Preserve*
3. *Washington Crossing Historic Park*
4. *Bowman's Tower*
5. Hughman Power
6. Pidcock Agency
7. Stanley Cleaners
8. *New Hope Eagle Fire Company*
9. Lisa J. Otto Country Properties
10. Cordials Bed & Breakfast
11. The Raven
12. Camel Walk
13. New Hope Photo
14. Interiors for Gracious Living
15. The New Hope Motel
    "The Motel in the Woods"
16. Asiantique
17. Weidel Realtors
18. Adam Shipiro, Weidel Realtors
19. 1st National Bank & Trust Co. of Newtown
20. Coldwell Banker Hearthside Realtors

21. Legacy Antiques
22. L'Avantage
23. Union National Bank
24. Monkey Hill
25. Best Western - New Hope Inn
26. Lyons Antiques
27. Gardner's Antiques
28. The Clock Trader
29. Kurfiss Real Estate
30. Magill Mini Storage
31. Brillman's Rental Barn
32. Hotel du Village
33. The Inn at Phillips Mill
34. *Phillips' Mill*
35. Rosade Bonsai
36. Paxson Hill Farm
37. *Bucks County Audubon Society Visitor Center*
38. Honey Hollow Farm
39. Rice's Sale & Country Market

Attractions/Points of Interest

to 5 pm. Information is available on an automated line at 215-862-5880, or from an information specialist at 215-862-5030.

Parking areas both public and private are sign posted. The New Hope-Solebury High School parking lot is open to the public on weekends throughout the year and daily during the summer. It is rarely full and though a few blocks from the center of the town, it is a pleasant walk.

If you are parking in town at a meter be sure to check the hours of operation as they vary from street to street. Most operate daily from 10 am to 9 pm and Sundays from noon to 9 pm. Some meters permit parking for periods of four hours or eight hours, depending on their location. The Borough does have meter persons and should you get a ticket, read the envelope carefully. If it is not paid promptly District Court costs are added.

The wall and markers speak for themselves.
Photo: Martin E. Kennedy

Solebury Township farm joins past and present. Photo: Martin E. Kennedy

SOLEBURY

New Hope Borough is surrounded by Solebury Township on three sides except on the east where it meets the Delaware River. In contrast to the one square mile of New Hope, Solebury Township encompasses an area of 14,078 acres or roughly 28 square miles. Originally a part of Buckingham Township, it appears to have been separated in about 1702. It is believed that the name comes from the village of Soulbury in Buckinghamshire, England, the original home of the Paxson family. The Paxson's were among the first and most influential settlers in the township and are believed to have given it its name. The first reference to its current spelling is on a 1720 lease, concurrently it appears elsewhere as Sole-

berry, Soulbury, and Solesbury.

At the southern end of the township two miles below New Hope are the northern grounds of Washington Crossing Historic Park which include Bowman's Hill Wildflower Preserve, the Thompson-Neely House, and Bowman's Hill Tower. The 100 foot observation tower was built in 1930 to commemorate the lookout of the American Revolution. Prior to the Christmas crossing Bowman's Hill, which rises 380 feet above sea level and is one of the highest points along the river, was used as a signal station and to observe enemy movements. For forty-six years the climb to the top of the tower was a popular attraction. The tower closed from 1976 until 1985 when it reopened with a newly installed elevator making it accessible to more than the most energetic visitors. On a clear day the tower commands a 14 mile view of Pennsylvania and New Jersey. The tower is open, with an admission charge, Tuesday-Saturday from 9 am to 5 pm, Sunday noon to 5 pm, with the tower road closing at 4:30. For more information call 215-493-4076.

Surrounding the tower the 100 acres of Bowman's Hill Wildflower Preserve offer endless hours of discovery on its 26 trails and habitat areas. The preserve was founded in 1934 by legislative act and through the years it has become acknowledged as the State Wildflower Preserve.

The Visitor and Resource Center houses the Twinleaf Shop, Sinkler Bird Observatory and Platt Bird Collection, and educational exhibits. Display gardens of showy native plants adjoin the entrance which is handicapped accessible. Daily wildflower walks are conducted from March through October. Special native plant sales are held on Mother's Day weekend and in September. They are both open on Saturday and Sunday from 10 am to 4 pm.. The grounds are open every day from 8:30 am until sunset. The Visitor Center is open from 9 am to 5 pm daily. For a complete schedule of events and activities call 215-862-2924 or write to Bowman's Hill Wildflower Preserve, P.O. Box 685, New Hope, PA 18938.

On the east side of River Road the Thompson-Neely House, now a museum, was requisitioned for

16 days during the 1776 campaign to serve as headquarters for Gen. Lord Sterling, Capt. Wm. Washington, Capt. James Moore and Lieutenant James Monroe. Lieutenant Monroe, then a boy of 18, was wounded capturing a strategic cannon in the Battle of Trenton but lived to serve the country as its fifth president. The earliest section of the house dates to 1702 and at the time of the Revolution was a structure one room deep and two stories high. Today in the museum you will see items contributed by local families, including the descendants of the Thompson-Neely's.

On Aquetong Road, just north of the park, one comes to the home and studio of the late George Nakashima Woodworker, S. A. Certainly Bucks County's most respected craftsman, for nearly fifty years he designed and produced his extraordinary works in wood, which transcend their description as "furniture," at the studio in Solebury. His artistry and philosophy are carried on today under the guidance of his wife, Marion, daughter, Mira, and son, Kevin. Like her father, Mira Nakashima-Yarnall's formal train-

Aaron Phillips 1756 mill, site of the Phillips Mill Art Exhibition. Photo: Martin E. Kennedy

ing was as an architect. She served as her father's assistant from 1970 and continues his design work with the same devotion to "nature's art" revealed through masterful woodworking. The showrooms at 293 Aquetong Road are open on Saturdays from 1 to 4:30 pm, except on holidays.

Returning to New Hope and following River Road north takes you to the tiny hamlet of Phillips Mill, named for the grist mill built in 1756 by Aaron Phillips. The mill was operated by four generations of the Phillips family until 1894 when the mill, race, miller's house, and adjoining farm were sold to Dr. George M. Marshall, a Philadelphia surgeon who described the site as "suggesting something classical, if not Greek." Marshall convinced his good friend, painter William Lathrop, to rent the miller's house across the road from the mill. Taken with the beauty of the area, Lathrop bought the house the next year. With this move the seed was plant-

ed for the New Hope art colony.

In 1898, Edward Redfield settled a few miles north in Center Bridge, because it was, he said, "a place where an independent, self-sufficient man could make a living from the land, bring up a family and still paint as he saw fit."

In 1907, Daniel Garber came to Solebury to live along the Cuttalossa Creek. Over the years Garber transformed his property into an American equivalent of Monet's Giverny, complete with sheep, goats, and other animals.

These three honored landscape painters were teachers as well as the first generation of Pennsylvania Impressionists. They were visited by friends and students who shared their admiration for the beauty of the surrounding countryside and the art community swelled rapidly. Among the many painters who visited and returned to stay were Henry B. Snell, William Taylor, Charles Rosen, Robert Spencer, and George Sotter. The canal towpath and the narrow strip of land between the river and canal held a special lure for the landscape painters and by the 1920s it was lined with artist's studios all the way from New Hope to Lumberville.

Morgan Colt, architect, artist and designer, came to the area in 1908. He lived on the towpath where he rebuilt the studio next to the Lathrop's house. Next, he completed the "old English" buildings that made up his Gothic Shops and lend a distinctive character to the hamlet. Today's Inn at Phillips Mill and the adjoining buildings are Colt's wonderful legacy to Solebury Township.

In 1928 a group of local artists headed by William Taylor met to consider buying the mill with the idea that it would give the art community a place to exhibit. In 1929 the mill was purchased for $5,000 by the Phillips Mill Community Association which initially held two exhibits a year as well as dances, plays, lectures, dinners, and concerts. William Lathrop was the first president of the association, with Ruth Folinsbee, wife of painter John Folinsbee, as vice president. 125 paintings and sculptures, all by members of the association, comprised the first Phillips Mill Art Exhibition in 1929. Among the members exhibiting that year were Garber, Redfield, Lathrop, Bredin, Snell, Sotter, Folinsbee, Coppedge, Baum, and Nunnamaker.

Seventy-two years later, the 2001 Phillips Mill Exhibition will be held from September 22 through October 28. It is open

Solebury Friends Meeting from behind. Photo: Martin E. Kennedy

Charles H. Mueller Co., bulb specialist, is a must-see sea of color in the spring. Photo: Martin E. Kennedy

every day from 1 to 5 pm with a small admission charge. Groups are encouraged to visit and should make advance arrangements by writing the Phillips Mill Community Association, P.O. Box 1, New Hope, PA 18938 or by calling 215-862-0582. See the calendar of events for other activities at Phillips Mill, including an annual photography exhibition, theatrical events, periodic special events, and Silver Dollar Production's annual Holiday Songfest in early December.

Going back to the intersection of River Road and Phillips Mill Road, today's Hotel du Village, a country inn with a fine restaurant, inhabits the old Holmquist School, started as a young woman's academy in 1917 by Miss Karline Holmquist. In 1925, a few miles up the road the Solebury School for boys was opened by Arthur Washburn, Robert Shaw,

writer Laurie Erskine and Julian Lathrop, William Lathrop's son. In 1949 the two schools merged with Solebury continuing today as a coeducational school.

A detour down Ely Road takes you to the Rosade Bonsai Studio, founded in 1970 by internationally recognized Bonsai teacher and lecturer, F. Chase Rosade. It is a center for learning the art of Bonsai and its permanent collection in the arboretum is one of the largest private collections of Bonsai in the country. Chase Rosade and his wife Solita, also a Bonsai expert, teach and lecture on the subject all over the world and offer a full schedule of classes, lectures, workshops and seminars at the studio for novices and advanced students of the art.

The studio is open Friday-Sunday from 11 am to 5 pm or by appointment during the week and in January. For a schedule of classes

and events write to Rosade Bonsai Studio, 6912 Ely Road, New Hope, PA 18938; 215-862-5925; or visit www.rosadebonsai.com.

The village of Solebury, at the Junction of Phillips Mill Road and Route 263, marked its 300th year September 6th, 1981. It was on that date that William Penn granted a deed to Nathaniel Harding, a basket maker of London, for 500 acres encompassing what is the village today. Like so many of the early deed holders, Harding never settled the land, and it was John Dawson, who bought the land from Harding's heirs, who is believed to have been the first settler in 1719.

The one room school house at the corner of Route 263 and Sugan Road was built in 1755 and

The towpath north of Phillips Mill. Photo: Martin E. Kennedy

St. Phillips Chapel was built as a one-room schoolhouse in 1864. Photo: Martin E. Kennedy

The pond and out buildings at Cutalossa Farm welcomes families who come to feed the animals.

Zebulon Pike, for whom Pike's Peak was named, was a student at the school for a brief time.

Continue past the school and turn right at the third intersection if you enjoy idyllic country. The road runs along the Cuttalossa Creek and eventually down to the river at Lumberville. This is the area where painter Daniel Garber lived midway between Sugan Road and the river. Today his home is Cuttalossa Farm, which raises baby doll sheep and is a favorite place for families to bring their children to feed the animals.

The Bucks County Conservancy, today the Heritage Conservancy, was incorporated in 1958 by a group of residents foreseeing the potentially rapid growth of the area. It provides a medium for the preservation of open space—particularly stream valleys, flood plains, and woodlands.

An affiliate of the conservancy since 1969, the Honey Hollow Watershed in Solebury is the first area in America to be treated as a watershed unit for the management of its natural ecology. The project was instituted in 1939 by six farmers whose lands were part of Penn's grants. In 1969 the Honey Hollow Watershed was named a National Historic Landmark.

The Bucks County Audubon Society, founded in 1969, is dedicated to conserving wildlife and habitats, promoting awareness of environmental concerns, educating the community about the interdependence of humans and their world, and furthering the wise use of land, air and water. Their major emphasis is environmental education, which is carried out through the operation of the Honey Hollow Environmental Education Center, located on the Honey Hollow Watershed National Historic Landmark. The Audubon Visitor Center, at 2877 Creamery Road, just off Route 263, is open on Saturdays from 9 am to 5 pm and on Sundays from noon to 5 pm. The site includes five miles of walking trails, bird

blinds, and environmental and natural history displays.

Earth Week is always celebrated by the Society and its annual native tree and plant sale is a big event. The Society has a full schedule of activities including natural history walks, workshops, field trips, and naturalist training programs. For more information call 215-297-5880.

Traveling west from New Hope on Route 202 you pass the Great Spring, or Aquetong Spring as it was called by the Lenni-Lenape. The spring came to be called Ingham's Spring for the family that owned the surrounding land from 1747 until 1849. The spring at one time provided sufficient power to run a paper mill, fulling mill, two merchant mills, four saw mills and an oil mill.

Continuing toward Lahaska, at Aquetong Road a detour to the right will take you to Rice's Sale, where, each Tuesday and Saturday, one may join the crowds flocking to this farmers market and flea market.

The Township has, over the years, been the home of many nationally known members of the literary and theatrical worlds. It was the combination of seclusion and proximity to New York and Philadelphia that attracted such luminaries as Moss Hart, Sam and Bella Spewack, Paul Bowles and Sheldon Cheney, among many others. Today the Township, as well as the entire area, is sought out by visitors and new residents for much the same reasons.

Heart of the home

Fine Crafts for the Home and Garden

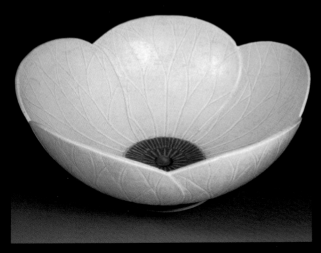

28 S. Main St.
New Hope, PA 18938

215.862.1880
heartofthehome.com

98

Michener Museum: "Art and Soul" of Bucks County

by Doris Brandes

In 1988, with the support of many dedicated citizens, the James A. Michener Art Museum opened in Doylestown as an independent, non-profit cultural institution dedicated to preserving, interpreting and exhibiting the art and cultural heritage of the Bucks County region. The museum is named for Doylestown's most famous son, the Pulitzer Prize winning writer and supporter of the arts who had first dreamed of a regional art museum in the early 1960s. Today the museum prides itself on being the "Art and Soul" of Bucks County.

In November of 1999, the James A. Michener Art Museum publicly announced the largest single gift in the institution's 11-year history. Marguerite and Gerry Lenfest gave the museum an extensive collection of fifty-nine paintings by important regional artists of the Pennsylvania Impressionist School. It is now home to the finest collection of Pennsylvania Impressionist paintings in public or private hands.

Ensconced in the museum's walled, lush "back yard" is an outdoor gallery, the Patricia D. Pfundt Sculpture Garden. Sculptures are on view in a natural setting that pays homage to the Bucks County landscape which has inspired countless artists. The museum hosts nationally touring special exhibitions and also showcases important regional artists.

George Nakashima (1905-1990) was internationally known for his innovative furniture designs as

Unveiling of Edward W. Redfield's painting, **The Burning of Center Bridge,** *at the Museum's 10th anniversary celebration in 1998. Photo Whitney Photography, courtesy of the James A. Michener Art Museum.*

In the sculpture garden, Woman Washing Her Hair, *by Joe Jenks, black granite, 1954. Gift from the grandson of the artist. Photo courtesy of the James A. Michener Art Museum.*

well as his meditative architectural interiors based on ancient principals of Japanese design. He created the Nakashima studio in Bucks County after World War II and soon established himself as one of the premier American woodworkers of the 20th Century. The Nakashima reading room is a permanent installation designed by his daughter Mira Nakashima-Yarnall. During the summer of 2001 a special display of George Nakashima and the Modernist Movement will examine Nakashima's influence on contemporary art and design. It features a core group of Nakashima works as well

as related works by several major European and American designers.

Another major exhibition featuring Abstract Expressionist paintings from the 1950s and '60s as well as recent acquisitions of works by regional artists not previously exhibited at the Michener opens on July 14 and continues through October 7, 2001.

The Education Department has a mission to involve the community in the visual arts through a diverse program which seeks to develop a lifelong involvement with the arts. In addition to school-year programs, there are a variety of summer activities for children on and off site. There is also serious attention devoted to inspiring people of all ages to become better acquainted with the wonderful collection. With each new exhibition, curators, historians, authors, artists, and sometimes the family of regional artists, are part of planned programs. On-going lectures, demonstrations, gallery tours,

continued on page 102

George Nakashima, Conoid Cushion Chair, *1961, walnut, hickory, cotton and upholstery. H. 33.5 x W. 34.25 x D. 35.25 inches. Collection of George Nakashima, Woodworker. From the exhibition, "George Nakashima and the Modernish Movement".*

101

Girl scouts "scouting out the art door", display their art-to-wear made at art camp. Photo courtesy of the James A. Michener Art Museum.

videos, and special events help the participant understand the meaning behind the works on view. Frequently the acquired knowledge leads to further interest for individuals, in which case, the Art Research Library can be accessed by appointment.

One of the most fascinating areas of the museum is a separate wing called "Creative Bucks County," It houses a multi-media, interactive exhibition which brings to life the work of the many visual artists, authors, playwrights, lyricists, and composers who have lived and worked in Bucks County. It includes individual displays on twelve of the county's best known artists, a video theater, and a comprehensive computerized database containing information on hundreds of Bucks County artists, both living and deceased. Just to name a few, the list includes Pearl Buck, Oscar Hammerstein, Moss Hart, George S. Kaufman, Edward Redfield, and Edward

Hicks. Many of these artists gravitated to Bucks County to escape the rigors of New York. Most of the painters were drawn by the bucolic setting, the farms, the river, and the special light by which they painted in the prized impressionist style. The composers, lyricists, and writers were drawn by the closeness to New York and the accumulating cultural community.

The Museum Shop specializes in acquiring the work of local artists. In addition to a wide range of books by/about Bucks County residents, the shop also sells local handmade crafts, from jewelry to pottery. Children especially love to buy items to remind them of their visit, and there is something in every price range to bring home. Adjacent to the shop is a small, but convenient café. Lunches are reasonable and so well thought of that locals frequently stop in just 'to do' lunch. The café is also open on Wednesday evenings for light fare.

Since the Museum opened in 1988, it has grown and developed into an important cultural center in Bucks County and beyond. Located in the heart of Bucks County, it is housed in a splendidly renovated historic site that formerly served as the county jail from 1884-1986. James A Michener liked to tell the story about his youth, growing up in Doylestown. "They used to say to me, "James, if you don't behave yourself, you're likely to end up in jail!" "Well, here I am", he proudly boasted at the dedication of the museum which bears his name.

Sticks

Handpainted original furnishings and sculpture

How to Furnish Your Home & Office in Style that Survives the Latest Fads

For the past two decades, this solid oak roll top desk has proven itself in style, quality, form, and function. It's been one of our best sellers since 1980, and still is. Maybe it's the way it's built. Maybe it's the design. And maybe it's the price tag. You're invited to see for yourself.

Brass & Oak Gallery

Furnishings for Home & Office

6 Penn's Purchase, Route 202, Lahaska, PA
215-794-7254   **www.brassandoakgallery.com**
OPEN DAILY • Delivery in PA, NJ, NY

Cento per Cento Italiano

(100% Italian)

Murano Glass   Venetian Glass   Coppers of Italy   Music
L'Erberio for the Bath   Gourmet Foods   Leather Accessories

CASA CASALE

Peddler's Village Shop #2 Lahaska PA ❖ 215-794-1474

Bringing the Outdoors Inside

One-of-a-kind hand painted indoor and outdoor furniture
in garden motifs from orchids and ferns
to butterflies and birdhouses.

Potting Benches ❦ Gliders ❦ Gazebos
Tuffits ❦ Hand Blown Glass from London
European Throws ❦ Silk Pillows

*Hand thrown bathroom sinks as featured in Country Living Magazine
and elegant marble sinks and counters.*

Shop #43, *Peddlers Village* Lahaska, PA 18931 ❦ 215-794-9969
www.ePaintedLady.com

The Place Where Every Day
Feels Like December 25th

Christmas & Candles

Our selection of the world's most beautiful Christmas collectibles
makes every day feel like December 25th. You'll find Christopher
Radko, Old World Christmas and Lynn Haney, just to name a few.
You'll also discover Yankee, Colonial, Williamsburg and Village
candles in every size, shape and fragrance at the very best prices.
Visit today for that Christmas feeling now.

Pine
Wreath & Candle Ltd.

A Radko Rising Star Store

Shop #70 at the Grist Mill *Peddler's Village*, Lahaska, PA 18931
215-794-7060 ▪ Toll Free 877-333-6968 ▪ Open Every Day

The Area Guide Gallery

Oranges, oil on canvas, H. 16 x W. 20 inches.

Lisa Mahan, *New Hope, PA*
Lisa Mahan works mainly in oils with a primary focus on color and light. Her subject matter ranges from the figure, interiors, landscapes, to the still life. Whether the scene is a scattering of plates and fruit on a tin-top table or a narrative urban scene at dusk, her focus is on the light at that particular time of day and its effect on the colors in the scene. Since 1996, Mahan has exhibited at numerous juried and invitational shows throughout the area, and is a founding member of Artist's Gallery in Lambertville, where her work can be seen regularly.

Jerry Cable, *Flemington, NJ*
Jerry Cable was born in northeastern Ohio and discovered his passion for art at an early age. Today his creative spirit thrives in a Hunterdon County studio, nurtured by the rich landscapes and historic buildings of the Delaware River countryside. Resonating with luminous rhythms of light and color, his paintings evoke mood and emotion. Since 1995, Cable has shown in 32 group exhibitions and has had 9 one-man shows. His works are in private and public collections across the United States and Canada. He is represented by Canal Frame-Crafts Gallery, Washington Crossing, PA and Travis Gallery, New Hope, PA.

December Solstice, oil on canvas, H. 16 x W. 22 inches.

Six Among Many:

A sampling of the range and professionalism of the area art community.

Rose Fleece Roost, oil on canvas, H. 30 x W. 44 inches.

Timothy Martin,
Sergeantsville, NJ
Timothy Martin first gained widespread recognition in 1993 when he was selected by Tiffany & Company to display artwork in their windows on Fifth Avenue. He says of his paintings, "I believe my interpretation of objects out of flowers, plants and animals is perfectly natural, no pun intended." Since the late 1990s, his work has been reproduced by fine art publishers as posters, giclee prints and note cards. A 1994-95 New Jersey State Council on the Arts Fellowship grantee, since 1998 Martin has participated in the *Inizio* exhibition mounted by the Phoenix Arts Group in Arizona. In 1999, Martin launched his own web site at www.timothymartin.com, which features reproductions as well as original gouaches and oils.

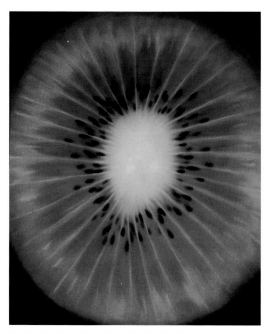

Untitled (Radiant), oil on linen, H. 78 x W. 66 inches.

Illia Barger, *Stockton, NJ*
Illia Barger was the 1999 recipient of the prestigious Pollock-Krasner Foundation Award for excellence in painting. In the same year, the exhibition, *Illia Barger: Sacrament,* was held at The Cathedral Church of Saint John the Divine in New York City to celebrate five paintings installed behind the High Altar and a site-specific, 48 foot long work-on-paper created for the central nave of the Cathedral. Barger has exhibited in Connecticut, New York, and New Jersey, and her work is in many private and public collections including the Greek Consulate in New York and the Selma Burke Museum of Art in Winston Salem, North Carolina. Her work can be found on www.artspan.com.

Jane Gilday,

Wrightstown, PA
Jane Gilday is a painter, musician, and writer, who has been based in the New Hope-Lambertville area for the last decade. She works in three primary directions: landscapes, decorative pattern pieces, and illuminations. Gilday paints onsite and from memory, with most landscapes emerging as syntheses of scenes seen and re-combined into imaginary, but

First Day of Spring, 2001, acrylic on wood, H. 31 x W. 21 inches.

archetypal, vistas. The "illuminated" aspect appears on frames, made by the artist, which are an integral part of the finished work. In the ancient tradition, frames are engraved, decorated, and often gold-leafed and glazed with washes of earth-tones. Gilday is represented by the Hrefna Jonsdottir Gallery in Lambertville, NJ.

Glen D. Harren,

Holicong, PA
Glen D. Harren describes himself as "an artist that responds in color and shapes to the world around me. I seek the extraordinary aspects of everyday life, whether in the color of a landscape or the simple dignity of the human form." Harren has exhibited widely in the greater Philadelphia area in group and solo exhibitions, and is well represented in private and public collections. The recipient of may awards, Harren's *Egg Whites in Lambertville*, shown here, won first prize in the Artsbridge at Prallsville Annual Juried Exhibition in 1999. His work can be seen at www.HarrenFineArt.com.

Egg Whites in Lambertville, oil on linen, H. 56 x W. 50 inches.

110

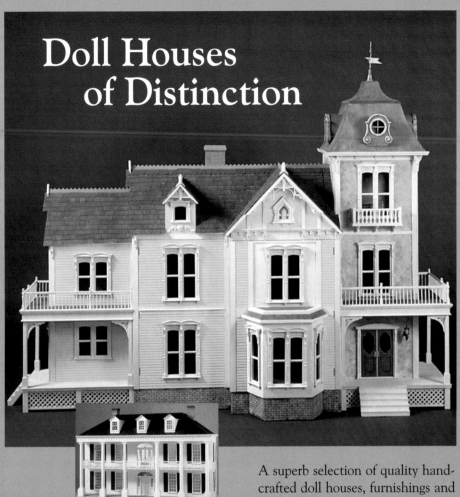

Doll Houses of Distinction

A superb selection of quality hand-crafted doll houses, furnishings and accessories by famous artisans of the miniature world for the discriminating collector as well as the beginner.

WORKSHOPS
THROUGHOUT THE YEAR

Miniature Curiosities

Shop #55, *Peddler's Village* Lahaska, PA 18931
215-794-9150 □ www.miniaturecuriosities.com

Down the hill from Lahaska's shopping centers. Photo: Martin E. Kennedy

LAHASKA

Traveling south along the York Road, Route 202, takes one over the same ground covered by the earliest travelers on the Swift-Sure Stage. The route takes you first to the village of Lahaska, through Holicong and on to Buckingham at the crossroads of Routes 202, 263 and 413. This short stretch of road offers an incredible assortment of experiences, from shopping, dining, and wine tasting, to treasure and history hunting. The four miles of road from New Hope to Lahaska are dotted with old stone houses, many of them inhabited by antiques shops. It is one of the first areas in Bucks County to be nationally known as an antique shopper's paradise.

The village of Lahaska is at the boundary of Solebury and Buckingham Township, which is the largest township in Bucks County and includes the villages of Lahas-

ka, Holicong, Buckingham Village, Buckingham Valley, Spring Valley, Mechanicsville, Forest Grove, Mozart, Wycombe, and Pineville. Geographically the township is primarily rolling fields and woodlands with Buckingham Mountain as its most striking topographical feature. The mountain is 545 feet above sea level and 250 feet higher than the surrounding valleys. The township's first settlers were English Quakers who came to the area around 1700 and settled on lands patented to William Penn, whose English home county of Buckinghamshire gives it its name.

As early as 1705 Lahaska was the site of the first Buckingham Friends Meeting, built to serve the residents of Buckingham and Solebury. In 1731 a second, larger building was erected and served until it burned in 1768. The

For Those Who Know That Happy Feet Make the Rest of You Feel Good

Swedish clogs are famous for their comfort and superior arch support, which in turn is good for your back, good for your legs, and of course, good for your feet. That's why people who spend long hours standing on their feet wear our clogs. So come in and make your feet happy. You'll soon discover that the rest of you will feel good too.

Available in sizes for kids, women, and men in a wide selection of fashionable styles and colors.

Built in 1769, Buckingham Friends Meeting served as a hospital during the Revolution. Photo: Martin E. Kennedy

current meeting house was built in 1769 and was used as a hospital during the Revolutionary War. On the grounds, the site of the original meeting house is marked, and the cemetery houses a "Strangers Plot", the resting place for many of the revolutionary soldiers who died there. Also on the grounds is a stone "mounting block" used by colonials to help them into the high farm wagons that transported the family to services over rough, sometimes muddy roads. Adjacent to the meeting house is the Buckingham Friends School, built in 1786, and still in operation as a private elementary school.

A post office opened in Lahaska in 1874, at which time the town was comprised of 15 houses, a store, hotel, coach factory and a few shops. The face of Lahaska changed little in the 80 odd years

that followed, except that stately old houses and barns were converted into antique shops with the owners living over the store, and the village became known as an antique center. When Earl Jamison created Peddler's Village in the early 60s, he set the tone for the modern growth of the village with clusters of shops springing up in old and new buildings.

From its beginning as the chicken farm of this writer's childhood, Peddler's Village has grown to cover over 42 acres of Solebury and Buckingham Townships. In the early days Mr. Jamison continued to operate the family business at Bountiful Acres, which had expanded from a typical roadside farm stand into a produce, plant and landscaping business. It was not at all unusual in those days to find him on a summer evening working on the kernel of the magnificent gardens you see in the village today. With the growth of the Village a series of country festivals were born that offer a special event for almost every month of the year. And the initiation of the Peddler's Village Dinner Theatre added yet another reason to visit.

While Peddler's Village was emerging, Lahaska was growing and changing beside it. More antique shops moved into the houses, barns, and small outbuildings that lined the short stretch of Route 202 that passes through the village. The two largest properties in the village faced each other across Route 202. On the north side of the road, Sterling & Son Antiques filled the barn while the family lived in the house on the old farm property. In the 1970s, the son, Wayne Sterling, began to develop the property into the Sterling Center, and the family business was joined, in renovated farm buildings, by antique dealers from around the area.

Across the road the second of the two large properties, which included a collection of old buildings, became Mary Fisher's Flea Market in the 60s. Through the 70s both properties grew; shops were added to the Sterling Center, and Mary Fisher's had become the Lahaska Antique Center with the addition of more dealers in a newly-built carriage barn and expanded flea market.

Just down the road, The Lahaska Antique Courte was created in three venerable structures in 1978. At the time the stretch of

Village guardian: Henry Harvey's tin man.

117

A lamp post marks an entry to Penn's Purchase.

The pond at Penn's Purchase.

Route 202 that runs through the village was a veritable antiques alley. All that has changed with only a handful of antiques shops still in Lahaska. The Courte continues to prevail in the rooms of the 1814 House, The Gilmore House, and the central barn, which had been the original home of the Midway Fire Company. The collection of twelve tasteful antiques shops are owned by professional dealers, many of them members of the respected Bucks County Antiques Dealers Association, who continue to offer a broad spectrum of American, Scandinavian, and continental antiques and artifacts, jewelry and fine art.

In 1985, Herbert Farber purchased both the Sterling property and the flea market and renamed them Penn's Market and Penn's Market II. While he made substantial improvements to the property, the mix of shops and the flea market remained basically unchanged for nearly a decade.

Then, in the fall of 1994, Lahaska underwent the biggest change since the inception of Peddler's Village. With Penn's Market II closed, ground breaking ceremonies took place on October 4th for the construction of a factory outlet village, to be called Penn's Purchase. After nearly ten years as the owner of Penn's Market, Mr. Farber witnessed a changing economic time during which many of Lahaska's antique dealers moved to nearby Lambertville, New Jersey. Working with local architects, George Donovan & Associates, and Gilmore

Associates, Inc., engineers, the project was designed to resemble a quaint village, complete with a pond, gazebo and clock tower. Penn's Purchase had its grand opening on Memorial Day weekend in 1995 with 35 outlets carrying brand name merchandise.

Linking old Lahaska to the new Penn's Purchase is the "Vanderbilt House," the only old structure incorporated into the overall plan. The 1880s cream Victorian house, once a boy's school, became known as Vanderbilt House in the 1940s when its owner purchased architectural antiques from the Vanderbilt estate in Long Island and added them to the building.

An exciting new space for the Harvey Galleries, the house looks down on the complex and Henry Harvey's Tin Man, perched on the porch roof, is the sentinel for the village. The move from Penn's Market has given the Harvey Galleries not only space for an outdoor sculpture garden, but the inspiration to turn each of the ground floor rooms into a gallery of its own. One room invites you to sit in a full-size, working time machine, and the largest has become the studio where you can enjoy coffee, chat with the artist and watch raw metal come to life as a piece of sculpture.

Just past the Lahaska Antique Courte, the Inn at Lahaska and McGowans' Buckingham Mountain Brewing Company, Bucks County's first micro brewery and brew pub, were also 1995 additions to the village. The inn dates to 1885, while the restaurant

appears to have been a slaughterhouse in earlier times. When it came time to find a name for their new enterprise, the McGowans dipped into the Area Guide Book for help. The restaurant's rear windows look out on Buckingham Mountain so that was a natural for the name; and Albert Large (see Buckingham) and his Wolf Rocks home appear on the beer menu as Hermit Albert's Pale Ale and Wolf Rocks Amber Ale.

Town square clock in Penn's Purchase.

119

Just south of Lahaska. Photo: Martin E. Kennedy

At the foot of the hill leaving Lahaska, a detour to the left takes you into horse country.

If you enjoy beautiful country, detour off Route 202 and lose yourself in rolling farmland dotted with restored 18th century stone houses and horse farms. Following Street Road into the country, one of these is now the Whitehall Inn, which holds three special events during the year that are open to the public. April brings a Chocolate High Tea; May a Baroque Tea; and June a Strawberry Tea. Each event is an elegant afternoon tea accompanied by chamber music.

Going back to Lahaska, Peddler's Village continues to grow, and, after 38 years, to change. From the very beginning Earl Jamison was aware that architecture and landscaping would be of major importance in establishing the identity of his village. Miles of herringbone brick paths were laid winding around this unique village. A number of local 18th century structures were purchased and moved to ideal locations sur-rounding the village green. By 1977, Peddler's Village had expanded to 42 shops and three restaurants. A consummate and creative entrepreneur, Earl Jamison and the village were soon recognized with landscaping awards and named one of the outstanding attractions in Pennsylvania by the state.

In 1986 Mr. Jamison purchased the Buttonwood Inn on the corner of Route 202 and Street Road and in November of 1988 ground was broken for the expansion that created The Spotted Hog, a 250 seat restaurant, 30 rooms for the Golden Plough, and more specialty shops on Street Road. Completed in 1989, the new street scene reflects his commitment to Bucks County history and is probably assumed by visitors to have been there for centuries.

In 1992, another round of expansion on the north side of Route 263 brought the number of shops to 75 and added an antique

121

Peddler's Village

...a beautiful place to shop and dine!

75 Quality Shops & Restaurants & the Golden Plough Inn

The Cock 'n Bull
Jenny's Bistro
The Spotted Hog
Hart's Tavern
Peddler's Pub
Casey's
Opening in May! The Painted Pony
European Conection
House of Coffee

Wearable Art • Specialty Foods
Jewelry & Fashion Accessories
Casual Wear • Women's Apparel
Home Furnishings & Accessories
One-of-a-kind Finds • Toys & Hobbies
Infant & Children's Clothing & Furniture
Kitchen Wares • Leather Goods
Collectibles • Footwear • Books
Dolls & Doll Houses • Bird Houses
Hand Crafted Works of Art
Paint-Your-Own Pottery

New! Opening this May! **Giggleberry Fair!**
Our new family "edu-tainment" center!

Route 202 & 263 • Lahaska, Bucks County, PA
www.peddlersvillage.com • (215) 794-4000

TAKE A RIDE BACK IN TIME ON OUR ANTIQUE CAROUSEL

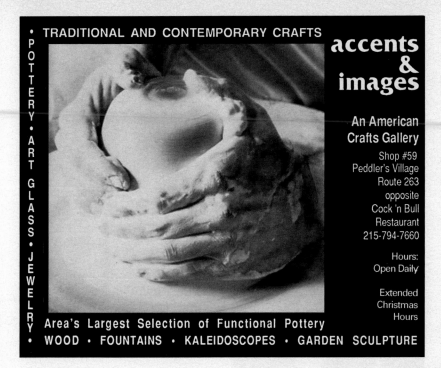
carousel. In 1998 the original carousel was replaced with one that fulfills Mr. Jamison's dream of owning a grander, more colorful carousel. His vision was to have a carousel that was fun, exciting, and visually stimulating to children, and at the same time elegant and appealing to the adult enthusiast.

In January 1998 he found an antique carousel in deplorable condition, stripped of its original figures, that he believed could be returned to its past opulent glory. With only six months to complete the restoration, Mr. Jamison hired local and national craftsmen to execute a project that would normally take a minimum of two years without replacing the figures.

Philadelphia Toboggan Company Carousel #59 was built in Germantown, Pennsylvania in 1922 and was one of the grandest carousels produced during the Golden Age of the Carousel. It was one of 89 created by the company, of which only 26 still exist. In storage for fifteen years, P.T.C. #59 was the company's showpiece at the 1922 National Association of Amusement Parks convention in Chicago. Originally installed in Schuylkill Park in Pottsville, Pennsylvania, it moved three times in its active life; first to Worcester, Massachusetts, then to Oklahoma City, Oklahoma, and finally to Panama City, Florida.

Master Carver Ed Roth from Long Beach, California was commissioned to carve 46 figures using the techniques employed by carvers at the turn-of-the-century.

His work for #59 was the subject of a documentary filmed for the Learning Channel. The figures include some of the greatest carousel figures from the past: Illions Supreme-style outside row jumpers with delicate manes and real horsehair tails, a Muller-styled Armored King Horse, and a rooster and bandana-bibbed pig personalized for Peddler's Village.

Several antique figures from Mr. Jamison's personal collection are featured alongside the newly carved figures. Reflecting his country roots, the crown of the carousel is adorned with hand-painted tulips and other flowers, and the shields feature restored oil paintings of farm landscapes.

The past four years have brought many changes. If you

Annual scarecrow contest. Photo: Peddler's Village

thought you knew the village but haven't visited recently there are pleasant surprises. Old shops are in new spaces, old spaces have been transformed, and the latest addition is an elevator in the Cock 'n Bull Restaurant which makes the second floor dining rooms handicapped accessible.

A new addition to the village last year was an operating windmill. It replaced the sand sculpture that had been a fixture each spring since 1997 when the village celebrated its 35th anniversary.

The Peddler's Village concept of free special events began more than three decades ago and these special weekends are occasions that draw thousands of people, many of whom return year after year.

This year's 32nd annual Straw-

At the Apple Festival. Photo: Peddler's Village

berry, Flower and Garden Festival was held on the first weekend in May. Highlights of the festival included strawberries—of course—in all forms imaginable, over forty crafters selling their work, the perennial pie-eating contest, and a traditional Maypole dance on the village green by the Dance Theatre of Pennsylvania. Peddler Pete, the horsey mascot of the village, and the Stiltwalker strolled the grounds greeting visitors and the sounds of music, from a brass quintet to a bluegrass band, filled the air throughout the weekend.

The holiday season in Peddler's Village opens each year with the Grand Illumination on the Friday before Thanksgiving. And grand it is when the switch is thrown and over 400,000 lights transform the village into an enchanted holiday world. Hot cider, warmed over an open fire in an old-fashioned kettle, toasted marshmallows, and the sounds of children's choirs add to the magic of the lights. The season's celebrations continue with twilight carriage

Winter in Peddler's Village. Photo: Peddler's Village.

rides, a fruit wreath seminar, country Christmas weekend, and weekend visits with Santa.

The calendar of special events, month by month, follows: January-April, Quilt Competition and Display; May, Strawberry, Flower and Garden Festival; June, Fine Art and Contemporary Crafts Show; July, Teddy Bear's Picnic; September, Scarecrow Festival and Jack-o-Lantern and Gourd Art Contest; September-October, Scarecrow Competition and Display;

Spring tulips are an annual attraction in the Village. Photo: Peddler's Village

November, Apple Festival; November-January, Gingerbread House Competition and Display; December, Christmas Festival.

Growing out of the festivals, the Peddler's Village competitions, Quilt in January, Scarecrow in September, and Gingerbread House in November, are popular with contestants and the public alike. If you are inspired to try your hand at any of these arts, the village offers seminars to help you get started.

For a complete schedule of these and other events throughout the year, as well as entry forms for the various competitions (which, by the way, offer great prizes), call 215-794-4000, or visit their web site at www.peddlersvillage.com.

When it opened in June 2001, Giggleberry Fair became the latest addition to the village. Billed as "pure edu-tainment," this new family oriented attraction combines two new components, Discovery Land, filled with educational activities and interactive games, and Giggleberry Mountain, the area's largest indoor obstacle course, with the popular Grand Carousel. For more information on Giggleberry Fair call 215-794-8960.

Leaving Lahaska and continuing down the hill, a turn left on Byecroft Road will take you past the fields of Paxson Farm that are the pastures for its fine thoroughbred horses. Returning to Route 202/263 and proceeding south will bring you to the village of Holicong, midway between Lahaska and Buckingham.

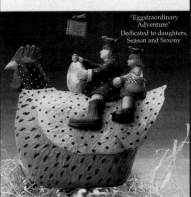

The gazebo on the village green.

LAHASKA • HOLICONG • BUCKINGHAM MAP

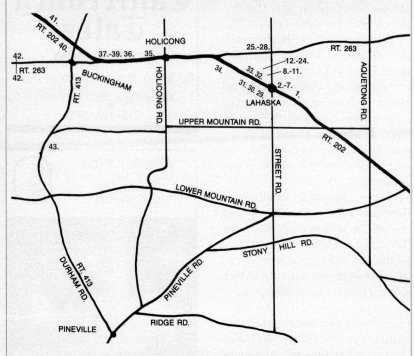

Lahaska-Holicong-Buckingham Map Key

1. 202 Market
2. The Courtyard - Peddler's Village
3. Jenny's Bistro
4. The Creative Child
5. Glass Masters
6. Pewter Plus
7. Casa Casale
8. Merchant's Row - Peddler's Village
9. Golden Plough Inn
10. The Spotted Hog
11. Zephyr Gallery
12. Village Green - Peddler's Village
13. Artisans Gallery
14. Canterbury Tales Book Shoppe
15. Cock 'n Bull Restaurant
16. Cookery Ware Shop
17. Country Accents
18. Creative Hands
19. Knobs 'n Knockers
20. Monroe Salt Works
21. Painted Lady
22. Peddler's Village Dinner Theatre
23. Pine Wreath & Candle, Ltd.
24. Upstairs Gallery
25. Wagon House Shops - Peddler's Village
26. Miniature Curiosities
27. Accents & Images
28. Sterling Leather
29. Coldwell Banker Hearthside Realtors
30. Penn's Purchase
31. Harvey Galleries
32. Penn's Purchase (across the road)
33. Brass & Oak Gallery
34. Scandinavian Touch
35. Country Homes
36. Union National Bank
37. Buckingham Green
38. Earth Foods
39. Bien Dormir
40. Baci Ristorante
41. Coldwell Banker Hearthside Realtors
42. None Such Farm and Market
43. Buckingham Valley Vineyards

Fabulous Leather...

Stone barn in Holicong.

HOLICONG

The tiny village of Holicong midway between Lahaska and Buckingham was significant to the Lenni-Lenape whose campsite at "Hollekonk" was located around a natural spring that still flows just off Holicong Road. The village took the name in 1881 when a post office was established there with J. Kirk serving as the first postmaster. In the 18th and 19th centuries it was a rural center with two schools, a tannery, a blacksmith's shop, a wheelwright's shop, a post office/general store, and a quarryman's house with a limekiln. The limekiln, which dates to 1732, is one of the few in the area that has been preserved.

Holicong is one of three villages in Buckingham Township that is listed on the National Register of Historic Places with Barley Sheaf Farm, c. 1740, as one of the eighteen structures included in its historic district. In 1936, the playwright and director, George S. Kaufman, bought the farm from Juliana Force, the director of New York's Whitney Museum. Kaufman called the farm Cherchez La Farm and was followed by a stream of Broadway personalities who came to Bucks County as visitors and summer residents. In the late 1970s the property was renamed Barley Sheaf Farm and opened as Bucks County's first bed and breakfast inn. With the opening of Ash Mill Farm in a 1790 manor house across the road from Barley Sheaf, Holicong became something of a 20th century bed and breakfast center.

A protected farm in Buckingham's award-winning agricultural preservation program.

BUCKINGHAM

Descending the hill out of Lahaska one views the Buckingham Valley with Buckingham Mountain in the distance. In 1775 Chief Isaac Still led his people, the last of the Lenni-Lenape in the area, off to settle along the Wabash River in what is now Indiana. As they departed, the chief announced to his people, "We are going far from war and rum." It is a sorry part of our history that both curses followed them.

During revolutionary times, Buckingham Mountain served as a hideout for the Doan outlaws, a notorious band of brothers and associates, who robbed patriots and worked as spies for the British. It is reported that on the night of Washington's move on Trenton, Moses Doan, the leader of the gang, and his cousin, Abraham, had sized up the situation and crossed at Morrisville to deliver a message warning Colonel Rahl, the Hessian commander at Trenton, of the imminent attack. As the story goes, the Doans found the colonel playing cards at a friend's house and delivered their message but it was never opened until the next day when it was found on the colonel's dead body.

The Lenni-Lenape name for Buckingham Mountain was Papcahesing, which translated means "at the place of the woodpecker." The mountain's major natural attraction is the Wolf Rocks, which

The General Greene Inn as it looked some 20 years ago.

fill a narrow, shallow gorge extending from the summit to the base on the steep northwest slope. A short distance below the summit the rocks were so arranged as to form a cave. An opening less than three feet square led to two small chambers, the larger being eight by ten feet wide and seven feet high. In this little rock home, Albert Large, the Hermit of Wolf Rocks, led the life of a recluse undiscovered for twenty years. The death of his mother, to whom he was devoted, and an unfortunate love affair drove him to the cave to forget and be forgotten. He was discovered living in the cave in 1858 when a passerby noticed smoke. Large made no attempt to conceal his identity and related some of his experiences to

his discoverers. One of the most fantastic was the story of being snowed in for six weeks. His discovery made the international papers of the day and turned Large into a celebrity. For a time he enjoyed the many visitors but slowly began to shun their attentions and returned to the life of a recluse.

The General Greene Inn in the village of Buckingham was built in 1752 by Henry Jamison who was granted a license that year for a "public house of entertainment." Jamison's widow married a man named Bogart and it was as Bogart's Tavern that the inn played an important role in the revolution. The first meeting of the Bucks County Committee for Safety was held there on July 21, 1775, and in 1776 it served as headquarters for General Nathaniel Greene. It was from Bogart's Tavern on December 10th that he dispatched the order to General Ewing to send "sixteen Durham boats and flats down to McKonkey's Ferry." These were the boats that Washington used for the Christmas crossing.

The Buckingham Boarding School was founded in 1830 by sisters, Martha Hampton and Hannah Lloyd. An 1832 advertisement for the school listed its curriculum as orthography, reading, writing, grammar, composition, geography, the use of globes, history, arithmetic, and elements of astronomy and natural philosophy. The cost per quarter was $23 with an additional 75¢ charge for fuel and candles.

By the spring in Spring Valley. Photo: Martin E. Kennedy

Continuing east on Route 263 takes you past None Such Farm and on to Furlong. The 18th century farm had fallen on hard times when William H. Yerkes, Jr. came there as a tenant farmer in 1926 and found the Victorian farmhouse being used to store grain. He bought the property in 1932, establishing one of Bucks County's most successful agricultural ventures. For fifty years the farm sold sweet corn to wholesalers and their trademark, "None Such," became known for quality. Two sons, William III and John, followed their father, becoming Pennsylvania Master Farmers in 1983, and continue to operate the farm today. In 1998, the Yerkes brothers placed the 217 acre farm in the State Farmland Preservation Program protecting it permanently from development. None

Such Farm offers pick your own crops in season and the market, built in 1978, sells produce picked on the day and their own additive and antibiotic free beef, as well as a full selection of farm market produce and plants.

Back at the crossroads in Buckingham, following Route 202 toward Doylestown one descends a hill into the tiny crossroads village of Spring Valley. The site of several mills and a corn-drying kiln, a detour into the country either left or right off the highway is an aesthetically rewarding experience in an idyllic setting.

A detour south on Route 413 will take you to Buckingham Valley Vineyards and Winery. Founded in 1966 by Jerry and Kathy Forest, this small, family operated enterprise is the oldest commercial vineyard and winery in the

Delaware Valley and is dedicated to producing Bucks County's best estate-bottled vintage varietal wines. One of Pennsylvania's first farm wineries, the original 15 acres of predominately French-American vines have been augmented with 20 acres next door. Production is about 40,000 gallons a year, with all of their wines corked, capsuled and bottle aged before being deemed ready to sell.

In 1999 the winery produced its first sparkling wine under the label, Forest Cellars Methode Champenoise. It was bottled as a Natural and a Brut, and was blended from Vidal, Cayuga, and Chardonnay grapes. Its first year was timed to coincide with the millennium and in the future 10,000 bottles a year will be corked.

Buckingham Valley wines are sold only at the winery and a visit should include time for a self-guided tour which will show you a combination of traditional and modern methods of wine making, from gallons of wine aging in small oak casks to modern stainless steel pro-

cessing and bottling techniques. A visit during September's harvest offers the opportunity to see the crushing, destemming, and pressing that are the initial steps in the production of all wines.

In 1998 the Forest family was honored as the Outstanding Winery Family of the Year at the Wineries Unlimited trade show in Lancaster, Pennsylvania. The show, which is sponsored by Vineyard and Winery Magazine for wine makers and grape growers from east of the Rockies, gives the annual award to families that have demonstrated success, achievement and leadership in the wine industry.

The house by the bridge. Photo: Martin E. Kennedy

CENTER BRIDGE

Traveling north on Route 263 from Lahaska takes you back to the river at Center Bridge. This tiny community, first called Reading's Ferry, like so many others along the river took its original name from the first ferry operator, in this case Colonel John Reading. The ferry was opened sometime between 1704 and 1711 when it is first mentioned in public records. The first inn is believed to have been built by Captain Daniel Howell, Reading's son-in-law who ran the ferry from 1731 to 1770. The inn was later run by William Mitchell who was the last owner of the ferry from 1796 to 1813.

In 1811 the "Center Bridge Company" was chartered by both states and included William Mitchell among its stockholders. The ferry ceased operation and from that time both the town and

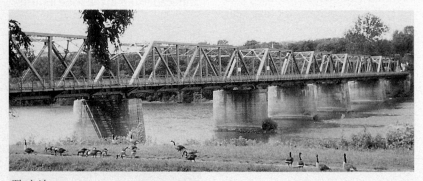

The bridge.

138

bridge became known as Center Bridge. The bridge opened in 1814 and was the first of three wooden covered bridges to span the river in this area. The bridge brought growth to the community and by 1871 the town had three blacksmiths, three carpenters, a physician, an undertaker, two wheelwrights, two shoemakers and a lime burner.

The original bridge was found to be faulty and at a meeting at Hunt's Center Bridge Hotel on December 5, 1829, the stockholders determined to rebuild the wooden super-structure. From its completion, the wooden covered bridge was constantly threatened by the river, as were all similar spans on the Delaware. In the flood of 1841 three spans, two

piers and the toll booth in New Jersey were washed away. George B. Fell, a Center Bridge storekeeper, walked out on the bridge to get a better view of the flood only to have the bridge collapse beneath him. Clinging to a piece of driftwood, Fell may have had the most adventurous river ride in history. He was pulled, exhausted, out of the river at Yardley.

The bridge was rebuilt and was the only one from Easton to Trenton to survive the great flood of 1903. In 1923 the bridge was struck by lightning and in a spectacular blaze was completely destroyed. At the time, Edward W. Redfield lived not far from the bridge and was witness to the fire. The next day he translated the image to canvas, leaving for poster-

The home of Edward W. Redfield, where he watched the bridge burn in 1923, and then painted the fire the following day.

ity his impression of the death of the wooden bridge.

Edward Willis Redfield first came to the area in 1887 as a student at the Pennsylvania Academy and returned in 1898 to make Center Bridge his home. A loner who never looked upon himself as part of the art colony, Redfield came here because, as he said, "it was a place where an independent, self-sufficient man could make a living from the land, bring up a family and still have the freedom to paint as he saw fit." He did all of those things as well as becoming one of America's most decorated painters. A member of the National Institute of Arts and Letters and the National Academy of Design, his bold, large canvases of the Delaware Valley and the Maine coast hang in museums around the world.

Like the bridge itself, the Centre Bridge Inn was struck twice by disasters. Emily Brit, reportedly a Russian countess, was innkeeper in 1932 when the inn burned to the ground on Halloween. In the late 40s the property was purchased by this writer's uncle, the late Patrick O'Connor, an artist living in New York who camped in the ruins for a summer with his wife, Marthe, and his son, Andrew. In 1952 the inn was rebuilt and reopened only to burn again in 1959. Resurrected again in 1961, the Centre Bridge Inn is today a beautifully appointed charming country inn.

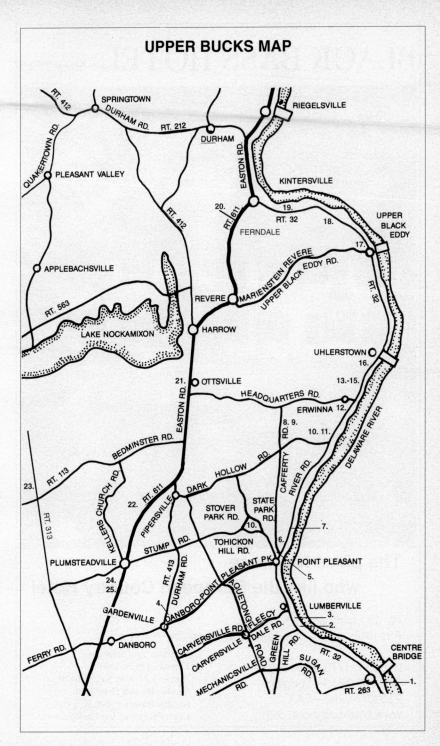

UPPER BUCKS MAP

142

The locktender's house at Lumberville.

LUMBERVILLE

Follow the river north and you will come to the village of Lumberville, a bit of the old world that seems not to change. Locked in by the canal, the river, and a ridge of mountains known as "the Coppernose," the heart of the village is comprised of two rows of beautifully maintained stone and frame houses, a church, the country store/post office, two inns, and a lumber yard. At a time when open space is nearly synonymous with development, the charm and purity of Lumberville are perhaps protected rather than locked in by its natural environment.

The first inhabitants of the village in the early 1700s were probably Swedes, but it is Colonel Joseph Wall, who settled here in 1785 and built two sawmills, who is generally credited with founding the community. It was known as Wall's Landing until 1814, ten years after the Colonel's death, when the village was renamed by Messrs. Heed and Hartley. Lumberville certainly would have seemed the logical name, from a marketing perspective, to the new owners of Wall's sawmill at the mouth of the Paunacussing Creek.

Lumbering and quarrying were the original industries and though their scale has diminished, both survive today. William Tinsman bought the same mill at the foot of the Paunacussing in 1869 and Tinsman Bros. Inc. continues to be run today by the fourth generation of his family.

The Cuttalossa Inn, at the south entrance to the village, stands on the site of Wall's other mill utilizing the mill ruins for

The footbridge at Lumberville with Bull's Island in the background. Photo: Martin E. Kennedy

outdoor dining. The current structure was built in 1833 and became a stagecoach stop at the end of the 19th century. On the National Register of Historic Buildings, the inn is a country restaurant in what can only be described as an incomparable setting. South of the inn, the Delaware Quarries Delaware Valley Landscape Stone division keeps alive Lumberville's other early industry.

Continuing north on River Road into the village, the 1740 House combines the charm of an old structure with a perfect view of the river and adds a large share of modern amenities. Over thirty years ago, the late Harry Nessler picked the site, which drops down from River Road to the level of the canal, and built the inn with original beams and stone walls from an old building preserved in one room. Migrating from New York to Bucks County, the inn was his home where he still greeted guests in his 90's. Harry loved the quiet of this country village, quoted

poetry, and genuinely invited patrons of the inn to be his house guests in Bucks County. Robert Vris, who shared the role of innkeeper with his grandfather for many years, continues the family tradition operating the 1740 House as a quiet place where the beauty of the landscape and congenial hosts make it a place to escape to, even if you only live twenty miles away.

The building that houses the Lumberville Store dates to 1770, and its use as a post office to 1835. The phenomenon of country store/post office is a bit of vanishing America worthy of note, and Gerald Gordon, the store's enterprising proprietor, stocks an ever changing mix of goods to satisfy the community's needs.

Lumberville boasts the only footbridge across the Delaware in the area, and it offers a rare and peaceful view of the river. At the end of the footbridge on the New Jersey side of the Delaware is Bull's Island, a New Jersey State Park. The park facilities include camping, a small boat launch, picnicking and a natural area that is home to a number of birds. It is of particular interest to birders as the nesting ground for Cerulean and Yellow-throated Warblers and other rarely-sighted song birds.

The charming stone house at the entry to the bridge was the locktender's house for Lumberville's Lock No. 12 on the Delaware Canal. Today it belongs to the Delaware River Joint Toll Bridge Commission and is the residence of a lucky employee.

Next to the locktender's house stands the Black Bass Hotel, a mainstay of village life since its opening in 1740. It has served many changing needs through the years, and in its serene old world charm there is not a hint of the rugged boatmen and rafters who where the earliest clientele. Appointed and run as a European country hotel, the Black Bass served as a rural retreat for President Cleveland, who came here to fish and find solitude.

For years Black Bass proprietor, Herbert Ward, struggled with the mixed blessing of having the hotel located right on the canal. In this case, so close to the canal that its foundation wall is a party wall with the western wall of the canal. Another 200 years were assured the hotel in the spring of 1996 when the state completed restoration of the canal wall. Perhaps a just bonus for the years of uncertainty, the foundation repairs brought with them the addition of a wonderful deck overlooking the canal and river.

Reflections from the past: The canal at Lumberville. Photo: Martin E. Kennedy

CARVERSVILLE

Following the Paunacussing Creek into the country away from the river you come to the village of Carversville. First surveyed in 1702, the community was served by wagon roads in 1730 and was a bustling village with five mills and the Roram Hat Factory. Known first as Mill Town, and then Milton, it became Carversville in 1833 when the first post office opened.

By the mid-1800s Carversville had developed a particularly artistic bent. Residents had been sending their children considerable distances to be educated and on the suggestion of Mrs. Elizabeth Stover, wife of Isaac Stover who ran the grist mill, the townspeople determined to build their own school. In 1858, it was built on the hill north of the Paunacussing Creek overlooking the town. The school opened with a faculty of eight and an enrollment of 93. Among the courses offered were ancient and modern languages, wax fruit and flowers, instrumental music, and needlework—zephyr, worsted, and embroidery.

During the same period stage lines connected the village with the railroads in Doylestown and with Bull's Island in New Jersey. Its commerce included two general stores, a creamery, ice cream parlor, hotel, dance hall, blacksmith, wheelwright, barber, saddler, harness maker, tinsmith and woodworkers. Later, as transportation improved, the commercial centers along the main roads thrived and not being one, Carvers-

The Carversville Inn. Photo Martin E. Kennedy

ville was again a quiet rural community by the turn of the century.

Today, an inn, general store, and the antique shops of Carversville comprise most of its commercial activity. In the early 1980s the village was placed on the National Register of Historic Places having been certified as historically significant by the Pennsylvania Historical and Museum Commission. This important recognition was achieved through the efforts of the Historic Carversville Society which was founded in 1971. The Society has produced a slide show, "A Walking Tour of Carversville," and sponsors Carversville Day, celebrated on a spring Saturday in the town square with craft and trade displays and lots of fun for everyone.

A sign of the plough. Photo: Martin E. Kennedy

GARDENVILLE

Leaving Carversville on the Carversville-Wismer Road takes you into the bucolic farmland of Plumstead Township. A detour to the west on the Point Pleasant Pike takes you to the tiny village of Gardenville. Located at the intersection of two early main roads, Durham Road and Ferry Road, Gardenville was a traveler's center of some considerable significance.

About the time the Durham Road was completed past Gardenville, the first tavern was opened here as the Sign of the Plough, probably around 1732, although the first petition for a license wasn't recorded until 1760. A common tavern sign in agricultural areas in the colonies and in England, the Sign of the Plough often

carried with it this advice: "He who by the Plough would thrive, Himself must either hold or drive."

Among the first settlers of Plumstead Township was a Quaker immigrant from England, one Thomas Browne, whose descendants settled near Gardenville. Around 1800 the town took their name and was known as Brownsville for a time. Later, when the tavern's innkeeper was the popular Charles Price, it became known as Price's Tavern.

A post office was established in the village on February 27, 1857, with John Schaffer as the first postmaster. Village names were anything but permanent in the early colonies, changing as they did with tavern owners and ferry owners. When a post office opened a town's name took on new significance. The post office name, which became a community's name, had to be approved by the Post Office Department and had to be different from any other post office existing at the time. It was in this setting that Gardenville was born.

A German woman with a gift for growing things had a large flower and vegetable garden in the neighborhood that was famous for the size, variety and beauty of its flowering plants. In the discussions about a name for the new post office, one villager, presumably an admirer of the garden, said, "Why not Gardenville?" Promptly accepted by the Post Office Department, the name remains though the garden is gone.

Around the turn of the century the village included a general store, furniture store, creamery, butcher, and the new Gardenville Hotel built in 1871.

Today Gardenville is home to a stained glass artist, general store, architectural craftsman, and the hotel. A fine furniture maker, caterer famous for his smoked salmon, country florist, and bed and breakfast inn round out the commerce of this crossroads village.

Chef Max Hansen

149

Looking like a bit of England on the edge of Gardenville, this impeccable restoration is the work, as well as the home, of architectural craftsman Sean Steuber.

PLUMSTEAD TOWNSHIP

Plumstead Township was probably named for Francis Plumsted, a London iron monger who acquired 2,500 acres from William Penn in 1683 for the sum of 50 pounds. There was an attempt to organize some 14,000 acres into a township in 1715, but the petition for the new township was ignored by the courts. In 1725, a new petition was introduced to the court, received approval, and the township of Plumstead was established. It begins at the Delaware River and forms a rectangle bordered by Doylestown and New Britain Townships to the west, Solebury and Buckingham Townships to the south, and Tinicum and Bedminster Townships to the north.

PLUMSTEADVILLE

Long before the Revolution, the hamlet of Plumstead comprised a tavern and a few scattered houses. The tavern was known first as Hart's Tavern, and is today's Plumsteadville Inn. Samuel Hart, who immigrated from England in 1716, settled in Plumstead Township and bought a large tract of land encompassing present day Plumsteadville. The original Hart house was a small stone cottage with one room on the ground level dominated by a large fireplace.

Samuel Hart and his eldest son James prospered. In 1751, James bought 400 acres of land adjoining his father's property. It seems that James built Hart's tavern as an addition on the front of the original cottage at about the same time he bought the land.

After the Revolution, the property came into the possession of John Rodrock, a man of much more than ordinary attainments; a Justice of the Peace and a figure of prominence in the Fries Rebellion. Maps of the period show that some time after 1800 the village became known as Rodrocks.

After Rodrocks, the village name changed to Fisherville. Why it was so named is unclear but it is quite certain that a "new post office" was established there under that name in November, 1832, with Levi Sellers as postmaster. It continued to be Fisherville until September 4, 1840, when John Delp was appointed to handle the mails, and the old name of Plumstead was resumed. The "ville" was tacked on in 1846.

PIPERSVILLE

Continuing the loop north takes you from Plumsteadville to Pipersville, just over the township line in Bedminster. A tiny crossroads village, it was first called Piper's Tavern in honor of the Revolutionary hero, Colonel George Piper. Visited by such influential men as Benjamin Franklin, Robert Morris and General Lafayette, the tavern was razed in 1884 to make way for a new structure. This "new" development was followed by the establishment of a clothing business in 1884, a library in 1877 and a chapel in 1886. ❦

Yesterday's barn. Photo: Martin E. Kennedy

The River: The heart of Point Pleasant. Photo: Martin E. Kennedy

Reflections: The Delaware Canal and towpath at Pt. Pleasant. Photo: Martin E. Kennedy

POINT PLEASANT

Back on River Road takes the visitor into an idyllic area of tranquil river villages, canal hamlets, state and county parks, covered bridges, and river valley farmland.

The river towns grew up early in the history of the country and were followed, with the building of the canal, by towns at the locks. The old inns and taverns were a necessity for the rafters and canal men who made the waterways work for them at a time when they were the only transportation routes for raw materials being shipped from the north to the industrially developing south. These men were among the most daring pioneers to participate in the development of the country and history tells us that they were a rough lot. It is ironic that the inns along the Delaware River and Delaware Canal, frequented by these men in the past, are among the most civilized and elegant dining and lodging establishments in the area.

As early as 1748 a grist mill was built on the Tohickon Creek and during the revolution ground not only grain for soldiers' bread but powder for their guns. Jacob Stover came to Point Pleasant in 1803 taking title to the grist mill for 10 shillings at a sheriff's sale. Situated on Cafferty Road, the "Point Pleasant Mill" was at the center of Stover's milling empire which dominated the grain trade in the valley and at one time consisted of twenty-eight mills. The property remained in the Stover family for 150 years with the grist

Waterways: Peaceful, contained, and powerful. Photos: Martin E. Kennedy

mill closing in 1912 and the saw mill in 1914.

The last of the Stovers to live on the mill property were the grand-daughters of Ralph Stover, Florence and Clara Louise. The unmarried sisters lived in the house until their deaths in the mid-fifties when the property was broken up and sold. The Stover "girls," as they were called by townspeople, are well remembered for their gift of the land for the Ralph Stover State Park and for the fine pipe organ that Florence gave to the village church. Florence was a musician and during her lifetime was the only person to play the church organ. Their home, the elegant manor house built by Joseph Stover, is today a country bed and breakfast, Tattersall Inn, which retains the style of the country squire for whom the house was built.

An important center piece in Point Pleasant was the old Point Pleasant Hotel, founded in 1782 when the town's two central stores were built. In addition to sheltering barge men, it was a way station for the Doylestown-Frenchtown-New York stage and has been the stopping point for at least two presidents. Both William McKinley and Grover Cleveland came here for the excellent shad fishing.

Over the canal bridge takes you to Bucks County River Country. For more than 30 years Tom McBrien has been introducing people to the Delaware River as a wonderful recreational resource. Canoes, rafts and tubes all offer the quiet pleasure of the river.

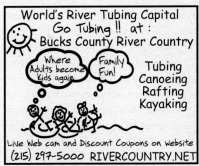
Point Pleasant is the site of two parks. The Ralph Stover State Park on Stump Road was founded in 1934 and encompasses 37 acres of Tohickon Creek valley. It offers camping, fishing, swimming and miles of wild unspoiled territory. The newer Tohickon Valley County Park, one mile west of Point Pleasant, has 45 acres which offer the same facilities as Stover Park.

Reflections: Summerhouses across the river from Tinicum. Photo: Martin E. Kennedy

TINICUM TOWNSHIP

Leaving Point Pleasant and continuing north on River Road you will be traveling into Tinicum Township's beautiful, pastoral countryside. A new organization, the River Road Business Alliance, was formed several years ago to promote this historic area. It is their goal to create interest in the River Road corridor while preserving the beauty that has made it one of America's "Top Ten Scenic Drives." For information on this special part of Bucks County contact the Alliance at P.O. Box 189, Upper Black Eddy, PA 18972; 888-BUCKS 32, or visit their web site at www.bucks32.com.

The area was the home of the Turtle tribe and in correspondence between William Penn and James Logan in 1699 is referred to as "an Indian township." The first large European landholder was the London Company which purchased a tract of some 7,500 acres. The area was settled by English and Irish immigrants who eventually displaced the Indians. Among the early families to settle here was the Marshall family. Edward Marshall was one of three walkers hand-picked to enact the infamous 1737 Walking Purchase.

The first of the historic inns you will pass along this route came into being when canal traffic was at its peak. Jacob Oberacker's Tavern catered to canal men who stopped to change mules and refresh themselves with beer and salt cakes. Today, the Golden Pheasant Inn, it is operated by Michel and Barbara Faure as a French country inn. The inn is the culmination of Michel Faure's life in the restaurant profession, which began at age fourteen in his native Grenoble, France. After eleven years apprenticeship he received the coveted title of chef de cuisine and in 1969 came to the United States.

After more than a decade of working for others, a life-long dream of operating his own restaurant was fulfilled and we are fortunate to have his restaurant and cooking school tucked away in this peaceful setting.

On the hill overlooking the Golden Pheasant is one of Tinicum's newest attractions. Sand Castle Winery is situated on two farms in a three mile strip designated as the central Delaware Valley viticulture area. In 1974, Joseph and Paul Maxian purchased the land and in 1988 the first wines had been pressed, aged and bottled on the premises. Completing the underground wine cellar first, the winery building above will be patterned after a 10th century castle in the Maxian's home of Bratislava.

A side trip into the country on Dark Hollow Road takes you to Stover-Myers Mill. Built in 1800, the mill is a fine example of an early turbine powered gristmill with adjoining "up and down" vertical style sawmill. The mill was in continuous operation until 1956 and in 1964 was purchased by the county and partially restored. The mill is open from June through August on Saturday and Sunday from 1 p.m. to 4 p.m. More information on the mill can be obtained by calling 215-757-0571.

Creative land use: a most unusual house on River Road in Tinicum.

A reflection from the past along the canal in Tinicum. Photo: Martin E. Kennedy

In the 1930s the Township hosted many famous figures from the New York art and literary scene, including Dorothy Parker and S.J. Perelman, and continues to be the home of an interesting collection of residents.

The combination of interesting inhabitants, beautiful countryside and significant history has made Tinicum a special place in Bucks County. The 126 acre Tinicum Park is one of the most active in the county park system with the planning and assistance of the Tinicum Civic Association. The park offers camping, lots of acres to hike, and is the site of many special events throughout the year. Annual events have included outdoor antiques shows, an art festival, dog shows, flower shows,

and a July 4th celebration featuring a concert by the Riverside Symphonia. See the Calendar of Events for more information on Tinicum events.

Just south of the Park, the Stover Mill Art Gallery, operated by the Tinicum Civic Association, is a wonderfully historic structure and offers changing exhibits by local artists. The gallery is open on Saturday and Sunday from 12 to 5 p.m. from April through December.

The Erwin-Stover House and the surrounding park land were bequeathed to the county in 1955. The oldest section of the house was built in 1800, with wings added about 1820 and 1860. The house, which has been restored and is open to the public, was the life-long home of John Stover,

Stover's Barn, at the center of activity in Tinicum Park. Photo: Martin E. Kennedy

Stover's Mill, Tinicum Civic Association Art Gallery. Photo: Martin E. Kennedy

first electric and telephone services in the township. The Erwin-Stover House is open June through August from 1 to 4 p.m. For information call 215-345-6722.

ERWINNA

Just beyond the park, Headquarters Road leads to the village of Erwinna. The village is on land originally owned by the London Company and was named, with the establishment of a post office, for Colonel Arthur Erwin who purchased the ground in 1769. The town was the headquarters for the superintendent during the canal's construction, hence the road's name. The primary commerce of the village was a boat building and repair yard.

At the corner of Headquarters and River Roads stands EverMay on the Delaware, a country inn in a stately Victorian house which was a popular resort in the late nineteenth century. Reports have it that the Barrymore family spent the summers here. To the delight of its owners, the renovation that created EverMay uncovered walnut trim, black walnut doors and original random width floors.

Following Headquarters Road to Cafferty Road will bring you to Van Sant Airport which offers all the services of a small country airport and where every weekend is like an unofficial fly-in. The airport offers biplane and glider rides, and hot air balloon flights. Van Sant was chosen as one of America's best turf strips by Private Pilot magazine. It was described as "a place to get

The Uhlerstown covered Bridge, constructed of oak in 1832, has windows on both sides and is the only covered bridge in Bucks County that crosses the Delaware Canal.

back in touch with the simpler side of aviation."

Back at the river, River Road Farms is on land acquired by Col. Erwin, with the help of George Washington in recognition of his service to the country. The farmhouse was built between 1720 and 1750, and the barn, which houses Chachka, is dated 1749. The farm's owner, Dick DeGroot, reports accounts of Hessian prisoners being ferried across the river here during the Revolution.

Continuing north on River Road one comes to Bucks Bounty Restaurant. Its designers were among the winners of the 1995 Excellence in Architecture Awards. One of the few fine restaurants along the river that is not in a historic building, Chef-owner John Vanderlinden asked his designers to create an image for Bucks Bounty that would stand on its own. Their solution, in keeping with the cuisine and the setting, is reminiscent of a rustic lodge with a ceiling portraying two bucks surrounded by Indian motifs in primary colors. The restaurant quickly became popular with residents of the area—its ambiance is comfortably informal and its sweetbreads are renowned.

UHLERSTOWN

A short side trip into the country brings you to Uhlerstown, a picturesque hamlet that was one of the locations used in the filming of *The Perils of Pauline*. First called Mexico, a name perhaps given to it by an imaginative canal builder, its current name comes from Michael Uhler, whose boatyard produced the successful Michael Uhler canal boats.

Upper Black Eddy

Continuing north into Bridgeton Township, one comes upon the river village of Upper Black Eddy. Located on the longest eddy on the Delaware River, its name apparently came from a combination of this physical feature and the Black family which ran the inn. It is further complicated by the fact that the Black family also owned property just below Point Pleasant at what was then called Lower Black Eddy. The village of Upper Black Eddy was a popular and busy overnight resting spot for the river rafters. Later, it was one of a number places along the Delaware where Grover Cleveland came to fish. If you wish to try your luck,, fishing licenses are available in town.

Just north of the river bridge, the restored stone structure that houses Robert Gavin's real estate office dates back to the days of the rivermen. It was a tavern run by the owner of the ferry that linked Upper Black Eddy and Milford, New Jersey. The tavern served as an overnight stop for boatmen waiting to deliver their goods to the mills in New Jersey.

More than a century ago Upper Black Eddy was a village of forty houses, three hotels, stores and shops. Along with its neighboring villages in Tinicum Township and the river islands in the area, it was a popular summer resort.

Burt Shepp's bird house.

163

Today the village is quieter with a few businesses along the river. The Bridgeton House, a gas station, Gavin's real estate office, Burt Shepp's Riverview Antiques, and Hairy Mary's garden and home shop comprise most of the commerce along River Road.

A side trip to the Ringing Rocks is definitely in order. Two miles west of Upper Black Eddy, this 65-acre park has a unique geological site comprised of an eight acre bed of mineral bearing rocks. The stones produce a ringing sound when struck with a metal object and are an enigma to geologists.

KINTNERSVILLE

North of Upper Black Eddy one enters an area known as The Narrows. In 1832 the Narrows were blasted to make room for the canal and the road. There were those who believed at the time that the beauty of the area was destroyed by the altered landscape. For those of us who only know "The Palisades of the Delaware"as they are today, it is hard to imagine a more beautiful setting.

Kintnersville was settled by the Kintner family around 1760. The family was active in the Continental Army with young Richard Kintner enlisting as a six-foot-two inch thirteen-year-old. A post office was established here in 1849 and by 1860 it was a busy community with twenty houses, hotel, store, lumber factory and large flouring mill.

A more quiet village today, Kintnersville is surrounded by the beautiful farmland of Nockamixon.

RIEGELSVILLE

Riegelsville's first settler was Wendel Shenk, who bought land in 1774 and opened the first road from Durham Furnace to the river. Shenk opened a ferry and the community became Shenk's Ferry.

Purchased in 1804 by Benjamin Riegel, known as "Benjamin Riegel, Farmer", the town honored him by taking his name. The Riegel homestead is an impressive riverfront house which served as the first village hotel. In 1838, abandoning the original hotel, Riegel built the current inn just one year after the ferry was closed and the first bridge opened. This bridge was damaged by the flood of 1903 and replaced with today's steel wire suspension bridge. The

new bridge was designed by John Roebling, famous as the designer of the Brooklyn Bridge.

The prominence of its early residents is apparent in the imposing houses along Route 32, and today's community retains that same quiet sense of importance.

NOCKAMIXON & ENVIRONS

Continuing north from Riegelsville takes you out of Bucks County and on to Easton in Lehigh County, the site of the National Canal Museum. Write to the museum at 30 Centre Square, Easton, PA 18042, or call 610-515-8000.

Going back to Bucks County, follow Route 611 into the farmland of Nockamixon Township. One of two townships whose names are of Indian derivation, the original form is not clear nor is the meaning. The petitioning of the township in 1742 followed the departure of Shawnee Indians by only 12 years.

Just south of Kintnersville the village of Ferndale was previously known as Rum Corner as it was the site of a rectifier and distiller. With the establishment of the post office in 1880 it took its present name, presumably from its sylvan surroundings.

Between Ferndale and Revere on Route 611 you'll find Bucks County Horse Park, the home of the Bucks County Polo Club. The polo season starts in mid-May and runs through early October with matches on Thursdays at 6:30 pm, and Sundays at 2. Polo Bucks County style is a bit different: the club calls it "polo for the people" and spectators are encouraged to tailgate. For the polo schedule of special events call 610-847-8228. For the horse show schedule call 215-847-8597.

Continuing south, take Route 563 west to Nockamixon State Park which encompasses 5,253 acres centered around the 1,450 acre man-made Lake Nockamixon.

By the stream in Ferndale.

Swimming, picnicing, fishing, hiking, and bridle and bicycle trails, are among the park's many recreational attractions. The Weisel Youth Hostel provides accommodations just north of the lake. Northeast of the state park, the smaller Lake Towhee County Park has sites for tent and trailer camping and a full complement of recreational facilities.

The Pearl S. Buck House, a National Historic Landmark.

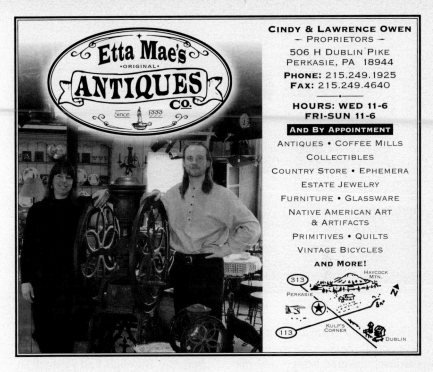
Past the parks, a detour south on Route 313 takes you to Dublin where a turn on Dublin Road will bring you to the Pearl S. Buck House, a National Historic Landmark on Green Hills Farm estate. It was the home of the late Nobel and Pulitzer prize-winning author and humanitarian, Pearl S. Buck, the only American woman to receive both awards. The 1835 stone farmhouse displays her awards and personal mementos collected in China. In 1964, she started the Pearl S. Buck Foundation for the welfare of displaced children of the world, which continues today at the farm as Pearl S. Buck International. For information on tours of the house, Pearl S. Buck International, *Bringing Hope to Children Worldwide!*, and other activities call 215-249-0100.

PERKASIE

Traveling northwest from the farm brings you to Perkasie. The town grew up around the country store, Bissey and Baringer, opened in 1870 by Samuel Hager. New houses and shops sprang up rapidly around the store and by 1871 Perkasie Post Office had been established. The borough incorporated in 1876 and was, at that time, the fourth largest in Bucks County. The name, Perkasie, appears to be a corruption of the Lenni-Lenape word Poekskossing, which translated means "where hickory nuts were cracked." Shellbark hickory trees were abundant along the stream that ran though the area and it is conjectured that the hickory nuts from Perkasie were prized for their particularly high quality.

Quakertown's Burgess Foulke House. Photo: Martin E. Kennedy

Today, this historic town has a wonderful park system with a carousel, covered bridge, and bik-

Liberty Hall in Quakertown.

ing and hiking trails. Olde Towne Day is celebrated in May and the Perkasie Borough Fall Festival in early October. For more information call 215-257-5065, or visit www.perkasieborough.org.

QUAKERTOWN

Quakertown Borough, in the center of Richland Township, was at the juncture of the main roads leading from Philadelphia to the Lehigh Valley. Perhaps originally called Richland, by 1803 when the first post office was established the town was known as Quakertown.

The borough is part of a 1,000 acre tract patented to Morris Morris in 1728. According to George MacReynolds in *Place Names in Bucks County,* "In 1832 Quakertown was described as 'a small neat town of a single street, containing about 40 dwellings, 2 stores, 3 taverns, and a Quaker Meeting House.'"

A welcoming corner at the Red Hill Church founded in 1766 in Ottsville.

Quakertown's rich heritage has been preserved through the stewardship of the Quakertown Historical Society. Founded in 1965, the society saved the first burgesses house from being razed and turned it into the Burgess Foulke House museum; preserved Liberty Hall, the house where the Liberty Bell was hidden when it was moved from Philadelphia to Allentown in 1777; and has turned Market Place, a barn built in 1897, into the Society's archives. A walking tour published by the society includes 35 properties in the town's historic district. Market Days, and a Christmas craft show are among the events held by the society. For more information call 215-536-3298, or write to P.O. Box 846, Quakertown, PA 18951.

OTTSVILLE

Returning to Nockamixon Park take Route 563 east back to Route 611. Turning south brings you to Ottsville, one of the oldest villages in Upper Bucks. First settled by Scotch-Irish Presbyterians, there are records of a log church here about 1738. The village was called Red Hill, for the red shale rock on which it stands, until 1814 when a post office was established. There was a Red Hill Post Office in Montgomery County, so the village name was changed to Ottsville, honoring the influential family of its first postmaster, Michael Ott.

Traveling south from Ottsville takes you back to Bedminster and Plumstead Townships en route to the county seat in Doylestown.

The Moravian Pottery and Tile Works. Photo: Martin E. Kennedy

DOYLESTOWN

Doylestown was named as one of The National Trust for Historic Preservation's "Dozen Distinctive Destinations" on their 2001 list of the best preserved and unique communities in the United States. For the list of 12, chosen from a field of 70, visit the National Trust's web site at www.nthp.org.

The news, which came on April 13th, resonated throughout the town, particularly among those who have spent countless hours working on downtown revitalization and historic preservation.

The National Trust's narrative on Doylestown begins: "A small town with a 250-year history, Doylestown, Pennsylvania, (population 8,575) rivals many large cities such as nearby Philadelphia with its world-class cultural facilities, elegant Victorian architecture, and historic attractions. Its commitment to the arts is exceeded only by its engrained preservation ethic."

"Americans are indeed fortunate to be able to visit these 12 communities," said National Trust President Richard Moe. "These are marvelously American locations that typify our country's small towns, close communities, and celebrated heritage. They are committed to preserving their historic landmarks, maintaining their unique character, and sustaining an economic base of small, locally owned businesses."

Looking back, Doylestown has served as the county seat since 1813, and is directly in the heart of Bucks County. The ground on which the town is built was first owned by the Free Society of Traders of London, and was part of a 2,000 acre tract purchased in 1724 by Jerimiah Langhorne. As

Gracious Lifestyle
Individualized Attention

Heritage Towers offers the best in Continuing Care Retirement with spacious residential apartments, personal care, and skilled nursing services.

Call our toll free number today to schedule a visit and experience first-hand all that we have to offer in retirement community living in Bucks County.

HeritageTowers
CONTINUING CARE RETIREMENT COMMUNITY

200 Veterans Lane, Doylestown, PA 18901
800-781-4301 • www.heritagetowers.com

The Mercer Museums. Photo: Martin E. Kennedy

early as the 1730s, Edward Doyle and his sons, William and Clement, from whom the town takes its name, were in residence here.

In 1745 William Doyle was licensed to operate a tavern and for the next thirty odd years the village was known as William Doyl's Tavern. Doyle owned the ground on both sides of the current intersection of Main and State Streets and there is uncertainty about the precise location of the original tavern. The Fountain House, circa 1804, on the northwest corner of the intersection is generally considered to be on the site of the original tavern and is a National Historic Site.

A post office was established here in 1802, with Charles Stewart as postmaster. Postmaster Stewart was responsibe for the first postal carrier route in the country. He would place the day's mail in the crown of his high beaver hat and

walk from door to door delivering letters to his customers.

Petitions to move the county seat from Newtown to Doylestown were presented to the legislature as early as 1784 by residents of the central and upper portions of the county who felt "great disadvantage of having the courts of justice held in a place very uncentral in said county, whereby the expense of attending on juries and other occasions fall unequally on the freemen of the county." At the time the court house needed to be rebuilt anyway, and the petition goes on to say, "the present time [is] a proper time to apply to your honorable House for leave to build a court house and prison on a better plan at Doylestown, a village nearly central, a place, remarkably healthy, and pleasant, situate at the crossing of several very public roads." Eight petitions were presented before the legisla-

172

The James A. Michener Art Museum.

ture passed the act on February 28, 1810 for the "removal of the seat of Justice in the County of Bucks from Newtown to a more central place." With the opening of the court on May 11, 1813, Doylestown became the county seat.

The Fountain House sets the tone for the many Federal, Colonial, and Victorian houses impeccably maintained by the residents and business community of Doylestown. Ironically, this relatively uniform feeling of the town's past is broken by the architecture of the current court house. An imposing round brick building, its construction caused a fair degree of controversy.

The most notable architectural landmarks, cited by the National Trust as establishing Doylestown's cultural identity, are three poured, reinforced concrete "castles" built by Henry Chapman Mercer. A noted anthropologist, archaeologist, historian, and writer, Mercer was an innovator and a collector. The magnitude and multiplicity of his accomplishments make "The Mercer Mile" almost incomprehensibe as the product of one man's endeavors.

Dr. Mercer began work on his home, Fonthill, at the age of fifty-two. He described the plan as "an interweaving of my own fancies blending with memories of my travels and suggestions from several engravings." Prints, engravings, tiles from around the world, and his own distinctive tiles literally cover the floors, ceilings, and walls of the forty-four room house. The museum is operated by the Bucks County Historical Society and open for guided tours only. Reservations are suggested and can be made by calling 215-348-9461. Fonthill is open all year Monday through Saturday from 10 to 5 and Sunday from noon to 5.

The adjacent Moravian Pottery and Tile Works, the second of the

three structures to be built, replaced Dr. Mercer's original studio, Indian House, which burned at about the time Fonthill was completed. Operated by the Historic Properties division of the county parks department, the pottery is a National Historic Landmark and a working history museum. Mercer's original formulas and techniques are used to reproduce his famous tiles, and visitors see original machinery, kilns, molds, tools, and tiles. The museum is open every day from 10 am to 4:45 pm. Call 215-345-6722 for information on special programs.

The last of the "castles" to be built, the Mercer Museum houses the collection, "Tools of the Nation Maker." (see article on page 216) Operated by the Bucks County Historical Society, the museum also houses the Spruance Library, which includes extensive research collections on Bucks County history and genealogy, and on the history of trades, crafts, and early industries. The whole year is filled with special activities at the museum, highlighted by the Mercer Folk Fest in early May. For more information and a full schedule of events call 215-345-0210.

Just across the street from the Mercer Museum is the James A.

Michener Art Museum (see article on page 100 for more on the museum). The museum opened in 1988 in the former Bucks County Prison with 6,000 square feet of gallery space. 1993 brought expansion and renovation that added 14,300 square feet to the exhibition, permanent collection, and photographic and print galleries. A reading room, classroom-lecture area, museum shop, tea room, and outdoor sculpture garden were also added.

The reopening brought with it the permanent exhibit, "James A. Michener: A Living Legacy," which celebrates the author's pro-lific career as a writer, public servant, art collector and philanthropist, as well as his life-long commitment to racial harmony. Michener's Bucks County office is installed at the museum and the exhibition includes a specially produced video, his Presidential Medal of Freedom and the original manuscript of "The Novel."

The Visual Heritage of Bucks County, also a permanent exhibition, traces the art of the area from Colonial times to the present with over 40 works representing the county's naive painters, Impressionists, Modernists and Abstract Expressionists.

Very **Personal Healthcare for Pregnant Women**

If you are pregnant or planning on becoming pregnant,
our independent team of OB-GYN specialists welcomes you
to experience a very caring, personal practice of healthcare
before, during, and after the birth of your child.
Our expertise in the field of obstetrics allows us to help you
through your pregnancy with comfort and ease,
even if you are considered at high risk. A pregnant woman
needs special care and that's what we do best.
Call for an appointment today.

**Jean O. Fitzgerald, MD, Tuan A. Le, MD
Nestor I. Sendzik, MD, Vivian Yeh, MD, Carolyn Ianeri, DO**

DOYLESTOWN
Women's Health
CENTER

708 Shady Retreat Rd, Suite 7, Doylestown, PA 18901
215.340.2229 • Day & Evening Appointments
Most insurances accepted.   **Doylestown Hospital**

Daniel Garber's 22-foot mural, "A Wooded Watershed," commissioned for Pennsylvania's Sesquicentennial Exposition in 1926, became a permanent installation at the Museum in June 1996, as did a group of Abstract Expressionist paintings from the collection of Mari S. and James A. Michener.

The museum has an extensive database which is an important research tool for students and historians studying the arts in Bucks County. The database includes biographical and visual material covering the area's visual, literary, and performing artists, past and present. Printouts of information from the database are available for a small fee.

See the Calendar of Events for changing exhibits, visit the museum's web site at www.michener artmuseum.org, or call the museum at 215-340-9800 for more information on programs, access to the database, and events throughout the year.

William R. Mercer, Jr. Henry Mercer's brother, also left an architectural legacy in his Aldie Mansion. Built in 1927, and named for the ancestral home in Scotland, it embodies all the essentials of Tudor architecture. A sculptor, Mercer himself created the fountains, benches, and wall plaques for Aldie's Italian garden. After a period of neglect, it has been restored to its former glory by the Heritage Conservancy. Today it houses the Conservancy's offices and offers tours open to the public and will arrange special group tours. Call the Conservancy

at 215-345-7020 for tour dates and times.

The Central Bucks Chamber of Commerce initiated "Bucks Fever" over a decade ago as a six-week celebration of visual and performing arts, festivals and history. What seemed to be an impressive roster of events in 1987 has grown to include over 200 events running from March through October.

Bucks Fever '01 was staged by some 80 organizations showcasing Bucks County's distinguished culture and history as well as its place as a renowned center for the arts. It is to the Chamber's credit that they have fostered this unique marriage between the business community and the arts with over 70 businesses contributing major funding and in-kind services to cultivate the arts in Bucks County.

To receive a calendar of Bucks Fever events, available in early spring each year, contact the Central Bucks Chamber of Commerce, 115 W. Court Street, Doylestown, PA 18901, 215-348-3913, or visit their web site at www.centralbuckschamber.com.

Two more recent organizations have been working to promote and maintain the rich history of Doylestown; the Doylestown Business and Community Alliance, and the Doylestown Revitalization Board which administers the town's Main Street Program.

The Alliance sponsors Christmas in Doylestown, the annual Food, Fun and Fitness Day at the end of May which features Bucks County's largest 5K Run, and the fall Doylestown Arts and Crafts Festival. It also organizes the

MAENNERCHOR FIELD
HOME OF THE
DOYLESTOWN DRAGONS
RUGBY CLUB

ESTABLISHED 1974

215-348-3817

Doylestown's commitment to art extends even to its rugby pitch.

hanging baskets in the spring and summer, historic street lighting, and the plaques that identify more than 100 historic properties. You can reach the Alliance at P.O. Box 1066, Doylestown, PA 18901, or call 215-340-9988 for information on events and historic sites.

As we reached the new millennium in January 2001, Doylestown was working to assure its place in the new century as an important historic, regional cultural center. The eight-month Bucks Fever celebration; Doylestown's participation in the Main Street Program; the Michener Art Museum's continuing growth; the Mercer Mile's dedication to history; all of these are only a small part of the community's commitment to preserve Doylestown as a friendly, dynamic county seat. The National Trust's announcement in April 2001 that Doylestown was one of its "Dozen Distinctive Destinations" for 2001 was an affirmation for the whole town.

Traveling east from Doylestown on the Old Easton Road, one comes to the village of Dyerstown, named for John Dyer, who built a mill here as early as 1720. Originally on the main road from Philadelphia to Easton, the early

DOYLESTOWN & ENVIRONS MAP

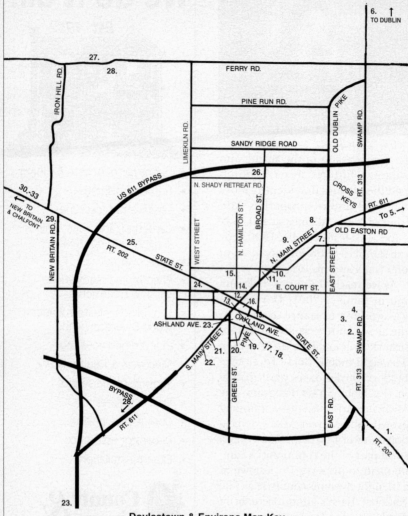

Doylestown & Environs Map Key

1. Best of France Antiques
2. *Bucks County Visitors Bureau
3. *Fonthill Museum
4. *Moravian Tile Works
5. Bucks Country Gardens
6. Coldwell Banker - Dublin
7. Weidel Realtors
8. Mt. Lake Pool & Patio Shop
9. Heritage Towers
10. Coldwell Banker
11. Kurfiss Real Estate
12. Class-Harlan Real Estate
13. Horn & Hardart Bakery Cafe
14. *Central Bucks C of C
15. Superior Woodcraft, Inc.
16. Roosevelts Blue Star
17. Doylestown Bookshop
18. County Linen Center
19. *James A. Michener Art Museum
20. *Mercer Museum
21. Weichert Realtors
22. Robert G. Gavin, Inc. Realtors
23. The Pewter Cupboard
24. Avalon Hair Design
25. *Doylestown Hospital
26. Doylestown Women's Health Center
27. *Shrine of Czestchowa
28. Evergreen Terrace
29. Delaware Valley College
30. Consignment Galleries
31. Michelyn Galleries, Ltd.
32. Los Sarapes
33. *Byers' Choice
*Attractions-Points of Interest

When only the best will do...

Private rooms with balconies and breathtaking views

Unparalleled personalized care

A Concierge to schedule your appointments

Superb attention to detail

Restaurant-style dining in an elegant setting

and so much more

Nursing Care at its finest.

For more information, call 215.340.5256

EVERGREEN TERRACE

777 Ferry Road, Doylestown, PA

JCAHO
Accredited

EQUAL HOUSING
OPPORTUNITY

success of the village is apparent
in its fine residential architecture.
The destiny of Dyerstown, with the
rerouting of Route 611 in 1939,
was to become a quiet village.

Traveling west from Doylestown, at its border with New
Britain, is the family estate of
W. Atlee Burpee, founder of the
Burpee Seed Company. Here a
piece of family history was preserved when his grandchildren
opened the estate as The Inn at
Fordhook Farm. The 18th century
stone house and the 62 acres surrounding it preserve a piece of important American agricultural history. Today the property is owned
by the Burpee Group of Compa-
nies which operates the inn and
uses the grounds for experimental
gardens.

184

New Britain's 1842 Pine Valley Covered Bridge.

NEW BRITAIN

Continuing on Route 202 into New Britain Township, one travels through an area incorporated in 1723 as a large township, originally about six-and-a-half miles long by four-and-a-half miles wide. The township's first settlers were predominantly Welsh, then Scots-Irish, and later Germans. The importance of roads in the area's development is clear and New Britain was well served by three; the Butler Pike, now Route 202; Limekiln Pike, now Route 152; and Ferry Road.

Patriots from New Britain Township were loyal supporters of the Revolutionary cause contributing wagons, blankets, and a local militia. The New Britain Militia served under George Washington at Trenton, Germantown, and Crooked Billet.

New Britain Borough was incorporated in 1928 covering an area of several square miles. General Lafayette made his headquarters here in a tavern called the Sign of the Horses and Wagon when the army was making its way from Valley Forge to Monmouth, New Jersey, in June 1778.

A detour into the country offers at least one surprise: the Pine Valley Bridge. Built in 1842 of white pine and hemlock in a lattice-type construction, it is one of Bucks County's eleven covered bridges.

Continuing north, the National Shrine of Our Lady of Czestochowa at the junction of Iron Hill and Ferry Roads has hosted millions of people including a President of the United States. The magnificent structure is open to the public and guided tours can be arranged by calling 215-345-0600.

CHALFONT

Back on the main road, the village of Chalfont grew up at the crossroads of Limekiln Pike and Society Road. Situated at the junction of the North and West Branches of Neshaminy Creek and Pine Run, the village took its early name from the owner of the mill. It was first called Butler's Mill for Simon Butler, a Welshman who built the first grist mill here in about 1720.

It isn't until 1869 when the North Pennsylvania Railroad Company changed the name of the station here to Chalfont that the modern name appears. The name comes from the village of Chalfont St. Giles in England, the town where William Penn found his wife, Gulielma Springett, in 1762.

Continue on Route 202 to County Line Road where a right turn will take you to Byers' Choice, Ltd., the home of the Caroler figurines. Among the most sought-after Christmas collectibles in the country, Byers' Choice began when Joyce Byers created the first Carolers at her kitchen table. By 1981 demand had outgrown the garage and Joyce's hobby incorporated as Byers' Choice, Ltd. The company moved to its current facility in 1994 and opened its Christmas Gallery.

In September 2000, Byers' Choice opened a new Christmas Gallery and Visitor Center. Visitors are instantly transported to Dickensian London as they stroll down life-size cobblestone streets peering into windows of establishments such as Fagin's and The Old Curiosity Shoppe. Inside the Olde Curiosity Shoppe the scale changes with hundreds of Carolers displayed in Victorian wintertime settings. Add to that the popular Observation Deck, where visitors watch Byers' Choice artisans handcrafting the Carolers, and the Byers' personal collection of handmade nativities.

A classic American success story, with more than 160 employees, Joyce still sculpts all of the faces and designs most of the clothes, while Bob handles the administration and heads the family's Byers Foundation. "We take pride in giving back to our community, and it is particularly rewarding that our giving has prompted others to do the same," says Bob Byers.

WARRINGTON

Today, the village of Warrington is in a busy urban area, however, it developed later in colonial days than its southern neighbors. When a township was established in 1734, it was called Warrington, a name borrowed from a town in Lancashire, England.

The village was the site of Craig's Tavern, which was granted a license in 1757. John Craig continued to hold the license for the tavern until 1773. An upstanding citizen, he is referred to on early documents as a grand juror and a member of the court for special service.

Over the years the village was known as Lukens Corner, Newville, Warringtonville and finally simply Warrington. The post office, which was established December 3, 1839, with Benjamin Hough, Jr. serving as the first postmaster, was in the village then known as Lukens Corner, and served all of Warrington Township.

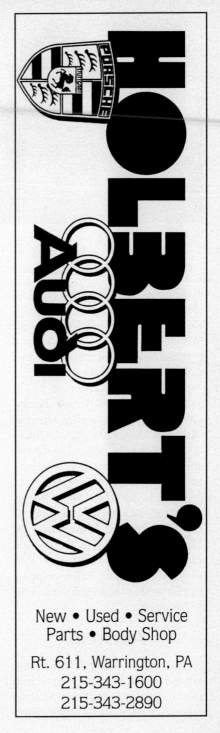

Farm just outside Furlong.

HARTSVILLE

A village at the intersection of the Old York Road and Bristol Road, it was named for Colonel William Hart, a revolutionary war veteran who established an inn called the "Sign of the Heart."

During the summer of 1777, Washington camped near Hartsville setting up his headquarters at Morland House. Morland House is owned by the Warwick Township Historical Society, which is restoring the farmhouse.

On February 14, 1854, Gideon Prior, the last surviving member of the Continental Army, died in Hartsville. On a trip from New Hampshire with South Carolina as his destination, Prior stopped in Hartsville and stayed to the end of his days.

FURLONG

Just south of Doylestown, the village of Furlong may have had more variations of its name than any other community in the coun-

ty. First mentioned as Baretown in an 1804 diary, the name is looked upon as a misspelling of Beartown. In 1825 it appears as Barrville, and in 1852 as Garville, surely a typographical error..

In 1757 Dr. John Watson bought the site on which an inn was built. The inn was sold to Thomas Carver, then Elisha Wilkinson, who changed the Beartown Inn's name to The Green Tree Tavern and ordered a new sign. It seems the sign painter was of little talent so the tree looked like a shrub. Green Tree remained the name until 1832, but it was commonly known as "The Bush."

With the establishment of a post office in 1832 the village name was changed to Bushington. A few years later, the Post Office called for a new name. The local postmaster discussed the problem with the postmaster in Doylestown. In the conversation he used the word furlong. His associate is reported to have interrupted to exclaim, "Furlong! There's your name," and so it is today.

WYCOMBE

The village grew up quickly when the Northeast Pennsylvania Railroad completed the lines in 1890 and opened its new Walton Station. Before that it had been a tiny hamlet around a grist mill on Mill Creek. With the railroad came new homes and shops, a newspaper, telephone exchange, natural gas line and an orchestra. In 1891 a post office was established with the name Wycombe.

Wycombe today is a country village surrounded by the farmland for which Bucks County is so famous. A collection of white clapboard houses, Wycombe Station, an old feed mill, tall shade trees and the Wycombe Inn, in the old town hall, make up the village, a quiet community off the beaten path.

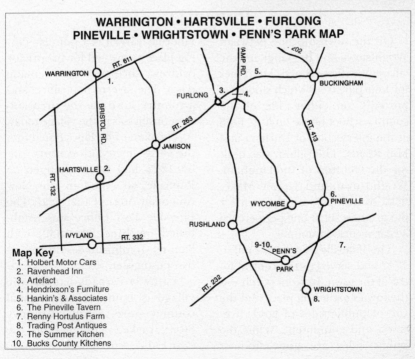

WARRINGTON • HARTSVILLE • FURLONG
PINEVILLE • WRIGHTSTOWN • PENN'S PARK MAP

Map Key
1. Holbert Motor Cars
2. Ravenhead Inn
3. Artefact
4. Hendrixson's Furniture
5. Hankin's & Associates
6. The Pineville Tavern
7. Renny Hortulus Farm
8. Trading Post Antiques
9. The Summer Kitchen
10. Bucks County Kitchens

189

Sign by the roadside in Wrightstown marks the start of the infamous walk. Photo: Martin E. Kennedy

PINEVILLE

On the township line between Wrightstown and Buckingham, the village was first named The Pines for four pine trees which stood, reportedly, on either side of the country school house built in 1768 at the intersection of Durham and Mill Roads. The school was built for the children of Buckingham, Wrightstown, and Upper Makefield Townships, with the rent for the grounds set at one peppercorn a year, a curious amount.

The Pineville Hotel was built in 1742 and served as the central focus of the town. Its front porch was the town's gathering place and the site of public sales of land, livestock, and equipment. While the public sales are gone, today's Pineville Tavern is a popular dining place renowned for proprietor Andrew Abruzzese's homemade pasta. The tavern, post office, and a country store are the predominant businesses in the village today.

The name The Pines lasted into the early nineteenth century, but by 1825 had been changed to Pineville, so called in the New American Atlas of that year. The Pineville Post Office was established on June 22, 1832, with Samuel Tomlinson serving as its first postmaster.

A tiny crossroads hamlet, the village is home to an unusual country store. Sandy's Country Store, tucked away behind the Post Office, specializes in homemade Scottish foods. The store's glass case holds an array of wonderful things you'll never find in a supermarket, but which bring fond memories of home to anyone from the United Kingdom who visits the store. The shelves are filled with simple British necessities like Bird's Custard mix. A sampler of Sandy Sinclair's wares would include Glasgow bridies, steak and kidney pies, pub sausages and sausage rolls, English Mars Bars, and shortbread.

Traveling south, between the villages of Pineville and Wrightstown, one passes horse farms, rolling fields, and old stone houses.

WRIGHTSTOWN

Midway between Pineville and Wrightstown at the junction of today's Routes 232 and 413, a village called the Anchor grew up around the Anchor Tavern. Built in 1720 by Joseph Hampton, a member of the Provincial Assembly of Bucks County and tax collector from 1757 to 1767, the inn burned to the ground a few years ago and with it went the last traces of the village.

Just south of the Anchor, the village of Wrightstown, settled in 1686, is best known as the starting point for Thomas Penn's infamous "Walking Purchase." Wrightstown was at the northern border of lands purchased from the Indians by William Penn in 1686 under an agreement alleged to have stated that the parcel would extend as far as a man could walk in a day and a half. The ground was not mea-

sured at the time of the purchase and by 1737, Penn's sons, Thomas and John, were anxious to acquire more land and insisted that the walk take place. Their tactics in the measurement amounted to thievery, ending peaceful relations with the Delaware Indians.

On the appointed day three walkers, carefully chosen for their stamina, set out on a trail that had been marked on a secret dry-run. By the end of the day the Indians were well aware that they were being robbed and declined to participate any further in this shameful event.

Although the Indians honored the agreement, they are reported to have expressed displeasure at every meeting with the colonials thereafter. This dishonorable act is believed to have brought about the 1750s alliance between the Indians and the French.

PENN'S PARK

At the center of Wrightstown Township, and its oldest village, Penn's Park was figured on the original map executed by William Penn's surveyor, General Thomas Holme. As early as 1716 it was known as Logtown, so named for the first houses which lined both sides of the road, all of log construction. The original name seems to have continued for nearly a century. In the 1825 atlas of Henry S. Tanner, the town is cited by a new name, Pennsville, which continued for nearly forty years. When the post office was estab-

Bucks County Kitchens, inc.
Penns Park, PA   215-598-3505
www.BucksCountyKitchens.com

lished in 1862, with T. Ogborn Atkinson as postmaster, the name was changed to Penn's Park, acknowledging its origins as one of William Penn's town squares.

CHURCHVILLE

Continuing south from Penn's Park one comes to the village of Churchville at the intersection of the Feasterville and Richboro

The library in Penns Park was built in 1872 as a school.

Turnpike Road (Route 232) and Bristol Road. With the opening of the North and Southampton Reformed Church in 1816, which joined the Low Dutch Reformed congregations from Richboro and Feasterville, the town became known as Churchville.

The village was first known as Smoketown, the origin of which is at least unusual. It is suggested that the name came from the early Holland Dutch colonists who settled the area. These early settlers brought with them their old-country habit of smoking long-stemmed pipes. As a group, the Holland Dutch were habitual smokers, and it seems that their non-smoking neighbors called the community Smoketown.

Bird in Hand Inn, site of a 1778 skirmish with the British.

NEWTOWN

The 5,000 acres that originally comprised Newtown Township and the Townstead are shown on land records from 1683 as part of a tract purchased by William Penn from the Indians on July 15, 1682. On a 1684 map by Penn's surveyor, Thomas Holme, the town plan is clearly defined with essentially the same boundaries as exist today. From 1726 to 1813 Newtown was the county seat, replacing Bristol because of its more central location. During that period the community grew into a prosperous government center leaving behind its origins as a farming community.

During the Revolution Newtown was an important center with Bucks County patriots organizing here in 1774. Washington spent time in Newtown preceding the Battle of Trenton and re-turned with Hessian prisoners when the battle was over. The town was an important supply depot. In 1778, a skirmish with a detachment of British soldiers behind the Bird in Hand Inn resulted in the loss of quantities of precious supplies, and left a number of Continental soldiers dead, wounded, and taken prisoner.

It was gratifying for the Newtown Joint Historical Commission when the historic district of Newtown Borough, containing 230 structures, was added to the National Register of Historic Places. The largest historic district in Bucks County, it encompasses the original 17th century village as well as the Federal and Victorian houses which fan out from it. The Bird in Hand Inn, which survived the British raid, stands as one of the oldest structures in the state.

Only the site of Washington's headquarters, at the corner of Sycamore Street and Washington Avenue, survives today. It was here, from the home of a widow, Mrs. Hannah Harris, that he wrote to Congress giving his official report on the victory at Trenton.

The Court Inn, headquarters of the Newtown Historic Association at Court Street and Centre Avenue, houses a library of historic documents, original deeds, and genealogical research materials. The building is open for tours and the library for research. For public hours and tour information call the Association at 215-968-4004. Originally the Half Moon Inn, its name was changed when the Court House was built diagonally across the street. Built by Joseph Thornton, Sr., the inn also housed Newtown's first library, sharing the space with Thornton's tavern.

Bird in Hand, erected prior to 1690, was originally the home of Shadrach Walley, considered by some the father of Newtown. It was licensed in 1726 by George Welch, who purchased the property from Shadrach Walley's son. Called "The Old Frame House" around the time of the Revolution, the Newtown Post Office was established here in 1820. About the same time, Edward Hicks painted a sign for the inn depicting Benjamin Franklin's saying, "A bird in the hand is worth two in the bush," and it has been known as Bird in Hand ever since.

Edward Hicks moved to Newtown from Langhorne in 1811.

Old Newtown. Photos: Martin E. Kennedy

Rows of brick and stone.

The Newtown Historic Association sponsors two annual events, including Market Day in mid-September. A walking tour published by the Newtown Business and Professional Association in cooperation with the Newtown Historic Association is a wonderful way to see the town and steep oneself in early American history.

The tour encompasses the entire town, listing nearly fifty structures which span the period from Bird in Hand's 1690 date to 1928 when the cornerstone was laid for the Newtown Title and Trust Company. Most of the buildings are impeccably maintained 18th and 19th century stone and brick houses, among them many small row homes typical of the period. A walk along Court Street, just a block from the commerce of today's State Street, is truly a walk

Internationally known for his primitive paintings, foremost among them "The Peaceable Kingdom," he is remembered locally as much for his commercial signs as for his paintings. From 1813 until his death he combined the life of a Quaker traveling minister with that of a painter, finding time to start a Friends Meeting in the town as well. On his death in 1849, four thousand people gathered in Newtown for his funeral.

Newtown Friends Meeting, founded by Edward Hicks.

back in time. For more information on town events call the Newtown Business and Professional Association at 215-968-0600 or visit www.newtownbpa.org.

On the edge of Newtown, Tyler State Park consists of 1,711 acres previously owned by Mr. and Mrs. George F. Tyler, of which one quarter is still farm land through agricultural leases. The park offers numerous recreational opportunities including a disc golf course, a small theater, overnight hostel service, and maintains a center for the Pennsylvania Guild of Craftsmen. Over one hundred members of the guild exhibit at the annual Tyler Springfest and Fallfest. For more information on the Guild of Craftsmen and the festivals, call 215-579-5997.

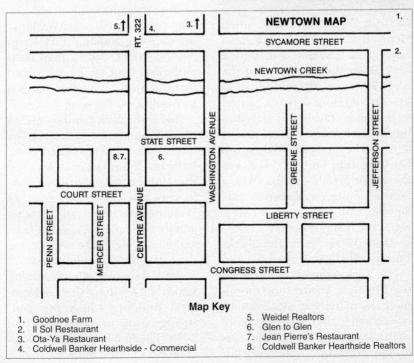

NEWTOWN MAP

Map Key

1. Goodnoe Farm
2. Il Sol Restaurant
3. Ota-Ya Restaurant
4. Coldwell Banker Hearthside - Commercial
5. Weidel Realtors
6. Glen to Glen
7. Jean Pierre's Restaurant
8. Coldwell Banker Hearthside Realtors

McConkey's Ferry Inn. Photo: Martin E. Kennedy

WASHINGTON CROSSING

The history of Washington Crossing began in 1684 when Henry Baker and his son Samuel came from England and settled here along the Delaware. In the mid-1700s ownership of much of the surrounding acreage passed to Benjamin Taylor and stayed in the Taylor family for many generations. The present Washington Crossing Inn, built in 1812, was the Taylor farmhouse. In 1829, a post office was established at Taylorsville, with John B. Taylor serving as the first postmaster.

As early as 1895, the Bucks County Historical Society had begun work at the site of the crossing placing a brownstone monument to mark the place where troops had gathered on the shore of the Delaware. In 1917, by Acts of Assembly, the Commonwealth of Pennsylvania authorized the state park. In 1918 the Washington Crossing National Park Commission, which had by then started buying land for a park, asked that the town's name be changed to Washington Crossing.

Today the park grounds and 13 historic buildings, including the original ferry inn, an 18th century farm and industrial complex, and the 19th century village of Taylorsville, help tell the story of Washington's important crossing and its consequences, and of farm and village life in the area during the half century that followed.

Near the point of embarkation stands the keystone shaped Memorial Building which was constructed using native fieldstone in 1959. The building houses a Revolutionary period museum and an

auditorium in which hangs an exact replica of the famous Emil Leutze painting "Washington Crossing the Delaware;" a museum shop; and in the east wing, the Washington Crossing Library of the American Revolution.

The Old Ferry Inn, at the bridge to New Jersey, has been restored with much of the original paneling and woodwork intact. Washington is believed to have eaten his evening meal at the inn on the night before the Battle of Trenton. Four additional buildings are open to the public. The Mahlon K. Taylor House is completely restored

and furnished to reflect his c. 1817 lifestyle. The Hibb's House and Blacksmith's House, both c. 1828-1830, were also Taylor houses. Tours and open-hearth cooking demonstrations are offered at the Hibb's House, and the herb garden on the grounds is an interpretation of an 1830s formal herb garden. The last of the four is the Taylorsville Store, which also housed the Taylorsville Post Office with Mahlon Taylor serving as Postmaster for almost 40 years. Open today as The Patriot, it continues the tradition as an old-fashioned general store.

The homestead of Bernard Taylor VII, today's Washington Crossing Inn. The original structure is shown to the left and center. Arched windows retain the architectural details of an open porch.

The lower grounds of the park include picnic areas and a lagoon which serves as a bird sanctuary and is a great place for ice skating when it's frozen.

Events in the park include Washington's Birthday celebrations in February, sheep shearing in May, militia encampments and art shows in the summer and fall, the Handweavers of Bucks County's annual show and sale in November, and the December reenactment of the Christmas crossing.

Generally park hours are 9-5 Tuesday through Saturday and 12-5 Sunday. For information on events and hours call 215-493-4076.

Just north of the park is The David Library of the American Revolution, a privately endowed nonprofit foundation devoted to the study of American history c. 1750-1800. Founded in 1959 by the late Sol Feinstone, a businessman, philanthropist, and collector of Americana, the library is open to the public Tuesday through Saturday from 10 to 5. For detailed information on the collections, fellowship programs, lectures, and exhibitions, call 215-493-6776

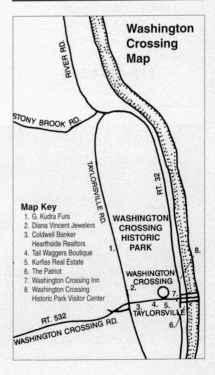

Washington Crossing Map

Map Key
1. G. Kudra Furs
2. Diana Vincent Jewelers
3. Coldwell Banker Hearthside Realtors
4. Tail Waggers Boutique
5. Kurfiss Real Estate
6. The Patriot
7. Washington Crossing Inn
8. Washington Crossing Historic Park Visitor Center

Monument marks the site of 1776 crossing.
Photo: Martin E. Kennedy

Crossing the river brings you to New Jersey's Washington Crossing State Park at the site of the landing. The New Jersey park has a visitor center, the Ferry House, an open air theatre, and the George Washington Memorial arboretum. For more information write to the Park at Box 337-A, R.D. 1, Titusville, NJ 08560 or call 609-737-0623.

Reenactment scene with the General's white horse.

Lakeside, 1728 home of ferry owner, Thomas Yardley. Photo: Martin E. Kennedy

YARDLEY

This quiet country community was founded in 1682 by William Yardley, an active participant in the early history of Bucks County. He was instrumental in the establishment of the first monthly meeting of Friends on the Pennsylvania side of the Delaware, founded the Orphans Court in 1683, and served on the original ruling body with William Penn. The town became known as Yardley's Ferry in 1722 when Thomas Yardley, nephew of the founder, established the first ferry.

The White Swan was a busy colonial tavern situated at the ferry crossing and at the crossroads of three major routes leading from Philadelphia, Falls, Attleboro, and Newtown. In 1835 the first wooden covered bridge was built at the site of the ferry, and

the tavern continued operating until 1892 when its license was revoked. Purchased by John J. FitzGerald for $15.00, the license was regained. He ran the White Swan as a family hotel until 1910. The old White Swan sign is now in the collection of the Bucks County Historical Society.

Already blessed with the beauty of the river, the creation of Lake Afton added to the picturesque charm of the village. According to George MacReynolds, author of *Place Names in Bucks County*, the lake was probably named by an early settler with a penchant for Scottish poetry. Overlooking the lake on two acres of lawn and garden is Thomas Yardley's Georgian manor house, "Lakeside," built in 1728.

During and after the Civil War the cost of sugar soared because

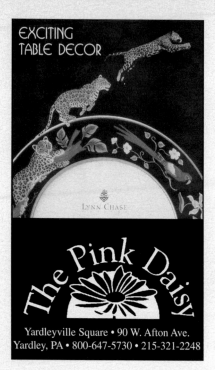
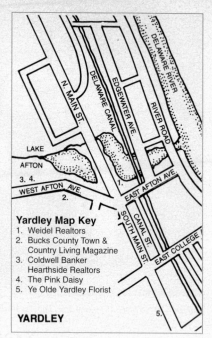

Yardley Map Key
1. Weidel Realtors
2. Bucks County Town & Country Living Magazine
3. Coldwell Banker Hearthside Realtors
4. The Pink Daisy
5. Ye Olde Yardley Florist

YARDLEY

the north was cut off from southern supplies. Yardley was planted in sugar cane and in 1868 a sorghum mill was fully operational.

In 1828 a post office was established at Yardleyville. In 1876, the Reading Railroad finished the New York Branch and the station and town became Yardley. In 1891, a Reading Railroad pamphlet advertised Yardley as follows: "There are pleasant walks and drives, excellent boating, bathing, fishing, good spring water and no malaria."

With enormous population growth in and around Yardley, commerce in the town reflects the need for service businesses and professionals, while maintaining its historic charm and a small but fine collection of shops offering necessities and interesting art and antiques.

MORRISVILLE

Continuing south, lower Bucks County is replete with 17th and 18th century sites. Just below Yardley, Morrisville is on land sold to John Wood by Sir Edmund Andros about 1680. It was referred to as the "Falls of the Delaware," then Colvin's Ferry until 1792 when Colvin sold the ferry to Robert Morris, the financier of the Revolution.

The stately Georgian mansion, Summerseat, c. 1760, was the home of Thomas Barclay when Washington was headquartered there from December 8-14, 1776. It was purchased in 1791 by Robert Morris, and then by George Clymer, both signers of the Declaration of Independence. The house was restored in 2000 and is open the first Saturday of each month. For information call 215-295-7339.

HISTORIC FALLSINGTON

Three miles southwest of Morrisville, Historic Fallsington is a credit to its residents' dedication to historic preservation. The early village includes 15 structures, c. 1685 to 1879, fanning out from the central Meetinghouse Square. Historic Fallsington, Inc., formed in 1953 by a group of concerned citizens, has acquired and restored six buildings since its inception. These six, together with five private homes, Falls Meetinghouse, the community center in an older meetinghouse, Fallsington Library, and All Saints Episcopal Church, comprise the core of the 300 year old village.

Historic Fallsington Day in early October features a house tour, craft demonstrations, special exhibits, and entertainment for the entire family. Historic Fallsington offers guided tours of four houses from May-October, Monday - Saturday from 10:30-3:30, and Sunday 1-4. For more information call 215-295-6567.

PENNSBURY MANOR

Returning to the river, one comes to the reconstructed Pennsbury Manor, the 17th century country plantation of William Penn. Administered by the Pennsylvania Historical and Museum Commission, Pennsbury Manor interprets the life style of William Penn, his family, and the Quaker colonists who staffed the plantation. In addition to the manor house, visitors will see a bake and brew house, smoke house, plantation office, ice house, stable, and barge house, complete with a replica of a river barge like the one Penn used to travel between Pennsbury and Philadelphia. The plantation includes 17th century gardens, orchards, and domestic animals that would have lived there in Penn's day. Guided tours feature an audio-visual introduction and a costumed interpreter.

A full schedule of activities are planned from March through December. For hours and details call Pennsbury Manor at 215-946-0400.

BRISTOL

Bristol, previously Buckingham, was founded in 1681 when Samuel Clift received a grant for 240 acres on the Delaware River. In 1697 Buckingham was laid out as a town, became the first seat of justice in 1705, and in 1720 was erected as the Borough of Bristol. Bristol prospered early and continued to be the county's economic center even after the county seat moved to Newtown. Bristol's fortunes continued until late in this century when it began to suffer urban decay. Then, in the 1980s, Bristol experienced a renaissance that blossomed around the opening of the Bristol Riverside Theatre with a professional theatre company in residence. For the company's season schedule, call 215-785-0100.

The Margaret R. Gundy Memorial Museum at 610 Radcliffe Street was established by the late Senator Joseph R. Grundy. The museum overlooking the river is an excellent example of a fine Victorian residence. Open Monday-Friday from 1 to 4 and Saturday from 1 to 3, groups should call 215-788-9432 for an appointment.

The Bristol Cultural and Historical Foundation, founded to preserve and promote the history and culture of the community, published a walking tour which includes fifty sites in the four neighborhoods listed on the National Register of Historic Places. For information on tours and events call 215-781-9895, or write to P. O. Box 215, Bristol, PA 19007.

LANGHORNE

Turning north and traveling back into the county, one comes to the Borough of Langhorne, a small modern community that has preserved its history as a part of everyday life. As with most colonial communities, it began as a crossroads hamlet which, because of its location at the junction of four highways, was at one time called Four Lanes End. In 1874, Langhorne Borough was carved out of Middletown Township and incorporated as Attleboro. In 1876, with the opening of Langhorne Station on the North Pennsylvania Railroad, the recently incorporated Attleboro followed suit and became Langhorne Borough.

A village of less than a square mile surrounded by dense suburban development, Langhorne maintains its identity through foresight, hard work, and continuing vigilance. Since 1970, local government has enacted historic zoning; purchased and saved a farm within the borough boundaries; and created an Arts Council, Recreation Board, Historical Association, and a Shade Tree Commission that has planted 155 trees.

A self-guided walking tour is available at borough hall and a stroll through the town will confirm its citizens' pride of place. Notable among the town's successes was the purchase twelve years ago of today's Langhorne Heritage Farm. The borough saved the farm from development and turned it into a public recreation area.

DIANA VINCENT'S artistic vision in jewelry design has won her international awards and put her on the pages of countless magazines. Her jewelry is showcased in the finest stores worldwide - yet her home is here in the heart of Bucks County where she shares with you her entire collection of 18k gold and platinum jewels.

In addition to her signature designs are many one-of-a-kind pieces, all exclusive to this area. Discover this local treasure and make it your own.

Business hours:
Tuesday-Friday: 10am-6pm
Saturday: 10am-5pm

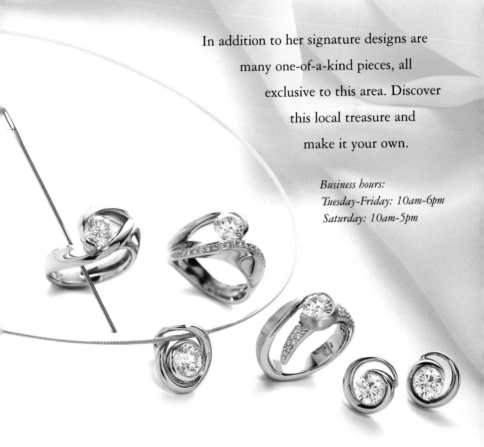

JEWELERS · DESIGNERS · PLATINUMSMITHS

1116 Taylorsville Road · Washington Crossing · PA · (215) 493·0969

BEST of FRANCE ANTIQUES, INC.

Design, Restoration & Appraisal Services Available

at Chestnut Grove Estate
3686 Route 202 South, Mechanicsville, Pennsylvania
Open Friday, Saturday, Sunday 11 am - 5 pm
(215) 345-4253

Come wander through the beautiful European inspired gardens on the grounds of Chestnut Grove Estate (c. 1890). The unequaled selection of magnificent marble and bronze fountains and sculpture offers a perfect focal point for your garden.

An architecturally stunning barn provides a splendid contrast to fine French antiques and accessories found inside.

Our professional woodworkers have extensively studied techniques of Ebinestes of the 17th and 18th centuries, and are experts in French conservation.

A friendly and knowledgeable sales staff is available to help you with your purchases.

In a concerted venture, we offer the world famous La Cornue Kitchens. Long coveted by the great chefs of Europe as the Rolls Royce of kitchens, the refinement and functionality of La Cornue can now be a part of your home.

Selecting from several exquisite porcelain enameled color finishes coordinated with your choice of a variety of metal fittings, makes each design an original work of art.

Toss some coins into the fountains and help make a child's wish come true. All donations go to the Make-A-Wish Foundation® Southeastern Pennsylvania Chapter.

Vineyards & Wineries of Bucks and Hunterdon

by Pat Tanner

When it comes to winemaking, everything depends on *terroir*. With rolling hills, moderate climate, and shale and limestone soils, Bucks and Hunterdon counties provide some of the best conditions on the East Coast. Vineyards here produce an amazing variety of wines–everything from traditional European wines made from vinifera grapes, such as chardonnay and cabernet sauvignon, to all-American Concord and Niagara, to French-American hybrids with names like seyval blanc, marechal foch, and chambourcin, which, prevailing wisdom has it, produce wines best suited to the *terroir*.

The essential grape: Ripe for harvest at Unionville Vineyards.

With a backdrop of lush countryside, stunning hilltop vistas, and the Delaware River, these vineyards and wineries, which are often nestled down country roads near historic towns, provide a beautiful setting for discovering what local winemakers proffer.

An aerial view of Buckingham Valley Vineyards.

All offer complimentary tastings in rustic or historic settings, which range from old barns with hand-hewn beams, to a 1719 manor house, to a massive stone cellar embedded 30 feet into the hillside. All are family operations – Pennsylvania passed its family wineries act in 1968, New Jersey followed in 1981– and each has its own distinctive personality. Many offer tours, and most encourage picnicking to take in the beautiful surroundings. Add to the mix concerts (under the stars or under a grape arbor), seasonal food and wine festivals, and you have a recipe for year-round pleasure. Drink up!

Buckingham Valley's automatic champagne riddling machine.

AMWELL VALLEY VINEYARD
www.amwellvalleyvineyard.com

Making wine is a science as well as an art, which might explain why Amwell Valley Vineyard in Ringoes, New Jersey has won so many awards over the years. Its founder is Dr. Michael Fischer, a scientist and patent award winner. The vineyard is owned by Dr. Fisher and his family. He was instrumental in getting New Jersey's winery act passed in 1981, and Amwell Valley became the first winery licensed under it.

State-of-the-art stainless steel fermentation and storage equip-ment can be found here, and a fully automated bottling line, but also a cozy tasting room with etched-glass windows that command a wonderful view of the Sourland Mountains. The 30-acre farm affords a view of the surrounding unspoiled valley.

Amwell Valley produces 19 wines, most of which are dry and French in style. All are grown, produced, and bottled on site. Among its award winning wines are chardonnay, a blanc de blanc sparkling wine, ruby port, Pleasant Ridge Blush, and Ravat, a dessert wine. Tours and tastings are conducted on weekends, and visitors are invited to picnic on two large decks that take full advantage of the view.

BUCKINGHAM VALLEY VINEYARDS
www.pawine.com

Although a laid-back attitude is the signature style of Kathy and Jerry Forest and their sons, there is nothing laid back about the success of their winery, which was one of the first started under Pennsylvania's winery act of 1968. From five acres in 1966, Buckingham Valley has grown to a 40-acre estate that produces 30,000 gallons

continued on page 276

Harvest festival at Unionville Vineyards.

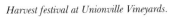

CUSTOM PROFESSIONAL DESIGN
Visit Our Fabulous Showroom
SALES ▪ INSTALLATION ▪ SERVICE ▪ MAJOR APPLIANCES

QUALITY
CUSTOM CABINETRY
INC.

PLAIN
& FANCY
CUSTOM CABINETRY

MacDonald
Kitchen and Bath Designs, Inc.
71 N. Main St., Lambertville, NJ 08530 ▪ 609 397 8500

A Sense of Whimsy Sets Mercer Museum Apart

by Victoria Memminger

The Mercer Museum in Doylestown, Pa., looks like a castle and that's the way it's supposed to look. Henry Chapman Mercer (1856-1930), its builder and founder of the collection the museum houses, was fourteen when his aunt sent him on a six-month tour of Europe where he fell under the spell of the castles there. The other two Mercer buildings open to the public, Fonthill and the Moravian Pottery and Tile Works, have a certain castle-like quality, too. If castles and unusual collections of just about everything you can think of are your cup of tea, then the Mercer Museum, built in 1913, should be high on your list of things to see in Bucks County.

The lobby does not prepare you for what's ahead. There's a glass case holding recent additions to the collection: a folk art landscape from 1890, a rifle from 1855, a molding plane with a card dating it sometime between 1790 and 1820. One item, though, gives you a clue that this may be a pretty quirky collection—that's the Cheerios box with a back panel celebrating the Central Bucks High School Football Championship of 1997. The gift shop is off the lobby—here you can buy a hand-carved ark complete with animals for $750 or you can spend 25 cents on a candy stick. The most popular items, according to one of the

The Castle. Photo: Milton Rutherford. Courtesy of the Mercer Museum.

women working there, are a $6.50 folk toy and pieces from the Redware Pottery Collection. The lobby also offers background on the museum and a place to watch a video that tells you what's in store once you leave the ground floor.

The centerpiece of the museum is the Central Court, up on the next floor. There's a very apt exhibit just outside the swinging doors that usher you into the court. It's a vampire killing kit, designed, the card says, for "those who travel to little known countries of Eastern Europe." The kit contains a pistol with the obligatory silver bullets, an ivory crucifix, powdered garlic, a wooden stake and special "serum." At first, museum officials believed that the kit was a genuine, if odd, artifact from the late 19th century. It was later proved to be a 1920s hoax, but once you push open those doors, Dracula's castle comes immediately to mind. Mel Brooks would love the place.

Here's just some of what you see suspended from the rafters and the side railings when you look up to the ceiling, six levels above you: a whaling boat, a sleigh, a huge bellows, an old fire truck, butter churns, chairs, cradles, carriages, a canoe, tables, and examples of every tool you could imagine (and some you couldn't.)

Literature from the museum will tell you that Mercer's legacy was a "significant collection of tools and artifacts that illuminate the history of pre-industrial America to circa 1850." That may well be true, but it is also a significant

The redware collection. Photo: John Hoenstine. Courtesy of the Mercer Museum.

collection of just about anything that interested Mercer, and that seems to be everything.

Ringing the Central Court, on each of the floors, are what look like old shops, rather than the standard museum cases. You look in the windows of these shops to see the exhibits, which are well lighted and clearly and succinctly described in the cards on the walls. There's a sense of whimsy about the place that is a pleasant change from the usual dry-as-dust atmosphere in a museum.

On a table near one of the "stores" there is a case with a sign identifying the contents as "Obsolete Artifacts, circa 1991." The contents include a black dial phone and a 45 RPM record.

A view of the ceiling from the Central Court. Photo: Scott E. Mabry. Courtesy of the Mercer Museum.

continued on page 218

Since Mercer was an archaeologist as well as a collector, builder, lawyer, and architect, the artifacts include things that he found interesting even if they are not American; e.g., 19th century brass candlesticks and needle cases from England, a West African two-stringed musical instrument.

Where would the average visitor linger? According to one of the staff, it depends on your interests. Household items? Try the exhibits on combs and buttons and the tools for making tortoise shell ornaments. Kitchen utensils? Chances are you had no idea of the variety of potato mashers, cheese molds, pitchers or pottery or what was used to make these things. If presses are your hobby, there's a flatbed printing press from 1830 and an enormous fruit press designed to produce wine and preserves.

There are cases full of pretty pale green glass bottles, a number of decanters, and what looks like an early mason jar. There's a fragment from the Old North Bridge in Concord, Mass., and a statue of Buffalo Bill, minus his left arm and right hand. There's also a cigar-store Indian.

You can learn about making dairy items, how to preserve meat and fruit, what a country store looked like. A partial list of subjects not mentioned here includes exhibits on shoemaking, architectural hardware, hats, pewter, wallpaper and fabric printing, tin ware, threshing, harvesting, coopering, and tanning and leatherworking. Obviously, the phrase "something for everyone" is not a cliché at the Mercer Museum. The women at the desk will tell you it takes between an hour and an hour-and-a-half to do the entire tour. If you can get through the Mercer Museum in that time, you're not paying attention.

❧

Engrossed, you can bet this family didn't finish their tour in an hour. Photo: Scott E. Mabry. Courtesy of the Mercer Museum.

218

NEW ART & ANTIQUES

WITH

STYLE

HUMOR

SPIRIT!

CHRISTMAS AND OTHER
HOLIDAY ANTIQUES
FEATURED YEAR ROUND.

GLASS SCULPTING
BY REX CRAVAT ON SITE.

Brion Galleries

1293 Route 179
3 miles northeast of downtown Lambertville, NJ 08530
609.397.7030 • Open Wednesday-Sunday
www.briongalleries.com

Transitions:

Observer
& Observed

There is an excitement about our new menu that makes dinner by the Delaware unspeakably desirable

Lambertville Station
since 1867

Do yourself a party favor! Make your next celebration a real splash at the Riverside Ballroom

Riverside
BALLROOM

Three new martini concoctions! Two nights of live music! One great bar menu! Zero reasons not to have fun!

Station Pub

Bridge Street and
the Delaware River

Lambertville, NJ

609.397.8300

www.lambertvillestation.com

THE LAMBERTVILLE WATERFRONT

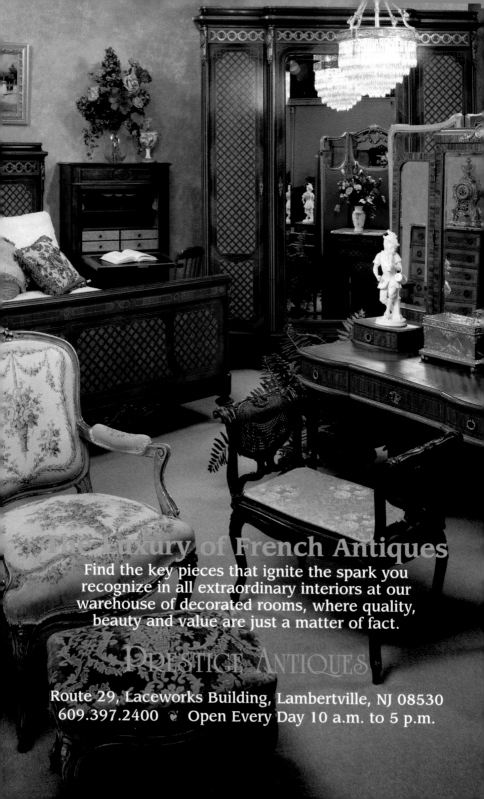

Called Coryell's Ferry in 1776, Lambertville retains a sense of its past. Photo: Martin E. Kennedy

WELCOME TO LAMBERTVILLE

Leaving Bucks County, Pennsylvania by crossing the river at New Hope, one arrives in Hunterdon County, New Jersey at Lambertville. Settled in 1705, Lambertville has the distinction of being one of the oldest communities in Hunterdon County and continues today to be its only city. The prosperity and development of the town were largely due to the efforts of its first settler, John Holcombe, who pressed to have the proposed main road from Philadelphia to New York pass through his lands. When the first leg of the road was completed it met the Delaware at Reading's Ferry, now Stockton, and it seemed that Holcombe's efforts were for naught. Col. John Reading had also lobbied long and hard to have the road pass through his lands, and it appeared that he had been dealt the winning hand. With the completion of the York Road across New Jersey to New York, Holcombe's fortunes changed. The

original road was rerouted at Lahaska to arrive at the river here, and Lambertville's future prosperity was assured. The city's location on the Delaware River, roughly at the midpoint between New York and Philadelphia, sealed its destiny in colonial America and has continued to influence its identity ever since.

In 1726, John Coates was granted a patent to operate a ferry here, which he sold to Emanuel Coryell in 1733, and it is as Coryell's Ferry that the community left its mark on colonial history. During the Revolutionary War, the town shared with its neighbor across the river not only the name Coryell's Ferry, but also the full impact of the war's activity in the area. On the evening before the Christmas crossing, Washington was escorted by Cornelius Coryell to the top of Goat Hill, just south of the village, to see for himself that the boats hidden on Malta Island in the Delaware could not be

Holcombe homestead, Washington's headquarters in 1777-1778. Photo: Martin E. Kennedy

seen by Cornwallis and his men.

Later that evening Lt. James Monroe was dispatched from Lambertville with fifty men to approach Trenton from the north in order to block a Hessian exit via the road to Princeton. In the ensuing skirmish he was hit by a musket ball and transported back to Coryell's Ferry to be treated. During the campaigns of 1777 and 1778, Washington crossed New Jersey twice, both times stopping to rest in Lambertville at the home of his friend Richard Holcombe, the son of John Holcombe. The stone farmhouse on the Holcombe Homestead is today a private residence, and can be seen from North Main Street adjacent to Homestead Farm Market at the edge of town.

Colonial development was dependent on access and in the late 18th century Coryell's Ferry was a major trading center because of its strategic location on the east-west highway and on the north-south route provided by the Delaware River. Early merchants bartered

227

Canal bridge on the edge of Lambertville joins towpath with farm museum.

manufactured goods for hickory nuts, grain, eggs, and butter, and all of the lumber used throughout much of the state was transported down the river to Coryell's Ferry, where it was sold and hauled away in wagons to surrounding communities in Hunterdon, Somerset, and as far away as Plainfield.

With the Holcombe's and Coryell's, the Lambert's played a significant role in the early history of the community. Joseph Lambert, son of Gershom Lambert who settled in nearby Sandy Ridge in 1740, followed the Coryells as ferry owner and kept a store and tavern. In 1812, U.S. Senator John Lambert, Gershom's other son, applied for a post office for the town. It was granted and opened in 1814 with Senator Lambert's nephew, Captain John Lambert, as the first postmaster. With the opening of the post office, the town's name was changed to Lambertville, thereby assuring a place in history for the family's name.

Ashbel Welch's engineering of the Delaware and Raritan feeder canal, which connected with the Trenton-New Brunswick canal, added a new link in the chain of development for Lambertville. In June 1834 the opening of the canal was celebrated with a barge ride from Trenton to Lambertville. It was a historic moment, with Governor Peter Vroom in attendance to help Welch honor the occasion.

The 22-mile long feeder canal runs from the Delaware River at Raven Rock to the main canal in Trenton. Six feet deep and fifty feet wide, it starts at seventy feet above sea level and falls through locks at Prallsville and Lambertville before entering the main

A fine row of 19th century brick homes. Photo: Martin E. Kennedy

canal. In the 1840s a cable system was devised to bring coal barges across the river from the Delaware Division Canal at New Hope and lock them into the feeder at Lambertville. A record two million tons of freight were moved on the canal in 1871, the same year that the Pennsylvania Railroad leased the system and began manipulating rates to the advantage of their railroad freight lines. After nearly forty years as a losing operation, 1932 saw the end of an era with the railroad defaulting on its lease and the state taking over the canal.

In 1974 the canal was designated a state park administered by the Delaware and Raritan Canal Commission, whose executive director not only reviews all projects slated for the canal but monitors 400 surrounding acres which drain into the canal. While earning two million dollars in state revenue from water sales, the canal and its towpath offer a bit of peace and quiet running through a rapidly developing area. The Commission recently restored the canal walls and the towpath through Lambertville, improving what was already a wonderful place to walk or bicycle.

The park offers a full slate of free nature and history programs for all ages. For current programs visit the park's web site at www.danddrcanal .com, or call either 609-397-2949 for the park naturalist or 732-873-3050 for the park historian. Programs range from basic orienteering and walks with the historian and naturalist, to an Arbor Day program dedicated to trees of New Jersey.

Returning to an earlier time, colonial manufacturing pursuits in Lambertville included a canning factory, brickyard, shoe factory, linen mill, and two rubber factories, one of which produced the

2 CANAL ST • LAMBERTVILLE, NJ
LUNCH AND DINNER DAILY
609 397 6477

THE FISH HOUSE

widely advertised "snag-proof" boots. In 1859 the Lambertville Iron Works was established and continued to operate for nearly fifty years.

At the turn-of-the-century, The Kooker Sausage Company thrived in what is today "The Porkyard." The old sausage factory beside the canal was redesigned some years ago by Lambertville native, designer, and more recently restauranteur, Jim Hamilton. Over the past thirty years Hamilton has left his mark on Lambertville in four projects that have sensitively preserved and creatively reused old spaces. The expansion of The Swan Hotel was the first, followed by the total reworking of The Porkyard and the small frame building beside it that became The Boathouse. Next came the renovation of the old Record newspaper building in front of The Porkyard. Here he preserved the

integrity of the old structure while creating second story apartments with balconies overlooking the canal and shops on the ground level. The fourth was the creation of The Fish House in an unused barn by the canal behind the store fronts on Bridge Street. As with the Swan Hotel, the reworking of these spaces combines Hamilton's familiarity with the historic city with a sense of the theatrical that comes from his background as a scenic designer.

Significant among the town's many historic buildings is the Lambertville House, built in 1812. Lambert's Inn, as it was then called, was the site of the city's first post office and was host to many famous guests, among them President Andrew Johnson and Generals Ulysses S. Grant and Tom Thumb. In the 1980s it fell victim to real estate speculation and neglect. The property was purchased by Bucks County developer, George E. Michael, who took

on the monumental task of bringing this grand old inn, the city's central landmark, back to life. Work began in November 1995 and in mid-April 1997 the Lambertville House reopened, fully restored in keeping with its place on the National Register of Historic Places. Standing empty for 11 years had taken its toll making the project as much reconstruction as restoration, and despite its near-ruin condition, Michael was able to save the first floor foyer, staircase, exposed stone walls, and fireplaces. The inn's 25 rooms combine the painstakingly preserved sense of history with modern amenities. Working gas-jetted fireplaces add a touch of old warmth while data ports link guests with cyberspace.

Just a block further on Bridge Street stands the James Wilson Marshall House Museum, listed on the New Jersey and National Registers of Historic Places. The house was the childhood home of

Resident Canada geese. Photo: Martin E. Kennedy

James Marshall, the man who discovered gold in a sawmill race in California in 1848 with John Augustus Sutter. It was their discovery that started the Gold Rush of 1849.

Owned by the State of New Jersey, the house is administered by the Lambertville Historical Society. Built in 1816 by Philip Marshall, James's father, the original property included a brick kitchen, wheelwright and wagon shop, barn, smokehouse, and other outbuildings. The museum is furnished from an 1834 household inventory with displays of photographs, maps and artifacts showing life in early Lambertville.

One of the exhibits in the museum was inspired by the town's annual Shad Festival. "Are we there yet? Gil's journey upstream," chronicles the history of shad fishing on the Delaware, with historic photographs, artifacts, and a lively text presented by the precocious fish, Gil. It tells the story of the shad and the important role they played in the commercial and recreational life of Lambertville; of the Lewis family fishery; of the river's recovery from pollution; and of the central role the river plays in the region.

The museum is open Saturday and Sunday from 1 p.m. to 4 p.m. on the second and fourth weekends of the month from May-October. The Society also offers one hour guided walking tours at 2 p.m. on those weekends. Museum admission is free; the walking tour is $5.00.

The Society's Autumn Open

*The A.H. Holcombe House, Lambertville's
preserved historic city hall.*

House Tour, to be held this year on October 17, showcases Lambertville's superb Victorian architecture, structures with unusual histories, historically accurate restorations, and buildings featuring inspired uses of space and furnishings. The tour includes approximately eight houses plus the Marshall House, Holcombe-Jimison Farmstead Museum, and the Kalmia Club. Tickets are $12 in advance, or $15 on the day of the tour. Call the Society at 609-397-0770 for 24-hour information on the tour and other Society events, or write to the Lambertville Historical Society, P.O. Box 2, Lambertville, NJ 08530. Advance tickets may be purchased by sending a check to the society with a self-addressed, stamped envelope.

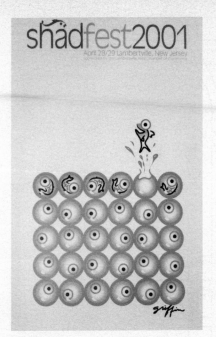

Shad Happens, *poster by Kevin Griffin, Studio 58, designer of many festival t-shirts.*

In 1986, the Lambertville Area Chamber of Commerce and the Lambertville Historical Society published a self-guided walking tour of the outstanding buildings in Lambertville and other points of interest. The tour map, which can be found in local shops, is a leisurely walk of about 45 minutes that begins at the Marshall House and returns to the center of town.

If architecture appeals to you, don't limit yourself to the twenty-two buildings on the tour. The residential streets, particularly north of Bridge Street, offer one wonderful building after another and you could spend days or even weeks looking at all of them.

The Museum at Holcombe-Jimison Farmstead, on Route 29 north of the city, is dedicated to

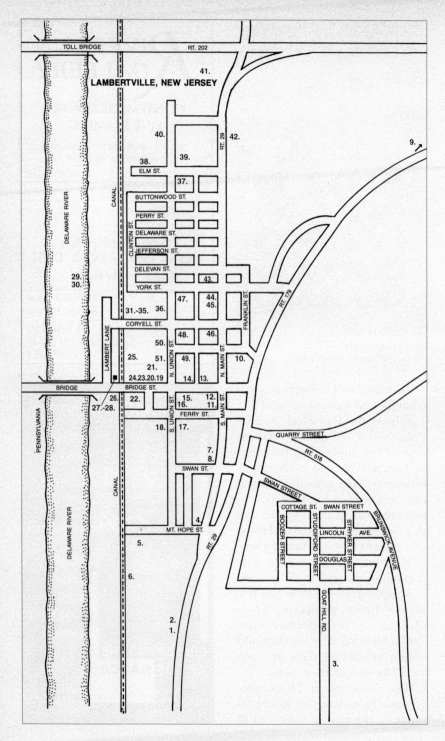

LAMBERTVILLE, NEW JERSEY

⚜ York Street House ⚜

Rekindle Your Romance Bed and Breakfast

In front
of your fireplace
or
over a candlelit
breakfast for two

42 York Street, Lambertville, NJ-

Non Smoking
Relaxed Atmosphere
Amenities, Robes
AC, Cable, Parking
As seen in *Getaways for Gourmets*
and, *America's Historic Inns*

serving bed and breakfast since 1983

609.397.3007 or toll-free 1.888.398.3199

Visit our website for information and packages

www.YorkStreetHouse.com

Lambertville Map Key

1. Prestige Antiques
2. Riverrun Gallery
3. Chimney Hill Farm Inn
4. Hydrangea
5. *Cavallo Park*
6. *Delaware & Raritan Canal State Park*
7. Swan Hotel
8. Anton's at the Swan
9. Brion Galleries
10. Stanley Cleaners
11. Celt-Iberia Traders
12. B. Adorned
13. *Marshall House Museum*
14. Riverside Symphonia
15. E.J. Lelie Agency
16. Welsh's Wines
17. Oxus River Gallery
18. Ota-Ya Japanese Restaurant
19. Lambertville House
20. Coda
21. Flying French Hens
22. Tesoro
23. Hrefna Jonsdottir Gallery
24. Weidel Realtors
25. The Fish House
26. Lambertville Station Restaurant & Inn
27. Dresswell's
28. G. Evans Ltd.
29. *Swan Creek Rowing Club*
30. *Lewis Shad Fishery*
31. The Porkyard
32. Antiques
33. Coryell Gallery
34. Hamilton's Grill Room
35. The Boathouse
36. Phoenix Books
37. Old English Pine
38. Niece Lumber
39. Best of France
40. Roxey Ballet Co.
41. *Holcombe-Jimison Farmstead*
42. Homestead Farm Market
43. York Street House
44. McDonald's Kitchen & Bath Designs
45. 49 North Main
46. Howard Mann Art Center
47. Van Horn McDonough Funeral Home
48. A Mano
49. Church Street Bistro
50. Miller-Topia Designers
51. Bear Apothecary Shoppe

Attractions & Points of Interest

preserving Hunterdon's agricultural heritage. Housed in the 1711 farm's bank barn, the collection includes old farm equipment, a country kitchen, rural post office, a doctor/dentist's office, blacksmith shop, print shop, and carpentry shop. The museum is open May-October on Sundays from 1 p.m.-4 p.m. and on Wednesdays from 9 a.m.-noon. The museum holds periodic special events and is available for tours by calling 609-397-2752 or 908-782-6653.

In 1982, the Chamber of Commerce mounted the first Lambertville Shad Festival built around the Lewis Shad Fishery, the last commercial shad fishery on the non-tidal Delaware River, Fred Lewis and his family continue a tradition begun by his father, William Lewis, who took over the fishery in 1888. Situated on Holcombe Island, the historical fishery was started by Richard Holcombe circa 1771. Shad fishing in the Delaware River, as well as in many other rivers along the Atlantic coast, is dependent on shad leaving the ocean each spring and making their way upstream to the

The Marshall House. Photo: Martin E. Kennedy

headwaters of the river to spawn.

The elder Lewis was a participant in the 1896 record catch of 19,203,000 pounds of shad in the Delaware River and Delaware Bay. Roughly half a century later the river was so polluted that there was no catch at all. Successful cleanup efforts by the New Jersey Fish, Game and Wildlife Division brought the shad back to the river, and in 1982 the catch was nearly 4,000.

Today a nationally recognized event, the festival is held on the last full weekend in April and draws thousands of people to celebrate the return of the shad, the vitality of the river, and the arts, crafts, and history of Lambertville. Among traditional events at the festival are a riverside shad supper, shad hauling demonstrations by the Lewis family, outdoor art, craft and food vendors, entertainment, historical tours, and lots of activities for children. The festival has spawned a number of collector's items, among them "O'Fish 'L' t-shirts, a stamp cancellation and cache, and the Shad Fest posters.

A high point of the festival is the poster auction that closes the weekend. The festival posters are

The Georgian Revival Massey Mansion, today's York Street House, was built in 1909 and appeared on the cover of "Better Homes and Gardens" in 1911. Photo: Martin E. Kennedy

original art by noted local artists and community members. This year's highest priced poster drew a bid of $2,400, nearly five times the entire proceeds from the first auction in 1982. It was Robert Beck's "Union Street and Bridge," which also set the record for the highest price ever paid for a Shad Festival poster. In twenty years the auctions have raised nearly $140,000 for art scholarships for area students.

Another group of annual spring visitors to Lambertville are recognized by an interpretive sign mounted at the entrance to the river bridge. The sign calls your attention to the colony of cliff swallows that nest under the bridge. They were discovered in 1982 when bridge repairs were being planned and the nesting colony was identified as the largest of this species in New Jersey. Repairs were scheduled to follow the nesting season and naturalists ingeniously designed artificial nests to replace those disturbed by the work. It wasn't until the next spring when the swallows returned and moved into the new nests that the project was deemed a success.

The newer Lambertville-New Hope Winter Festival has grown in scope and popularity since its inception five years ago. Its goals are to provide a healthy, invigorating, experience and to demonstrate that the two towns are as exciting in the winter as in the summer. Proceeds from the festival, which totalled nearly $18,000

in 2001, are distributed to various non-profit groups.

Winter Festival 2001 was a great success, opening with an SRO concert by John Sebastian and Sally Taylor. Winter Festival 2002 will take place on February 1-3 with events on both sides of the river. Highlights of the weekend are the Friday night concert, the Chili Cook-Off on Sunday, the village snowfolk art competition, and ice carvings that delight viewers even after the festival. Visit www.winter-festival.net or call between October to March at 215-862-2974.

The last three decades saw major changes in Lambertville.

When the People's Store closed as a department store and reopened with three floors of antiques, no one expected to see most of downtown's shops filled with art, antiques, and restaurants. It happened, and today the city is among the most important and respected art and antiques centers in the northeastern United States and well known for its restaurants.

As the business community changed so did the city's cultural identity. The founding of the Riverside Symphonia, and the recent move by the Roxey Ballet, would never have happened in the old industrial river town.

The sky's the limit for this porch.

A porch with its feet on the ground. Photo: Martin E. Kennedy

The creation of the Riverside Symphonia gave Lambertville its own professional orchestra dedicated to providing world-class music in a local setting at prices affordable to all. Since its inception over a decade ago, it has become a vibrant part of the community performing classical repertoire in the acoustically excellent St. John the Evangelist Church with distinguished guest soloists and conductors. For information on the Symphonia's subscription series, family concerts, and special events, visit www.riversidesymphonia.org, or call 609-397-7300.

The founding of Artsbridge in 1993 proved that among the artists of the area there is a strong sense of community. The group is open to artists and art lovers alike with basic membership a nominal $20.00. After eight years, Artsbridge has well over 300 members, holds meetings which explore the creative process on the third Wednesday of each month at Riverrun Gallery in Lambertville, and publishes a newsletter as well as collections of member's writing in "The Writers Gallery." In 2000 Artsbridge opened its own gallery in the Linseed Building at Prallsville Mills in Stockton. The mill is also the site of the seven-year-old Artsbridge National Juried Exhibition held each April. For more information on membership, activities, and programs, call 609-773-0881 or visit www.artsbridgeonline.com.

The newest addition to the Lambertville cultural scene is the

Roxey Ballet Company and its Mill Ballet School. Founders, Mark and Melissa Roxey, both had distinguished careers in American dance as members of the Joffrey Ballet and Dayton Ballet, among others, before returning to Melissa's home town in Hunterdon County in 1994 with a mission to advance and preserve the art of dance. In 1994 they founded the Hunterdon County Youth Ballet at Prallsville Mills in Stockton, and in 1996, The Mill Ballet School. The company grew rapidly receiving high praise from all who were touched by it, and in 1999 moved to its current state-of-the-art facility at 243 N. Union Street in Lambertville, and adopted the name, Roxey Ballet Company, to reflect the founders vision of a world-class dance organization.

Today, the school has 400 students and the company draws large audiences whenever it performs. It has brought dance to young students in the local schools, and, through its "Wheels in Motion" program in conjunction with the Matheny School and Hospital, to children and adults with complex physical and neurological disabilities. For more information call the company at 609-397-7616, or the school at 609-397-7244.

Perhaps the most notable fact in Lambertville is that new hasn't replaced old, it has simply augmented it. Here, where industry thrived before much of the nation had broken ground, you will find simple country pleasures mixed with urban sophistication.

Today's Harvest Moon Inn inhabits the impressive Jersey sandstone structure erected in 1811 for the Amwell Academy, a popular educational institutional in its day.

RINGOES

From its first settlement around 1721, Ringoes position at the junction of Indian paths leading from Trenton and Lambertville made it a natural meeting point. When the York Road was completed, it became an overnight stop for the Swift-Sure Stage. John Ringo, believed to be the first settler, built a log tavern which served as his home and as public quarters. The only resting place for miles, it was guaranteed success making Ringo a very rich man. He lived in constant fear that the British would take his fortune and buried the money revealing its whereabouts to no one.

Following Ringo other settlers came to the Amwell Valley, bought

land and built their homes. Among the earliest houses was that of Peter Fisher, who built a log cabin on ground he purchased in 1729. Peter Fisher came to this country on a ship that was blown off course and landed in Philadelphia rather than its intended destination of New York. Setting off with a traveling companion, Peter Johann Rockefeller, Fisher planned to walk to New York. Whether fatigue or the beautiful countryside of west Hunterdon stopped them, both men ended their travels when they reached Ringoes.

Though John Ringo's log tavern no longer exists, its modern day counterpart is housed in the impressive Jersey sandstone structure erected in 1811. Across the road stands the Landis house, perhaps the oldest house in the county. It was here that the Marquis de Lafayette recuperated from an illness contracted at Valley Forge. Ringoes' location, on the Indian trails and the York Road, made it a busy colonial community. The stage line shifted in the early 19th century leaving Ringoes off the beaten path. Its destiny was to become the quiet rural village of today.

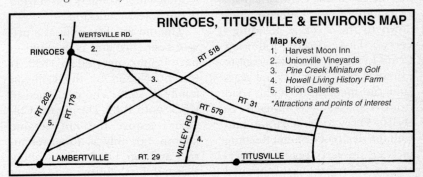

RINGOES, TITUSVILLE & ENVIRONS MAP

WERTSVILLE RD.
RINGOES
RT 518
RT 202
RT 179
RT 579
RT 31
VALLEY RD
LAMBERTVILLE
RT. 29
TITUSVILLE

Map Key
1. Harvest Moon Inn
2. Unionville Vineyards
3. *Pine Creek Miniature Golf*
4. *Howell Living History Farm*
5. Brion Galleries

*Attractions and points of interest

The historic Prallsville Mills are situated in the Delaware and Raritan Canal State Park in Stockton and are operated by the local Delaware River Mill Society.

STOCKTON

Traveling north from Lambertville on Route 29, the road follows the river to the country town of Stockton, first called Reading's Ferry for Colonel John Reading. Credited with being the first settler of Hunterdon County, he operated the ferry around 1700, and in 1703 was made the Indian agent for the area.

Reading played a major role in laying out the original Old York Road. It was through his efforts that in 1711 the road ran from Philadelphia to Lahaska and down to the river at Reading's Ferry. This route, following Lenni-Lenape trails, was meant to extend to New York. Several years later the main spur of the road from Lahaska was moved to Wells's Ferry at New Hope, and with the death of Colonel Reading in 1717, the ferry ceased to operate. In 1731 the ferry reopened but never regained its early importance as it was no longer on the main route from Philadelphia to New York.

The town remains today much as it was in the eighteenth century. For all its small size and rural nature, the town is presided over by a fine old country inn. The Stockton Inn, established in 1710, is the one that Richard Rodgers immortalized in song. *There's a Small Hotel with a Wishing Well* was written when Rodgers was staying in the hotel in Stockton.

The inn was first built as a private residence and is believed to have been converted in 1832. It was purchased by the Colligan family in 1922, who continued to run it until 1983. During the Colligan's tenure the inn became famous, not only as a fine restaurant and inn, but for the wishing well and the Colligan's pets—Saint

Bernards and deer! The murals on the dining room walls were painted during the depression by local artists, R.A.D. Miller and Robert Hogue, in trade for food and drink. The Stockton Inn is dominated by character, both that of time and of the Colligan family. Sold in 1983, the commitment to those intangible qualities which set Colligan's apart continues.

A newer conversion from private residence to inn is the Woolverton Inn. Built in 1793 by John Prall and later remodeled by Maurice Woolverton, the structure is a blend of 18th and 19th century architecture. Owned from 1957 to 1972 by St. John Terrell, producer of the Music Circus in Lambertville, the house hosted many celebrities while Terrell lived there. It is one of few local homes that can boast that George Washington's re-creator slept here. It was during this time that St. John Terrell first created the role of General Washington in the Christmas crossing reenactments at Washington Crossing Historic

Park. Today guests are invited to share the historic house with its young enthusisastic innkeepers and enjoy the resident sheep and the quiet country setting.

Stockton's place in history may lie in the contributions of its native sons. John Deats, an inventor of no small consequence, gave the farmer the Deats plow and the Deats corn sheller. John's son, Hiram, had a factory in Stockton in 1852 that manufactured threshing machines, reapers, mowers and corn shellers. The poultry business thrived in Hunterdon County, and it was a Stockton hatchery man, Joseph Wilson, who shipped the first day-old baby chicks.

An exciting development in Stockton was the formation of the Delaware River Mill Society to preserve and promote the Pralls-ville Mills. Since the society's founding, the mill has become a cultural and environmental center attracting participation from throughout the state. Through their efforts, the site was placed on the National Register of Historic Places in 1973, and in 1974, the entire property became a part of the Delaware and Raritan Canal State Park. A splendid biking and hiking path on the old railroad bed runs north along the canal

The herb garden at Prallsville Mills.

A successful preservation project.

from the Mill to Bull's Island and on to Frenchtown.

John Prall, Jr. became owner of the property on May 1, 1794, and with his settlement the area became known as Prallsville. The main mill was built in 1877 by I. Stout Stover on the foundation of the original mill. The current complex consists of four principal buildings: the main mill, which is open to the public, the granary which was attached about 1900, the small linseed oil mill, and the saw mill in the red frame building. The oldest of the buildings is the linseed oil mill which was recorded by John Prall's grandson as being used as a post office, general store and for Sunday services.

The Prallsville Mills are open to the public on Sundays from 1 to 4 from Memorial Day to August 25th. Guides explain how the grist mill worked and there is an opportunity to tour a garden of industrial herbs. The roster of events this year includes the Mill's annual antique show, art and sculpture shows, and concerts. For more information write to P.O. Box 298, Stockton, New Jersey 08559, or call 609-397-3586.

Artsbridge, the Lambertville based arts organization, finally had a home when the Linseed Building at the Prallsville Mills became its headquarters and gallery in the fall of 2000. The gallery is a cooperative that offers monthly exhibits of work by roughly eight Artsbridge members. Gallery hours are Thursday through Sunday from noon to 6 pm. For information call 609-773-0881.

❧

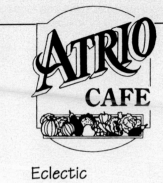

Alone on the river. Photo: Martin E. Kennedy

Road sign marks a place in history.

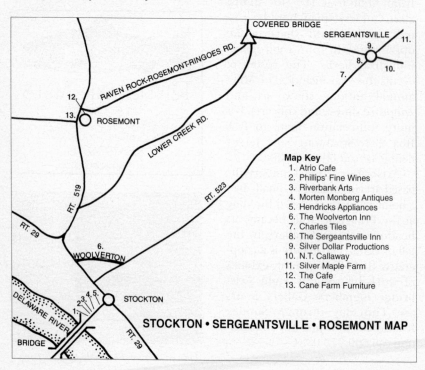

COVERED BRIDGE

SERGEANTSVILLE

11.

9.

8.

10.

RAVEN ROCK-ROSEMONT-RINGOES RD.

7.

12.

13. ROSEMONT

LOWER CREEK RD.

RT. 519

RT. 523

RT. 29

6.
WOOLVERTON

2 3 4 5.
1.

STOCKTON

DELAWARE RIVER

RT. 29

BRIDGE

Map Key
1. Atrio Cafe
2. Phillips' Fine Wines
3. Riverbank Arts
4. Morten Monberg Antiques
5. Hendricks Appliances
6. The Woolverton Inn
7. Charles Tiles
8. The Sergeantsville Inn
9. Silver Dollar Productions
10. N.T. Callaway
11. Silver Maple Farm
12. The Cafe
13. Cane Farm Furniture

STOCKTON • SERGEANTSVILLE • ROSEMONT MAP

Green Sergeant Bridge, New Jersey's last covered bridge. Photo: Martin E. Kennedy

SERGEANTSVILLE-ROSEMONT

Drive into the country up from the Delaware Valley and you will find yourself reminded of Hunterdon County's agrarian beginnings. The rolling fields and picturesque barns belong to farms where life has changed little in the three hundred years since colonial settlers first tilled the land.

Resting peacefully in the midst of this serene farmland is the village of Sergeantsville. The village was first settled by one Mr. Thatcher about 1700 and later named for Charles Sergeant, a revolutionary soldier.

It is hard to believe today that this tiny hamlet was once the center of a massive peach industry. About 1850, Dr. George Larison planted an orchard of 3,000 trees. By 1862 the trees were bearing fruit and shipments were made by rail to New York. By the 1860s special trains were shipping from

Sergeantsville to Lambertville, Bordentown and South Amboy.

In a single day in 1882, 64 carloads were shipped from here, and by 1889 Hunterdon County had two million peach trees and sold almost one million baskets of fruit. Peach growing stimulated other local industries, such as basket making, and employed hundreds of people.

About the turn of the century the San Jose scale appeared in Hunterdon County and nearly wiped out the industry. By 1959, two million trees had diminished to a mere fifteen thousand.

The Sergeantsville Inn in the center of the village speaks of an era when the local tavern was the focal point of rural life and served as a meeting place for a multiplicity of purposes. This tavern was one of the many where patriots gathered to fan the fires of revolution.

To the contrary today, it is a charming quiet country inn.

Fred Miller, a then-familiar face from his Lawn Doctor commercials, moved to Sergeantsville in 1983. He commuted to New York to work until 1987 when he founded the professional theatre company, Silver Dollar Productions, whose musical events have become a tradition in the area.

The company has covered nearly all musical bases in the past fourteen years and has over two dozen programs in its repertoire: The Golden Age of Operetta, Big Bank Memories, Gershwin, Berlin, Porter, Rodgers, Hammerstein, Kern, Arlen, Mercer, grand opera highlights, an all-Italian program, special holiday celebrations, and 19th century patriotic and barbershop material.

His latest addition was a six-part Lectures-in-Song series on "The Great American Songwriters," presented in full at the Philadelphia Art Alliance and the Hunterdon County Library. The success of this series prompted Miller to create a second six-part series on "The Great Lyricists."

The Copper Penny Players, now in its 20th year, is Miller's class for non-professional singing enthusiasts who come from as far away as Philadelphia and Princeton. Students practice solos in ten weeks of classes before appearing in a live revue. Musical talent or experience is not a prerequisite, only the desire to sing. For information on classes, private parties, or a schedule of upcoming performances, call 609-397-8700.

Just down the Ringoes-Rosemont Road west of Sergeantsville is Green Sergeant's Bridge, the last of 75 covered bridges that once stood in New Jersey.

Continuing on you come to the village of Rosemont, settled in 1719 by William Rittenhouse. The family homestead served friends, neighbors, and visitors as the Rittenhouse Tavern from 1757 until

got wine?

The Sergeantsville Inn
10 minutes from NewHope
609-397-3700

1870 when the temperance movement saw to it that its doors were shut, never to reopen.

During the Revolution, when machine oil was in short supply, the family ran a tannery near Prallsville. A local tale suggests that when a freshet stranded several sturgeon in the nearby creek, the tanners deduced that fish oil could replace machine oil. The tale goes on to say that the tanners were tempted to try the fish and that this marked the beginning of sturgeon eating in Hunterdon County. The predominant feature of Rosemont today is Cane Farm. Phil Cane transformed the family chicken farm into shops that house, among others, the local post office and his own Cane Farm Furniture. An old craft continues here, with handmade recreations of early American and custom

furniture still being made at the farm. A remodeled chicken coop serves as one of the largest country furniture showrooms to be found. Antiques, clocks, bookbinding, a sculpture garden, and The Cafe round out the commerce of this tiny village.

The Cafe at Rosemont in the old Rosemont Country Store is at once unusual and exactly what you hope you'll find in the farmland of Hunterdon at a country crossroad. The setting is as unpretentious as it comes and the surprise is the food. Called full-flavored by The New York Times, the restaurant was rated "very good" in a Times review in July 2000. A favorite spot for breakfast and lunch Tuesday through Sunday, The Cafe serves dinner Wednesday through Sunday.

The bridge at Frenchtown.

FRENCHTOWN

If you go back to the river from Rosemont and continue north you will come to the village of Frenchtown. Like so many other river communities, Frenchtown was the early site of a ferry. The service dated from about 1741, when it was known as London Ferry. Later, it was called Mechlenburg Ferry, Tinbrook's Ferry, Prigmore's Ferry, Sherrerd's Ferry and Edwin's Ferry. It was looked upon as a site of such strategic importance during the Revolution that in 1778 the Council of Safety of New Jersey agreed to exempt ferry owner John Sherrerd and his three employees from militia duty.

In 1776 a tract of land surrounding the ferry was purchased by Mr. Thomas Lowrey, the son-in-law of Samuel Fleming, for whom Flemington was named.

Lowrey built a grist mill, saw mill and a home in the village that was then known as Sun Beam. The mills continued to operate into the early 1900s grinding corn into meal for Hunterdon County's poultry farmers.

In 1794 a tract of 893 acres the township of Alexandria was purchased by Swiss aristocrat, Paul Henri Mallet-Prevost, who came to America fleeing a French order for his arrest. Prevost's Paris banking career came to an end during the French Revolution when he was suspected of saving many of his countrymen during a massacre of the Swiss. The local population assumed him to be French, thus the town around his home came to be known as Frenchtown.

In the early 1800s, growth in the village followed that of the

Beyond The Looking Glass

Gallery of Internationally Acclaimed
Master Printmaker and Painter

Charles Klabunde

Paintings   Drawings
Limited Edition Etchings

33 Bridge Street . Frenchtown, New Jersey
908.996.6464
Artist Studio Visits by Appointment

other river towns. Oak and hickory from local woodland was suplemented by timber brought down the river to supply the sawmills, and Frenchtown's shops manufactured wagons, harnesses, wheels, rims, spokes and hubs.

In a comfortable hour's walk one can explore the Frenchtown Historic District, listed on the National Register of Historic Places, which is made up of mills, an old brick tavern, Greek Revival hotel, and Victorian houses and commercial buildings. One of the oldest is today's Frenchtown Inn, the earliest section of which dates to 1805 when it was built by Prevost and was known as The Old Brick Tavern. In 1838, the present hotel was completed and renamed the Rail Road House in anticipation of the Belvidere and Delaware railroad line extending from Trenton to Frenchtown.

The first bridge at Frenchtown was built in 1844 and with it the town became a gateway to Pennsylvania. The current bridge, built in 1930, is still considered a primary asset of the town.

In 1849 Samuel B. Hudnit laid out streets and offered building lots for sale on the farm just above the village. While sales began slowly, a rumor that the Pennsylvania Railroad was going to move its shops to Frenchtown caused sales to become brisk. In the *Hunterdon County Master Plan, Sites of Historic Interest*, published in 1979 by the county, Frenchtown is described as having "the unique quality of being one (perhaps the only) 'speculator or development

towns built in Hunterdon County.'"

Like other 18th and 19th century industrial towns, Frenchtown fell victim to the mid-20th century migration of industry and commerce to more urban areas. The last three decades saw the transformation of Frenchtown from a post-industrial river town into a special place where new residents, new businesses, and visitors, all came because of the natural beauty of its quiet setting on the river. Its own unique character developed as the store fronts on Bridge and Race Street became home to antiques shops, art and craft galleries, and a proliferation of restaurants and cafes.

Artists have been coming to Frenchtown since the 1930s. The writer, Nathanael West, completed *Miss Lonelyhearts* in a rented room here, and in 1930 Kurt Wiese, best known for his illustrations for the original *Bambi* book, moved to Frenchtown and stayed until his death in 1974. He illustrated over 300 children's books, including eighteen which he wrote and illustrated, for which he won the Caldecott Medal and the Newbury Award. A painter as well as an illustrator and writer, Weise exhibited at Phillips Mill outside New Hope and in local galleries.

Charles Klabunde's Beyond the Looking Glass Gallery offers the

Frenchtown's old Odd Fellows Hall. Photo: Martin E. Kennedy

most unexpected experience in Frenchtown. One is transported "beyond the looking glass," both by the art around you and by the artist, who willingly shares the passions that drive his work—personal visions interwoven with forgotten myths, lost innocence, and the magic of wonder. A painter and master printmaker, he has been compared with Bosch, Durer and Blake; and the Metropolitan Museum, National Gallery, and Philadelphia Museum, are among the major museums where his work is part of the permanent collections.

In the fall of 1999, after more than thirty years of working in New York, Charles Klabunde moved his studio to Frenchtown across the street from the gallery.

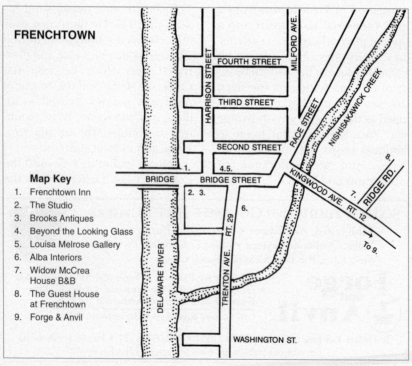

FRENCHTOWN

Map Key
1. Frenchtown Inn
2. The Studio
3. Brooks Antiques
4. Beyond the Looking Glass
5. Louisa Melrose Gallery
6. Alba Interiors
7. Widow McCrea House B&B
8. The Guest House at Frenchtown
9. Forge & Anvil

With the new studio in place, he began work on an important series of six etchings titled "Studies of the Revolutionary Mind." Klabunde describes the series as a commentary on the 20th century's flirtation with nihilism, an analytical study of the disintegration of the revolutionary mind as it moves from the search for idealism to madness. He believes that art defines reality by mirroring society, and can portray visually those darker aspects of society that can neither be spoken nor written. The series of black and white etchings, reminiscent of Goya's "Disasters of War," can be seen in the gallery as a boxed folio complete with Klabunde's commentary.

Surrounding the businesses on Bridge Street is a charming small village, the natural beauty of the river, and a walking path that invites you to slip away. Plan a stop in Frenchtown: visit its artists, be touched by its history, enjoy a taste of past, present, and future in the quiet of a river town.

A walk by the river. Photo: Martin E. Kennedy

Milford on the Delaware, the quintessential river village. Photo: Martin E. Kennedy

MILFORD

The first saw mill and two houses were built in Milford about 1760. The mill burned and the town became known as Burnt Mills. One Thomas Lowrey of Flemington bought several large tracts of land in the vicinity including Burnt Mill Farm. In 1798 Lowrey contracted to have the grist mill and a saw mill built along the river. Shortly thereafter Julius Foster built another saw mill.

Just above the mill a ferry was licensed to cross the river and was called the Lowreytown Ferry. The name changed to Burnt Mills Ferry, and later to Mill-ford Ferry. By 1820 it had settled at Milford.

The ferry was abandoned in 1842 when a bridge was built across the river. The bridge added bustle to the small community as it gave the farmers and industry over the surrounding mountains access to the Delaware Canal in Pennsylvania, and opened new markets for their goods.

In 1844 the roster of businesses included 3 stores, 3 taverns, 12-15 mechanic shops, a flour mill and 2 saw mills. The residential community included 45 dwellings, 2 churches and a school.

Milford's major industry is the paper mill at the south entry to town. Begun in a converted grist mill in Finesville by Reigel Paper, which later opened four other local mills, it was one of its largest. With four owners in its history, it was taken over this year by Curtis Paper Company.

In 1911 Milford incorporated as a borough by a vote of 126 to 20, separating from Holland Township so that it could control its own destiny and purse strings. In the first year the new council appropriated funds for street lighting and a water supply for

CHESTNUT HILL ON THE DELAWARE

BED AND BREAKFAST
908-995-9761
www.chestnuthillnj.com
Victorian e-mail: ChHillInn@aol.com

Lovely accommodations in Victorian Elegance

63 CHURCH STREET • PO BOX N • MILFORD, NEW JERSEY 08848

fire protection, both concerns that still appear on local agendas today.

Milford has blossomed over the last few years and, in addition to being a beautiful river town, is the home of a number of interesting restaurants, specialty shops and the charming bed and breakfast, Chestnut Hill on the Delaware.

With its picturesque setting overlooking the river, Chestnut Hill offers traditional bed and breakfast lodging on Church Street. The ambiance at Chestnut Hill is Victorian elegance, and owners, Linda and Rob Castagna, maintain that sense of civility in every aspect of the operation of the inn. This extends even to Linda's handwriting, which makes receiving a letter from Linda, written in fine, florid calligraphy, a reminder of a past time, and a pleasure.

Milford's major employer today is The Baker, the trademark of the Adams Bakery Corporation. In 1976 The Baker was one young man with extraordinary baking credentials and the idea to create a fabulous loaf of bread using today's technology but keeping old-fashioned quality and goodness intact. It had the aura of

another time. The Baker now serves local villagers twelve varieties of breads and rolls from an old-fashioned retail shop. That one young baker has fifty co-workers and loaves of bread are distributed all around the Delaware Valley, throughout New Jersey, Baltimore, Washington, New York City, Boston and Connecticut

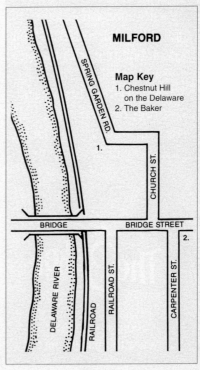

MILFORD

Map Key
1. Chestnut Hill on the Delaware
2. The Baker

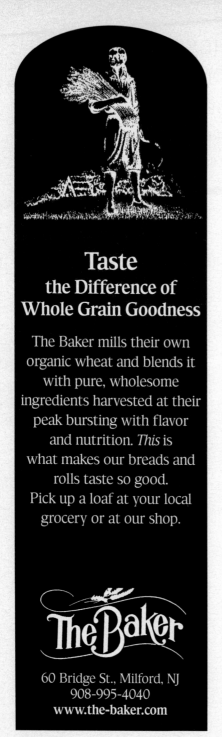
Across the street, The Ship Inn restoration brought a fine Victorian building back to life. The 1860's building maintains the original tin ceiling, beams and handmade brickwork. In past times it housed a bakery and then an ice cream parlor with a speak-easy in the back during Prohibition.

As the first brewpub in New Jersey, The Ship tapped its first home made draft beer on January 15, 1995. The Ship specializes in British ales using 3 beer engines as well as the standard draft method to complete its authenticity as a British pub. This family run business has installed a 7 barrel system from Peter Austin and uses traditional open fermentors and top fermenting Ringwood Yeast. Brew day is usually Tuesday or Thursday and short tours are available. For further information call (908) 995-0188.

The annual "Christmas in Milford", chaired by Melissa Harrison, Milford Guild president, is a warm, festive occasion shared by the local community and visitors alike. Milford opens the holiday season on the second Friday in December with the arrival of the animals for the unusual live manger scene. Santa, Mrs. Claus, and the elves make a spectacular arrival at 6:00 p.m. each year, and the whole town turns out to welcome them with a community open house. Visit Milford online at http://milfordnewjersey2000.tripod.com.

North of Milford along the river are the cliffs of Milford Bluffs, an important ecologic area protected by the Nature Conservancy.

ALEXANDRIA TOWNSHIP

Traveling west back through rural farmland on the southern slope of the Musconetong Ridge you will come to Alexandria Township. Little changed by time, the villages of Mt. Pleasant, Little York, and Everittstown are rich in history, and Everittstown has been listed on the National Historical Register.

Turning into the rural farmland outside of Everittstown will bring you to Alexandria Airport. An example of American pioneer spirit, the airport is on land still owned by the descendants of Reuben A. Williamson, who, in 1876, came to farm 126 acres in Alexandria Township.

Reuben Williamson's heritage goes back to the original founder of the family in New Jersey, who came here from Germany. His mother, Charity Clifford Williamson's grandfather served in Captain Horton's company in the Revolutionary War and was with Washington for the crossing of the Delaware in 1776.

PITTSTOWN

Pittstown is located at the intersection of two major Hunterdon County roads, the north south Route 579 and the east west Route 513, both of which follow Indian paths the were there long before the community was settled. Once mentioned as the county seat of Hunterdon, the village is listed on early maps as "Huffs" or "Hoffs Mills." The Capoolong Creek that runs through the village was an attraction for early settlers and they soon established three of the oldest churches in present day Hunterdon in the vicinity of Pittstown. The oldest, Saint Thomas Episcopal, established in 1723, lies to the southwest; the Bethlehem Presbyterian, organized in 1730, is located to the northeast on Route 513; and the Quaker Meetinghouse, built in 1733, is on Route 579 to the southeast.

Pittstown played an important part in the Revolutionary War through the efforts of Moore Furman, who served as Deputy Quartermaster General for New Jersey. Furman had purchased most of the village prior to the Revolution and had changed its name from Hoffs Mills to Pittstown. Tradition says that Furman changed the name in honor of William Pitt, the British statesman who spoke up for the rights of the American Colonists.

Still a rural business community, Pittstown has experienced "changing times." What was once a thriving feed mill has become an outlet for recreational vehicles and the nail factory and mill is a lumber yard. The village now boasts a bank, interior decorator and Sky Manor Airport.

18th century stone mill, home of the Hunterdon Museum of Art.

CLINTON

The town of Clinton, tucked away in the dip of a valley created by the confluence of the South Branch of the Raritan River and Spruce Run River, is a quintessential American small town. The business district encircles the intersection of Main and Leigh Streets and on a quiet spring afternoon you'll find shopkeepers standing under the cherry trees chatting in front of their stores. At the west end of Main Street a two hundred foot wide waterfall separates two old mills, both of which have been restored and put to modern use. It isn't surprising that film crews have been using Clinton as a stage set for years.

This wonderful scene out of *Our Town* is surrounded by three major highways, Route 31, Route 22 and Interstate 78. When the last leg of the interstate was completed several years ago, it made the trip from New York City only

a short one hour drive to Clinton.

In the mid-eighteenth century the Easton and New Brunswick Turnpike passed through Clinton and David McKinney built a mill on the river's west bank about that time. It was replaced by a woolen mill in 1812. Near the time of the Revolution, Daniel Hunt bought a tract of land along the river on the east side and built a crudely constructed stone grist mill.

Called Hunt's Mills at that time, Clinton had two taverns, Bonnell's and Jones's, which were recruiting sites for the Continental Army. In 1775 a regiment of "minute men" was formed at Bonnell's Tavern.

The town took its current name from New York Governor DeWitt Clinton in 1825 and was incorporated in 1865.

The business community is an eclectic collection of small independent enterprises that work together as the Clinton Guild to promote and preserve the community. Fine craftsmanship and a sense of style are evident in the shopkeepers choice of merchandise, and in the careful maintenance of the historic streetscape.

A special event sponsored by the Guild is the annual Dickens Days weekend, held in late November, when the whole town turns into a festive village. December brings the annual Christmas parade with wonderful floats and fun for all.

The 1810 Hunt's red mill is the contemporary home of the Hunterdon Historical Museum. (see article on page 282)

2001 marks the 38th year the museum has been open to the public. In 1974 the Red Mill was listed on the National and State Registers of Historic Places and in 1977 the Museum received accreditation from the American Association of Museums.

More information on the Hunterdon Historical Museum and its schedule of events may be found in the Calendar of Events or by calling 908-735-4101.

Across the river, the Dunham/Parry Mill was in operation from 1832 until 1949. Functioning as a

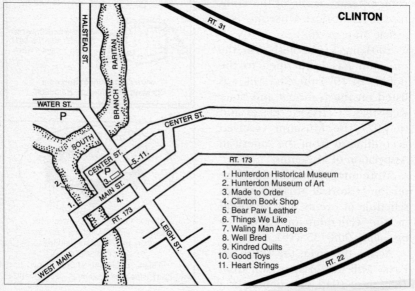

CLINTON

1. Hunterdon Historical Museum
2. Hunterdon Museum of Art
3. Made to Order
4. Clinton Book Shop
5. Bear Paw Leather
6. Things We Like
7. Waling Man Antiques
8. Well Bred
9. Kindred Quilts
10. Good Toys
11. Heart Strings

nonprofit organization since July 1952, the Hunterdon Museum of Art's (see article on page 278) broad based range of services is guided by its mission "to provide education and participation in the arts" for the entire community.

For more information and a full schedule of events call 908-735-8415.

Two state parks located near Clinton afford the visitor to this beautiful area an opportunity to hike, camp, swim and otherwise enjoy the area's natural resources. Spruce Run is just north of town and Round Valley is to the southeast just a few miles on Route 22.

Natural beauty and historic perspective, fine shops filled with exciting wares, craftsmen at work, as well as a wonderfully informed and friendly atmosphere make a visit to Clinton, whether from near or far, an occasion to remember.

An unusual porch. Photo: Martin E. Kennedy

Lebanon Township

The Borough of Glen Gardner is located on the western edge of Lebanon Township. Before its incorporation in 1919, the area was known as Eveland, after John Eveland, who built and kept a tavern here as early as 1760. By 1820, the name had changed to Clarksville, after Joseph Clark who ran the general store.

By the late 1860s the town's name had changed to Glen Gardner. Snell's *History of Hunterdon and Somerset* describes Glen Gardner in the 1880s as having three churches, one Academy, a hotel, two gristmills, a frame factory, four stores, a coal and lumber yard, several shops and a railroad depot.

The 516 acre Voorhees State Park near Glen Gardner is the site of the New Jersey Astronomical Association's observatory. For information on tours of the observatory call 908-638-8500. The park includes individual and group camp sites, a paracourse fitness circuit, fire rings, hiking, a nature area, and is open all year. For park information call 908-638-6969.

The village of Annandale was first known as Clinton Station, the name it held until 1873 when John T. Johnson, president of the Central Railroad, renamed the village after a town in his native Scotland.

A charming small village, the center of Lebanon has changed little in the past century and its Dutch Reformed Church is one of the oldest churches in the county. The records begin in 1769, however, the church is cited as early as 1747.

Lebanon's museum. Photo: Martin E. Kennedy

New Hampton

This charming riverside village on the banks of the Musconetcong River has quietly slipped into the twentieth century with little change from its early beginnings. .

Among New Hampton's famous native sons is Daniel Morgan, who was born in 1719 on Forge Hill Road. At the age of 20, Morgan moved with his family to Virginia where he later joined the colonial army as a teamster, rising to the rank of Brigadier General.

The Lebanon Township Museum is housed in the old New Hampton one-room school, built in 1823. This living history museum invites school children to spend a day in a nineteenth century school where they are taught elocution, history, arithmetic, reading and participate in a spelldown.

The museum is open Tuesday and Thursday from 9:30 to 5 pm

Oldwick Community Center. Photo: Martin E. Kennedy

and Saturday from 1 to 5 pm. Admission is free. For information on lectures and craft classes, write to R.D. 2, Box 645, Hampton, NJ 08827, or call 908-537-6464.

TEWKSBURY TOWNSHIP

Tewksbury Township's earliest settlement was in the late 1720s on a tract purchased from the Indians in 1710 by the West Jersey Society. The first settlements appear on a direct line from Potterstown to Pottersville, as settlers moved west from Somerset and Middlesex Counties.

In 1740, James Logan, William Penn's secretary, owned most of the land in Tewksbury and divided it into farms which he let to others on 110 year leases. Tewksbury was separated from Lebanon Township in 1755, then gerrymandered to Somerset County in 1844, and returned to Hunterdon the following year.

Among the villages in Tewksbury, Mountainville is a rural hamlet that maintains the original character of its early nineteenth century beginnings. Sixteen of its twenty-nine old buildings are figured on the Cornell map of 1851. With Oldwick and Pottersville, it is protected by Historic District legislation.

OLDWICK

Oldwick came into being as New Germantown. Its settlers were part of the same group that came from Europe and took up residence in Germantown, Pennsylvania. The land they chose to tame was bountiful terrain, although secluded and ringed by mountains.

The village was the center of the first Lutheran congregation in the area, established in 1714. In 1749 the Zion Lutheran Congregation purchased land at the intersections of Potterstown and Fox Hill Roads to build their church. The land that was not needed by the church itself was divided into lots which comprise the core of the town today. The church, still holding services today, stands as the home of New Jersey's oldest Lutheran congregation in continuous service.

The commerce of the town is centered around the historic

Tewksbury Inn and the busy General Store of Oldwick. Steve Roth certainly filled a need, and did it very well, when he expanded the General Store to include not only the original country store, but the adjacent dining rooms. An interesting selection of antiques, art, books, and gifts round out the offerings of the small business community.

A recent addition was the opening of Collections in the building that for so many years was home to The Pink Sleigh. Joyce and Rick Brady, owners of the Tewksbury Inn, turned the space into a charming collection of shops throughout the house which specialize in antiques and collectibles. Shopping at Collections is like strolling through a lovely house.

A very special establishment is The Magic Shop, which benefits the Bonnie Brae Foundation. Started by Lib Schley and Mari Watts, each Easter the shop is magical with a bit of fantasy called the "Rabbit's Hole", reached through a blackened tunnel surrounded by lighted scenes from the animal world. Also a special place at Christmas, Santa Claus meets children in the barn. The Magic Shop is open Monday through Saturday from 10 to 1 and 2 to 5. During June, July and August the shop is closed on Mondays. For more information on Santa's appearance or to learn more about the Rabbit's Hole call the shop at 908-439-2330.

Leaving the town one moves into beautiful countryside which rises gently to become the hills of Hunterdon. The area has for years been a center for cider making with two cider mills and large numbers of apple and peach orchards.

The Cold Brook Preserve encompasses historic Oldwick and an area of 298 acres surrounding it. The Preserve is made up of acquired farmland and conservation easements. It includes scenic rolling fields, orchards, and old farm pastures, in addition to a contiguous easement along the Cold Brook.

READINGTON TOWNSHIP

Settled as early as 1710, the nearly 45 square miles of Readington Township was a large agricultural community. The first resident is believed to have been Adrian Lane, who came to the vicinity of today's Readington Village around 1715.

The township includes the villages of Centerville, Three Bridges, Pleasant Run, Potterstown, Reading Mills, Readington Village, Stanton, Whitehouse and Whitehouse Station.

On the boundary of Readington Township, Solberg Airport is the site of the Quick Chek New Jersey Festival of Ballooning, which takes place in 2001 from July 27-29.

This year's festival includes the Quick Chek Eagle, the GPU Polar Bear, and the Energizer Bunny, Entertainment features Mary Wilson & The Supremes and KC & The Sunshine Band

For a full schedule of events, times, and tickets, call the festival office at 800-HOT-AIR-9.

go higher

Where do designers and production pros go for the highest quality graphic arts services? They come to us —

Bucks County Digital Imaging.
For prepress, scanning, color digital printing, large format signs and displays. We combine high-tech equipment with old fashioned service and expertise. We offer FREE pick-up and delivery* and turnaround to meet your most demanding schedules.

Give us a call to receive our current price list and catalog of services or to schedule a pick up at **215-757-3600**.

*For qualified accounts in our trading region — call for details.

Wineries
continued from page 213

Katy and Jerry Forest in the Buckingham Valley cellars.

of wine a year. Kathy Forest's favorite is their chardonnay, although she admits, "it was sales of our Concord and Niagara that put my kids through college." Like several other area wineries, Buckingham Valley has joined the "nouveau" tradition, offering both a semi-dry medium red called Nouveau and a semi-sweet white called Nouvelle from November to January.

Visitors approach the winery, located just south of Buckingham, Pennsylvania, via a long drive flanked on either side by vineyards. Picnic tables outside the tasting room provide another means of relishing the view across the spacious lawn. Buckingham Valley's relaxed ambiance extends to self-guided tours and a pour-your-own sampling of the dozen or so wines. Lucky visitors are treated to occasional spontaneous live music, a holdover from Jerry Forest's guitar-playing college days.

FRATELLI DESIATO VINEYARD
www.winepa.net

Visitors are often greeted with a hearty, "Benvenuto!" at Desiato Vineyard, the newest addition to Bucks County's wineries. That is because this family operation creates small batch, handcrafted wines in the Italian style on their twelve sun-drenched acres. Not afraid to experiment, the Desiato brothers have even been known to incorporate into their wines the berries and cherries that grow wild on their hilltop property outside Pipersville, Pennsylvania next to Ralph Stover Park. Desiato wines have fanciful names, such as the light, dry table wine made with cabernet franc grapes they named Caspita. Dolce Vita is a sweet and fruity red table wine, and what better name for a Pennsylvania Champagne than Serenata?

An Italy-in-Bucks-County ambiance permeates the rustic barn, where, with traditional Italian music playing in the background, weekend visitors sample wines, nibble on complimentary snacks of imported provolone, olives, and

continued on page 297

The winery at Unionville Vineyards.

$\mathcal{H}$ow is it some people can live in the same house for years and still lose themselves in the kitchen?

Just a little look at our distinctive kitchen designs may give you a very good clue.

Hankins & Associates Inc.
KITCHEN AND BATH DESIGN

TEL: 215.794.5930   FAX: 215.794.5931
Visit our Web Site for Cooking Class Information
www.i-kb.com

Outreach Key to Hunterdon Art Museum's Success

by Doris Brandes

Since 1952, the Hunterdon Museum of Art has enjoyed growth and prestige in the landmark stone grist mill on the South Branch of the Raritan River. Located centrally in the artistically developing, historic town of Clinton, New Jersey, it offers an extraordinarily beautiful environment in which to view art. The site is but the introduction to a facility which houses exhibitions of modern and contemporary art, ranging from the cutting edge to the traditional, and featuring established as well as emerging artists. The museum mounts about a dozen exhibitions each year and presents a series of other programs.

In 1779 through 1789 wheat was ground in the mill on this site for Washington's soldiers when they were encamped nearby. It was rebuilt in 1836 and shortly afterwards it had become a sausage factory and a blacksmith's shop. There was a great fire in the town of Clinton in 1891, at which time the roof of this central building ignited. Eventually, a group of public spirited citizens recognized its historic value and purchased it to be used as an art center. The building was placed on the State and National Historic Registers in 1981, but it didn't stop the great flood of the South Branch of the Raritan River in 1984 from causing enormous structural damage.

Tim Nussbaum, Listening, *1998, acrylic on resin, edition of 9. From Degrees of Figuration Exhibition. Photo courtesy of Hunterdon Museum of Art.*

The following year an extensive rehabilitation and renovation project was begun. At last, major flood control systems were installed, waterproofing of the foundation and installation of museum-standard environment, security controls, and barrier-free accessibility updated this important site. In 1997 the Trustees of the Art Center voted to change the name to the Hunterdon Museum of Art.

The museum's print collection, named after printmaker/ donor Anne Steele Marsh, was the catalyst which helped create the standards for the designation as museum. The print collection consists of more than three hundred prints made since the 1930s. Noted artists and other donors have contributed to this collection and it has been lauded by jurors and collectors alike. Eligible institutions and corporations are able to rent prints from this impressive collection for display in their establishments.

The Hunterdon Museum of Art has always sought to promote further interest in art for the community by offering classes in a variety of media to students of all ages. A summer art camp is offered for children as young as three-and-a-half, specially designed to awaken creativity. The offerings are extremely imaginative. The museum likes to refer to these workshops as, "An Art Odyssey," in which the finest artists in their fields are selected for faculty. Teens have an opportunity to learn while helping the younger children. Adult studio courses are frequently scheduled at times convenient for those with children registered in the camp. Adult courses are held throughout the year.

The dramatic setting of the mill invites regional use as the scene for private events. The walls are always aglow with art and the waterfall outside provides the nourishing sound of nature alive. Children's parties are a special feature which offer parents choices from a variety

Summer camp students with masks they made. Photo courtesy of Hunterdon Museum of Art.

of projects which entertain and educate the youngsters while they celebrate and have fun.

An exhibition this past December and January emphasized the strong identification of the museum with its home state. Thirty five artists who were 1999 and 2000 recipients of fellowships from the New Jersey State Council on the Arts exhibited the best of New Jersey art in categories of painting, works on paper, sculpture, photography, media, crafts and new/emerging genres. Each year there is a Members Exhibition in the spring, and this year's National Juried Print Exhibition is the museum's forty-fifth. It will be on view through July 22, 2001.

Director Marjorie Frankel Nathanson is looking ahead to the summer season and the rest of 2001 "with the hope that it will be a year of continued success and growth."

The stone mill. Photo courtesy of the Hunterdon Museum of Art.

Art
& Life:
A Dance
between
Earth &
Sky

Perfectly Suited for Your Country Lifestyle

Handcrafted period-inspired home furnishings, comfortable
sink-into sofas, decorative whimsical accessories . . . room after
charming room of objects that make your country house a home.

Cane Farm Furniture
SINCE 1965

Rt. 519, Rosemont, NJ (North of Stockton) • 609-397-0606
Open Fri. & Sat. 10-5, Sun. 1-5 & by Appointment

Historical Museum Preserves Hunterdon's Past

by Victoria Memminger

A narrow, graceful river with an energetic waterfall, banks lined with willows, a view into a small, tidy village—for sheer bucolic tranquility, you can't improve on the view from the Hunterdon County Historical Museum in Clinton, N.J.

The museum complex, which includes seven buildings you can go into and an equal number of sites to look at, has been there since the 1960s. It's centerpiece, the Red Mill, has been there since 1810.

"We're more than just the Red Mill, though," said Amy Caputo, the educational director of the Museum. "Because we have nine acres, people often think this is a park with a pretty old barn, but there's a lot to see here."

That's true, but because of its size and proximity to the parking lot, the Red Mill is the place to

A student tries her hand at rolling a hoop. Photo courtesy of the Hunterdon Historical Museum.

start. It also houses the gift shop, where you can pay as much as $60 for cobalt blue glassware from Williamsburg, Va., and as little as 25 cents for candy or a small toy. The majority of the goods is priced somewhere in between.

The water wheel still works in the Mill and among the exhibits surrounding it are displays of the various tools needed to shape the building through its evolution from a woolen mill to one that produced, successively, plaster, grist, talc and graphite, and peach baskets. Naturally enough, there is a 2,000 pound millstone, but there are also old bicycles, something that looks like the ancestor of the go-cart, tools for corn husking and cultivating. The walls are hung with old signs. There is a large col-

The Red Mill.

lection of butter churns and equally large number of baskets. One display area is devoted exclusively to spinning and weaving and has old looms and carders. On the top floor is an exhibit sure to delight children: a replica of the Mill, doll-house size. When a visitor commented on the number of items in each area, Ms. Caputo nodded. "There are more than 40,000 artifacts in this complex," she said.

The land behind the Red Mill was owned for three generations by a family named Mulligan, who ran it as a limestone quarry from 1848 to 1964. The first building to see is the quarry office, which would boggle the minds of today's ergonomic planners. Built in the early part of the 20th century, the Mulligans' headquarters was smaller than many a built-in closet in today's custom-built homes. It houses the original desk, three

Museum's basket collection includes peach baskets made at the mill.

plain wooden chairs, a stove for heating the room, a mounted deer head, an Oliver typewriter (which does not remotely resemble any other typewriter you have ever seen) and a hat rack that offers a nice cinematic touch—a man's battered felt hat, very like ones worn in movies of the 1930s, hangs on one of the hooks.

The next stop will be the blacksmith's shop. On the way there you will pass the stone crusher, the screenhouse, and the lime kilns— all essentials in the quarry business. The blacksmith shop, built some time before 1873, was first used as a wagon shed and may have been the first quarry office. Today it is a working blacksmith shop, run by a real blacksmith every day that the museum complex is open. The tools date from 1750 to 1950 and the blacksmith uses the old tools in the demonstrations he gives. Your nose will attest to the shop's authenticity; there is a not-unpleasant lingeringn odor of smoke and hot metal.

The two-family tenant house that the Mulligans built in 1860 for their employees is historic proof that the good old days were not necessarily good for everyone. Each family had a kitchen and a parlor downstairs and two bedrooms upstairs. There was no heat except for the kitchen stove and no indoor plumbing; until the 1940s, there was no electricity.The parlors have been turned into a replica of a general store of the period and the space also includes a post office, which was typical of

continued on page 284

many general stores during that era. The merchandise in the store includes all manner of dry goods, shoes, clothing, hats, dishes—it looks a lot like any number of antique shops that dot the countryside today. Ms. Caputo said that the items were mostly antique, though reproductions were included to create the proper atmosphere. This is true of the kitchen, as well. A small room with dilapidated furniture and plain pottery, the most noticeable item is a kickstart washing machine, which was dragged out to a dock on the river where the laundry was done and then hung on lines between the trees. It must have been a thankless job, since grey quarry dust tended to cover everything in sight.

Down the road from the tenant house is the schoolhouse, which was built in 1860, but is not original to the property; it was moved here from a neighboring township when the museum complex was established. The school was heated by a central stove and held 50 children. The desks in front are very small, indicating they were for the little children—towards the back of the room, they are larger. The school probably went from first to eighth grade, and it was crowded—children had to sit three to a bench and where there were no desks, they were put on benches against the back wall.

The last stop is the log cabin, which was built for the Bicentennial celebration in 1976. It's an amazingly good replica, and gives a clear picture of what family life must have been like during the Revolutionary War period. It's one room, and not a big one. There is a large stone fireplace with a loft above it, which is where the children slept on straw. There is a small four-poster bed, some ladderback chairs, a breadbox doing double duty as a nightstand, a table, and a spinning wheel. Ms. Caputo said that, like the general store display, the furniture and accessories here are a mixture of authentic and reproduction.

There is plenty to see outdoors at the Museum, too. The herb garden, the spring house, the wagon shed, the corn crib are all worth a look. It is the buildings, though, that give you a feeling of what life was like between 1810 and the early 20th century. The Hunterdon Historical Museum is an interesting and educational way to spend a couple of hours.

❧

Interpreter Daniela Johnson teaches a class in the schoolhouse. Photo courtesy of the Hunterdon Historical Museum.

Exquisite Variations on the Theme of Tile

Exquisite custom designs in stone, marble, granite and limestone for creating grand backdrops in the place you call home.

Traveling
Without Reservation

A well-planned trip begins
with the right luggage.
inside and out
t should
suit your needs.

And with our
huge selection of
quality brands and
knowledgable service
you'll be packing for
your next trip
with ease.

TUMI ■ SWISS ARMY
ANDIAMO ■ TRAVEL PRO
HARTMANN ■ SAMSONITE
BRIGGS & RILEY ■ RICARDO
ATLANTIC

The Luggage Factory
76 Hwy. 202, Ringoes, NJ 08551 (3 mi. S. of Flemingtor
908-788-4810 ■ www.luggagefactory.com

On the edge of Flemington, the barn on the Johann Kase Homestead, land bought from William Penn's sons in 1738, is a reminder of the town's agricultural beginnings.

FLEMINGTON

The 105 acres that comprise Flemington were originally the territory of the Lenni-Lenape Indians. In 1712, as part of a land parcel of 9,170 acres, the Flemington acreage was acquired by William Penn and Daniel Coxe.

In 1756, Samuel Fleming purchased part of that land and built his home which still stands on Bonnell Street. "Fleming's Town" was born. The house, known as "Fleming Castle," served as an inn and stage depot and was frequented by patriot leaders and the Hunterdon men who distinguished themselves in the Revolution.

When the Civil War came, the people of Flemington showed their colors as true Yankees. In a single evening following the Southern attack on Fort Sumter, the residents of Flemington raised $5,000 for the soldiers of the Union.

The surrounding fertile farmland dictated that the beginnings of Flemington would be essentially agricultural. Early German and English settlers engaged in industries dependent on farm products: spinning, weaving and milling. As time passed poultry and dairy farms superseded crops in agricultural importance. When our nation's capital was still in Philadelphia, the Capners of Flemington sold cheese to Martha Washington. However, this was the exception until the late 1800s when dairying became a profitable enterprise.

In 1785 Flemington was chosen as the county seat of Hunterdon,

an area which was then much larger than the county today. The Historic Hunterdon County Courthouse was built in 1826 following a fire which destroyed the original building. In 1998 a new courthouse was completed and the old structure became an historic site. In 2000 the exterior of the courthouse was restored to its appearance in 1930.

In 1935 the courthouse was the center of worldwide attention during the trial of Bruno Richard Hauptmann, accused of kidnaping and murdering the son of aviator Charles A. Lindbergh. Each summer since 1990, "The Trial of the Century" has been reenacted in the Hunterdon County Courthouse. The reenactment is based on actual trial transcripts and will be presented this year on week-ends from September 28 through October 21. "History Comes Alive," Flemington's celebration of its past takes place during the same period. For details and events call Century Productions at 908-782-2610.

By 1980 sixty percent of the Borough of Flemington had been included on the New Jersey State Register of Historic Places, and is now on the National Register. The town is replete with architectural treasures including Colonial, Federal, Greek Revival, Italianate, Queen Anne, Gothic, and Second Empire Victorians.

Industry

The 1800s saw Flemington prosper as new industry developed and older industries expanded. Old grist mills, which had

Law offices of Samuel L. Southard, Governor in 1832. Photo: Martin E. Kennedy

previously only milled grain for stock feed, turned into large-scale flour milling businesses. Iron foundries, copper mines, glass factories, and potteries were among the early industrial successes. By 1889 there were over 54 trains a day passing through Flemington.

Hill/Fulper/Stangl Pottery

Of these early industries the pottery on Mine Street continued operating until the 1970s when it was purchased by Pfaltzgraff. The original Hill Pottery operated from 1814 to 1860 producing utilitarian redware and drain tiles. In 1860 Abraham Fulper bought the pottery, which passed to four of his sons in 1881. It was during the Fulper tenure, which continued until 1934, that the company was an important contributor to the

American Arts and Crafts Movement. The company's art pottery venture, begun in 1906 by William "Dutch" Fulper II, was noted for its secret glaze formulas. In 1915 Fulper was awarded the Gold Medal of Honor at the Panama Pacific Exposition in San Francisco. When Dutch Fulper died in 1928, Fulper was the only Art Pottery east of Ohio.

In 1935, J. Martin Stangl, who had joined Fulper in 1910, took over the company, which continued as Stangl Pottery until his death in 1972. In 1929 the Fulper pottery burned but was rebuilt through the efforts of civic minded residents who would not see one of the largest employers in the town disappear. By this time the major plant was in Trenton but some art pottery continued to be

FLEMINGTON

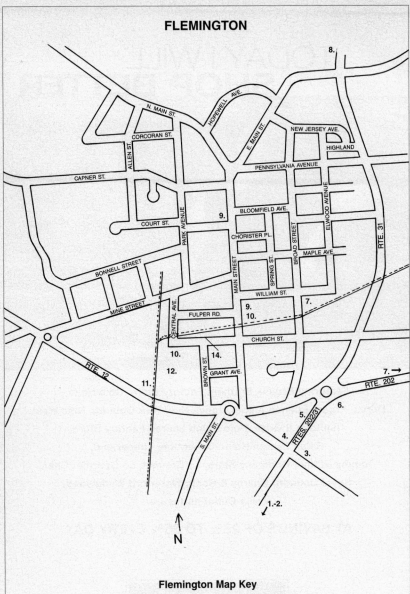

Flemington Map Key

1. The Luggage Factory
2. Verducci's
3. Rugs to Riches
4. Distinctive Dinettes
5. Hunterdon Marble Works
6. *FBA Information Center
7. Weidel Real Estate
8. *Hunterdon Medical Center
9. *Historic Hunterdon County Courthouse
10. Liberty Village
11. *Black River & Western Train Station
12. *N.J. Tourist Information Center

*Attractions & Points of Interest

produced in Flemington until 1935 when the Mine Street pottery became a distribution point.

Today, a museum display within the walls of a kiln preserved in the Pfaltzgraff Outlet includes work from the Hill, Fulper, and Stangl Potteries. Efforts to establish a pottery museum in Flemington are being headed by the Stangl/Fulper Collector's Club. For information on their activities, write to The Stangl/Fulper Collectors Club, P.O. Box 538, Flemington, NJ 08822.

Black River & Western RR

Railroad history in Flemington ran pretty much the same as everywhere else. From the first run by the Flemington Railroad Company in 1854, it rose to a peak in 1889 when three lines ran 54 trains a day into Flemington. Later, when independent rail lines seemed doomed to extinction, railroad buffs took over and you can still thrill to the sound of a steam whistle in some places.

One of these places is in Flemington where the Black River & Western Railroad successfully winds its way between Flemington and Ringoes. The railroad hosts a variety of special events throughout the year beginning on opening day, two Sundays before East-

Fleming Castle. Photo: Martin E. Kennedy

Historic Hunterdon County Courthouse.

er, when all children ride the train free. See the Calendar of Events for special events throughout the year or call the railroad at 908-782-6622 for information on regularly scheduled trains and prices.

Flemington Today

A significant change for this country county seat was its emergence as a factory outlet center in the 1970s. Before that Flemington had been a fairly typical courthouse town with the bulk of its activity centered around county government. Three exceptions to that rule had drawn people to Flemington for years, Flemington Cut Glass, Stangl Pottery and Flemington Fur. The development of the Liberty Village Colonial Shopping Plaza, followed by outlets throughout the town and on Route 202/31, added a new dimension to Flemington.

Northlandz, a recent attraction, is the world's largest miniature railway with 125 trains running on 8 miles of track. Called by visitors a "wonder of the world," the one mile tour is an indescribable experience. For information, call 908-782-4022.

Historic Flemington is a community that has worn many hats, from the Lindbergh trial to Liberty Village, from art shows to sidewalk sales, from greeting neighbors to welcoming visitors, and it has worn all of them very well. Its predominant character, however, continues to be that of a historic county seat filled with architectural treasures and a main street that is presided over by the Historic Hunterdon County Courthouse.

Wineries

continued from page 276

wine pretzels, and peruse shelves stocked with vinegars, pastas, and spice blends, all for sale. La dolce vita, indeed.

KING'S ROAD WINERY
www.kingsroad.com

From the stone cellars of a century old barn in Asbury, just west of Clinton, New Jersey, come the wines of King's Road. Mixing state-of-the-art technology with age old practices like oak barrel aging, King's Road produces 20 wines a year from vinifera and French hybrids - including a late-harvest riesling that caused the *Star-Ledger* to dub winemaker Nicolaas Opdam "top vintner in the state." The emphasis here is on easygoing wines that pair readily with food–a penchant reinforced by the winery's *weinstube* where light fare such as cheese and smoked fish platters are offered for sale. Some of the easy-drinking wines here include Weekend White, a semi-dry blend of chardonnay and seyval blanc, Beach Sand Blanc, a light wine popular in summer, and Sunburn Blush, which the winery advises pairing with pizza and hot wings.

The sunny tasting room is open Wednesdays through Sundays. Although the barn's hand-hewn beams and fieldstone walls make for a lovely setting, it is the panoramic view of the surrounding country-side–the vineyard sits at the bottom of a stunningly beautiful valley–that wins over visitors year round. Add to that music on weekends and picnicking on the grounds.

NEW HOPE WINERY
www.newhopewinery.com

Sandra Price has a very personal take on her winery. "Wines are fun and meant to be enjoyed all the time, so we create what we would want on our table every night," she says of her enterprise, located between New Hope and Lahaska, Pennsylvania. When Price opened in 1995, the vines were in such bad shape she was forced to uproot them and is planning to plant five acres of new vines. In the meantime she buys grapes from select Pennsylvania growers.

Among the 25 wines made at the winery are everything from concord to chardonnay, and a fair number of fruit wines. Two of the more unusual include Almondiera, flavored with fresh-pressed almonds, and a blackberry wine available each December.

Tastings are conducted in a big red barn that includes a collection of antique bicycles. Picnicking is encouraged, including at tables in the flower-filled, stone-walled courtyard for which the center-piece is a fountain of Bacchus pouring "wine" into an old cask.

POOR RICHARD'S WINERY
www.intac.com/~poorrich.com.

Changes are afoot at this Frenchtown, New Jersey winery, which recently changed hands. But Richard Dilts, the original winemaker, is still there, and three of his wines won medals at the 2001 New Jersey competition. With its sunny location, this mountainside vineyard promises good things to come. The winery is open on weekends for tastings and tours.

continued on page 298

ROSE BANK WINERY
www.rosebankwinery.com

When he took over what had been the In and Out Winery in October of 1999, Dave Fleming's prior experience was growing 400 acres of fruits and vegetables. He has learned viticulture fast, with the help of the winery's previous owner, Mike Selesnick. "It's lots of work but lots of fun," he says of his 11 acres planted with French-American hybrids and native American grapes.

In renaming the winery Rose Bank, Fleming returned the property to its original land grant name, wherein no one less than William Penn himself deeded it to his daughters. The estate consists of a 1719 dressed-stone manor home, an adjacent barn dating to 1835, and a 1720 carriage house, home to the wine shop and tasting room. A flock of Baby Doll Southdown sheep graze in the pasture next to the vineyard, which is located half a mile north of the Newtown, Pennsylvania by-pass.

Of the dozen or so wines at Rose Bank, Fleming's favorite is De-Chaunac, a hearty red made from a French hybrid, although house specialties are Rose Bank Blush and Spice, for which ginger, cinnamon, and cloves are added to a fruity wine.

RUSHLAND RIDGE VINEYARDS
www.rushlandridge.net

Atop scenic Rushland Ridge, Lisa and Ed Ullman have lovingly tended four acres of vines since 1991. "We're wine growers, not a winery," says Ed Ullman, who emphasizes that the twelve or so wines he makes and sells out of each year

come exclusively from grapes he grows. Rushland Ridge is perhaps Bucks County's smallest winery, producing only 2,000 gallons. Known especially for his chardonnay and cabernet franc, Ed Ullman says his aim is to make "good, drinkable wines," which he sells each weekend out of his pine-paneled tasting room, where a wood burning stove adds country charm and warmth in the cooler months.

Located between Jamison and Rushland, Pennsylvania, the vineyard is completely family run, which means visitors are sometimes treated to impromptu tours of the cellar and vineyards, and tastings are more or less pour-your-own. The Ullmans are considering planting an additional 15 acres in the near future, and are building their website.

SAND CASTLE WINERY
www.sandcastlewinery.com

Bucking the prevailing wisdom that French hybrid grapes are the most suitable for making wine in this area are brothers Joseph and Paul Maxian, who make all their European-style wines using only vinifera grapes, which they grow on their 72-acre estate in Erwinna, Pennsylvania. Chardonnay, Johannesburg riesling, cabernet sauvignon, pinot noir–all the varietals from the major wine regions of France and Germany are represented.

The Maxian brothers emigrated from Czechoslovakia in 1969. In 1974 Joseph, a geologist by training, bought the property that became Sand Castle, recognizing that it had all the right properties for a vineyard: gently

continued on page 299

sloping hillsides located high above the valley, rocky soils, and river frontage. In 2000, their Chardonnay Classic was awarded a silver medal in the Pennsylvania Wine Competition.

That hilltop location a quarter-mile up a mountain escarpment affords visitors a spectacular view of the Delaware Valley, and allows Sand Castle to have its massive wine cellar 30 feet underground. Seasonal events, music concerts, and wine and food courses enhance a visit to this unique winery.

UNIONVILLE VINEYARDS
www.unionvillevineyards.com

Halfway between Flemington and Lambertville is one of New Jersey's premier wineries, Unionville Vineyards. First opened to the public in 1993, Unionville is a consistent winner of gold medals, and both the *New York Times* and wine authority Hugh Johnson have declared it the best winery in the state. A former dairy barn houses the winery, where glass walls allow a view of the winemaking operations. The oldest part of the barn dates to 1858, and visitors to the tasting room often admire its hand-hewed post-and-beam construction.

Unionville's wines feature a fox hunting theme. The Hunter Series sports a label showing a different fox scene each year, painted by artist Jeff Echevarria. The Windfall Series produces wines from riesling and sevyal blanc grapes. A third series relies on traditional European vinifera grapes, such as cabernet sauvignon and chardonnay. Unionville came away with a record eleven medals (out of eleven entries) at the 2001 New Jersey Wine Competition.

The tasting room is open four days a week; tours are conducted on most weekends. Picnicking is encouraged at tables set out in front of the barn, as well as at Unionville's many seasonal festivals, including its summer concert series called "Jazz Under the Stars."

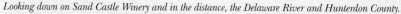

Looking down on Sand Castle Winery and in the distance, the Delaware River and Hunterdon County.

Cycling

continued from page 26

wide as they lead through woods and farmland. Though not a comprehensive list, these are some of my favorites: Cuttalossa and Fleecydale Roads in Solebury Township, which follow the Cuttalossa and Paunacussing Creeks; Ridge Road in Buckingham Township, which takes you through open farmland in a peaceful valley; Alexauken Creek Road near Lambertville, which runs right next to Route 202, though you'd never know it; Lower Creek Road near Stockton, the same road I "discovered" on my bike soon after I moved here; Creek Road just outside of Frenchtown, which starts near a public playground and follows the Nishisakawick Creek to the little town of Palmyra; and, finally, Raritan River Road between High Bridge and Califon, which is well off the beaten path but is probably the most dramatically scenic of any of these. The road follows the South Branch of the Raritan River as it tumbles through Ken Lockwood Gorge.

If you do go exploring on these or other back roads, please remember that even on relatively quiet country roads, cars pose a potential hazard to cyclists and pedestrians. Keep an eye out for approaching autos and remember to walk on the left, facing oncoming traffic; cycle on the right, riding with traffic. When you ride a bike, always wear a helmet.

Ready to get going with your own catalog of scenic places in Bucks and Hunterdon Counties? I hope that this information will be just a starting point—and that you'll enjoy adding to your list as much as I have over the years.

Wickechoeke Creek near the start of Lower Creek Road in Stockton. Photo: Martin E. Kennedy

Between fields. Photo: Martin E. Kennedy

2001-2002 CALENDAR OF EVENTS

Many organizations, societies and communities in the area hold demonstrations, tours, lectures and a variety of activities, other than those included in the calendar. The volume of these will, of course, vary seasonally but they do occur throughout the year. A telephone call can be remarkably rewarding and lead to a great deal of enjoyment.

2001–2002 Continuing Events

EVENT & LOCATION	DATE, PHONE
Annual Summer Festival of Music and Drama Open Air Theatre, Thurs.-Sat. 8:30 p.m. Washington Crossing State Park, NJ	July-Aug. 609-737-1826
Bristol Lions Concert Series Bristol Lions Park Gazebo - Sundays 6 p.m., Bristol, PA	July-Oct. 215-785-2582
Brown Bag It With The Arts Concert Series Bucks County Courthouse Lawn, Doylestown, PA Noon Wednesdays	July-Aug. 215-348-3913
Monthly Bucks County Folk Song Society Jam Wrightstown Friends Meeting, Rt. 413, Wrightstown, PA First Sunday every month, 6:30 to 10 p.m.	First Sunday 215-579-4540
Churchville Nature Center 501 Churchville Lane, Churchville, PA	Year 'round 215-357-4005
Classic Hollywood Summer Movies, County Theater 20 E. State St., Doylestown, PA, Wed and Mon.	Thru Sept. 215-345-6789
Concert In The Park Series Barclay School, Warrington, PA Sundays 7 p.m	July-Aug. 215-343-9350
D&R Canal State Park, Bull's Island Campground, Raven Rock, NJ. Family Fireside Programs, 8 pm	July-Aug 609-397-2949
Guided Canal Walks, Lambertville Lock behind the Inn at Lambertville Station, Lambertville, NJ, Monthly	2nd Sunday 732-873-3050
Ghost Tours 2001: the Mystery and History of New Hope Main & Ferry Streets, New Hope, PA	June-Nov. 215-957-9988
Howell Living History Farm 101 Hunter Rd., Titusville, NJ. Weekend Farm Events	Year 'round 609-737-3299
Hunterdon County Park System 1020 Route 31, Lebanon, NJ	Year 'round 908-782-1158
Lambertville Historical Society Guided Walking Tours James A. Marshall House Museum, Bridge St. Lambertville, NJ 2nd and 4th weekend, 2pm	May-Oct. 609-397-0770
Music Under The Stars Concert Series, Deer Path Park, Readington, NJ, Thursdays, 7 p.m.	July 908-782-1158
Parry Mansion Museum Tours, New Hope Historical Society, New Hope, PA	April-Dec. 215-862-5652
Newtown Business Association Newtown, PA	Year 'round 215-968-7550
Newtown Historical Society Newtown, PA	Year 'round 215-968-9004
Outdoor Sculpture Program, James A Michener Art Museum, 138 S. Pine St., Doylestown, PA	Year 'round 215-340-9800

Pennsbury Manor	Year 'round
400 Pennsbury Memorial Rd., Morrisville, PA	215-946-0400
Summer Concert Series In The Parks-Sundays, 7 p.m.	July-Aug.
Core Creek Park, Rte. 413, Middletown, PA	215-757-0571
Peace Valley Park, 230 Creek Road, New Britain, PA	
Twilight Serenades	May-Sept.
Sandcastle Winery, River Road, Erwinna, PA	800-722-9463
Warwick Community Park Summer Concert Series	June-Aug.
Warwick, PA	215-343-6100

2001

EVENT & LOCATION	DATE, PHONE
George Nakashima and The Modernist Moment	6/9-9/16
Michener Art Museum, 138 S. Pine St. Doylestown, PA	215-340-9800
45th Annual National Juried Print Exhibition	6/10-7/22
Hunterdon Museum of Art, 7 Lower Center St., Clinton, NJ	908-735-8415
Exhibition: Mohammad Omer Khalil	6/10-7/22
Hunterdon Museum of Art, 7 Lower Center St., Clinton, NJ	908-735-8415
Concert Under the Stars - Riverside Symphonia,	6/30
Tinicum Park, Erwinna, PA. 8 pm	215-862-3300
The Best of Bucks, Bucks County Guild of Craftsmen	6/30, 7/1
Stover Mill Gallery, Erwinna, Pennsylvania	610-294-9420
2001: An Art Odyssey, Summer Camps at Hunterdon	6/18-8/24
Museum of Art, 7 Lower Center Street, Clinton, NJ	908-735-8415
Southampton Days 2001 and Country Fair	7/2-7
Tamanend Park, Second Street Pike, Southampton, PA	215-355-1714
July 4th Celebration	7/4
Bristol Borough Business Assn., Bristol, PA	215-788-4288
225 Anniversary Celebration, Washington Crossing	7/4
Historic Park, Washington Crossing, PA	215-493-4076
Fonthill's Old Fashioned Fourth of July Celebration	7/4
E. Court St. & Swamp Rd., Doylestown, PA. 12-5 p.m.,	215-345-9461
Children's Theater, "Pinocchio"	
7/6 at Pearl S. Buck Foundation, Perkasie, PA,	215-249-0100
7/7,13 at Bristol Riverside Theatre, Bristol, PA	215-785-0100
Town & Country Players:	7/6, 7, 13-15,
"Social Security"	20, 21
Rt. 263, Buckingham, PA	215-348-7566
Langhorne Players: "As Bees in Honey Drown"	7/6-8, 18-21
Tyler State Park, Newtown, PA	215-860-0818
Bluegrass Concert	7/7
Hunterdon Historical Museum, 56 Main St., Clinton, NJ	908-735-4101
Tower Tours For Families	7/7
Fonthill, E. Court St., Doylestown, PA	215-348-9461

Walking Tour of Doylestown, 2 pm. Foundation for Architecture, meets in front of Michener Museum	7/8 215-569-3187
Soclair Music Festival, Eighth Blackbird Soclair Brooks Farm, Lebanon, NJ. 4 p.m.	7/8 908-236-6476
Living History Theater: "God Save The Queen" Pennsbury Manor, Morrisville, Pennsylvania	7/8 215-946-0400
River, Rills and Sunlight: Drawing and Painting at Phillips' Mill. Ages 13-18. Sponsored by Michener Art Museum and Phillips' Mill Community Association	7/9-20 215-340-9800
Wickline Casting's Film & Television Day Camp Dancers Extrordinaire, 135 S. Main St., Doylestown, PA	7/9-20;7/23-8/3 215-739-9952
Great Art Travelers at the Michener Art Museum 2-week programs, 1/2-day sessions, Mon.-Fri.. Session I: July 9-20; Session II: July 23–Aug. 3; Session III: Aug. 6-17. Ages 8-13 mornings, Ages 6-8 afternoons. Michener Museum, Pine St., Doylestown, PA	7/9-8/17 215-340-9800
ArtSplash at Tohickon Park, Pt. Pleasant, PA by Michener Art Musuem, 1 pm to 2:30 pm	7/9-13 215-340-9800
Historical Craft Summer Camp Mercer Museum, 84 S. Pine Street, Doylestown, PA	7/9-8/17 215-345-0210
Summer Camp: Great Art Travelers: Visual Art, Music and Language Arts sponsored by Michener Art Museum and Delaware Valley College. 2-week program Ages 6-12, 8:30 to 5:00, Delaware Valley College, Doylestown, PA	7/9-7/20 215-340 9800
Summer Archaeology Camp, Level I Level II Fonthill, E. Court St., Doylestown, PA	7/9-13; 7/16-20 7/23-7/27 215-348-9461
Watercolor Workshop at Historic Fallsington Fallsington, PA	7/9-13 215-295-6567
Arts and Crafts Camp I Arts and Craft Camp II Pennsbury Manor, Morrisville, Pennsylvania	7/9-13 7/30-8/3 215-946-0400
Under The Stars Outdoor Film Series, "The General" Mercer Museum Quadrangle, (indoors if rain) Pine St., Doylestown, PA. 8:30 p.m.	7/10 215-345-0210
Perkasie Summer Concert Series Menlo Park, Perkasie, PA. 7-9 pm	7/10, 17, 24, 31 215-257-5065
Demonstrations by the Society for Creative Anachronism The Bucks County Free Library, Northampton Library	7/10 215-348-0332
A Little Night Music: Charles Fambrough and Friends James A. Michener Art Museum, 7-8:30 p.m. 138 South Pine St. Doylestown, PA	7/11 215-340-9800
Summerfest Mercer Museum, 84 S. Pine Street, Doylestown, PA	7/11 215-345-0210
Bristol Riverside Theater, "14 years of BRT Musical Highlights", Bristol, PA	7/12-14, 21, 22 215-785-0100
Musical Fireworks, New Hope Library Event at Lambertville-New Hope Rescue Squad, Lambertville, NJ	7/13 215-862-2330
Summer Saturdays, Art Classes for pre-schoolers Michener Art Museum,138 Pine St., Doylestown, PA	7/14-8/18 215-340-9800
Children's Theater: "Jack and the Beanstalk" 7/13, 27 at Pearl S. Buck Foundation, Perkasie, PA 7/15, 21 at Bristol Riverside Theatre, Bristol, PA	215-249-0100 215-785-0100

Teddy Bear's Picnic
Peddler's Village, Lahaska, PA
7/14, 15
215-794-4000

The Spirit of Abstraction
James A Michener Art Museum, Pine St., Doylestown, PA
7/14-10/7
215-340-9800

Tinicum Art Festival
Tinicum Park, Rte 32, Erwinna, PA
7/14, 15
610-294-9420

Open Hearth Cooking: The Dairy
Pennsbury Manor, Morrisville, Pennsylvania
7/15
215-946-0400

History Camp I
History Camp II
Pennsbury Manor, Morrisville, Pennsylvania
7/16-20
8/6-8/10
215-946-0400

Under The Stars Outdoor Film Series: "A Hard Days Night"
Mercer Museum, Doylestown, PA
7/17
215-345-0210

Main Street Theatre: "The Sound of Music"
Quakertown, PA
7/18-8/4
215-536-3545

Historic Barn Tour, Bucks County Audubon Society
6324 Upper York Road, New Hope, PA
7/20, 21
215-297-5880

Scottish Heritage Festival
Graeme Park, Horsham, PA
7/21
215-343-0965

Children's Theater: "Aladdin"
7/20 at Pearl S. Buck Foundation, Perkasie, PA
7/22 & 7/28 at Bristol Riverside Theatre, Bristol, PA
215-249-0100
215-785-0100

Big Band Salute to WWII Concert
Hunterdon Historical Museum, 56 Main St., Clinton, NJ
7/21
908-735-4101

Open House, Bowman's Hill Wildflower Preserve,
Rte 32, 2.5 miles south of New Hope, PA. 10-4
7/21
215-862-2924

Red Mill-Mulligan Quarry Day
Hunterdon Historical Museum, 56 Main St., Clinton, NJ
7/22
908-735-4101

Under the Stars Outdoor Film Series:
"Pat and Mike", Mercer Museum, Pine St., Doylestown, PA
7/24
215-345-0210

Just for Families: Colonial Cooking
Pennsbury Manor, Morrisville, PA
7/26
215-946-0400

New Jersey Festival of Ballooning
Solberg Airport, Readington, NJ
7/27, 28, 29
973-882-5464

Bucks County Choral Society: Carmina Burana
New Hope Performing Arts Festival, Stephen Buck
Memorial Theater, W. Bridge St., New Hope, PA
7/28
215-862-1699

Revolutionary War Days
Hunterdon Historical Museum, 56 Main St., Clinton, NJ
7/28, 29
908-735-4101

Early American Craft Demonstration: Woodcarving"
Mercer Museum, Pine St., Doylestown, PA. 2-4 p.m.
7/28
215-345-0210

Jacqueline Ann Clipsham, The Art of Children's Books:
Illustrators of Hunterdon, Hunterdon Museum of Art,
7 Lower Center St., Clinton, NJ
7/29-9/9
7/29-9/9
908-735-8415

International School of Performing Arts Summer Music
Festival 2001, Delaware Valley College and
New Hope Solebury High School
7/30-8/12
215-794-3767

Teen Summer Art Studio
Fonthill, E. Court St., Doylestown, PA
7/31-8/3;
8/6-8/10
215-348-9461

Under The Stars Outdoor Film Series: "Jaws"
Mercer Museum, Pine St., Doylestown, PA
7/31
215-345-0210

2001

EVENT & LOCATION	DATE, PHONE
Festival of Lights Bristol Borough Business Assn., Bristol, PA	TBA 215-788-4288
Cool Happenings Clinton Guild, Clinton, NJ	8/3 908-735-8614
Children's Theater: "Pirates of Penzance" Pearl S. Buck Foundation, Perkasie, PA	8/3 215-249-0100
Tower Tours For Families Fonthill, E. Court St., Doylestown, PA	8/4 215-348-9461
Zydago: The Voo Dudes Hunterdon Historical Museum, 56 Main St., Clinton, NJ	8/4 908-735-4101
"Lego" Robotics Workshop Mercer Museum, Pine St., Doylestown, PA, 2-4 p.m.	8/6-17; 8/20-24 215-345-0210
Under The Stars Outdoor Film Series: "To Kill A Mockingbird", Mercer Museum, Doylestown, PA	8/7 215-345-0210
Main Street Theatre: "Godspell" Quakertown, PA	8/8-25 215-536-3545
Bristol Riverside Theatre: "Love, Luck, & Ladies" Bristol Riverside Theatre, Bristol, PA	8/9-11, 17, 18 215-785-010
Children's Theater: "Little Bo Peep" Pearl S. Buck Foundation, Perkasie, PA	8/10 215-249-0100
Langhorne Players: "Painting Churches" Tyler State Park, Newtown, PA	8/10-12, 16-19, 22-25 215-860-0818
Town & Country Players: "Mary, Mary" Rte. 263, Buckingham, PA	8/10, 11, 18-20 25-26 215-348-7566
45th Annual New Hope Auto Show New Hope-Solebury High School, New Hope, PA	8/11, 12 215-862-5030
New Hope Celebrates the Auto Show: Outdoor Art Show on the grounds of show, New Hope, PA	8/11, 12 215-862-5030
Soclair Music Festival - The Elements Quartet Soclair Brooks Farm, 4 p.m., Lebanon, NJ	8/12 908-236-6476
Motorcycle Show Hunterdon Historical Museum, 56 Main St., Clinton, NJ	8/12 908-735-4101
Canal Boat Dinner Friends of the Delaware Canal, New Hope, PA	8/12 215-862-2021
Annual Peach Festival 321 Cedar St., Bristol, PA, 3-6 pm	8/12 215-781-9895
Living History Theater: Quaker's Understanding of the Native American, Pennsbury Manor, Morrisville, PA	8/12 215-946-0400
Under The Stars Outdoor Film Series: "2001: A Space Odyssey", Mercer Museum, Doylestown, PA	8/14 215-345-0210

Middletown Grange Fair Fairground, Wrightstown, PA	8/15-19 215-968-2192
Children's Theater: "Broadway Musical Revue" Pearl S. Buck Foundation, Perkasie, PA	8/17 215-249-0100
Town & Country Players: "Alice in Wonder" Rte. 263, Buckingham, PA	8/18-25 215-348-7566
Oldies Rock n' Roll Concert Hunterdon Historical Museum, 56 Main St., Clinton, NJ	8/18 908-735-4101
Perkasie Olde Towne Day: Under the Lights Historic Downtown Perkasie, PA	8/18 215-257-5065
Hands-On History Day Graeme Park, Horsham, Pennsylvania	8/19 215-343-0965
Musical Fireworks, New Hope Library Event at Lambertville-New Hope Rescue Squad, Lambertville, NJ	8/24 215-862-2330
Young People's Dramas Phillips' Mill, Rte. 32, New Hope, PA	8/24, 25, 26 215-862-0582
Annual Antique Show, Delaware River Mill Society Prallsville Mills, Stockton, NJ	8/25, 26 609-397-3586
Early American Craft Demonstration: Plant Uses Mercer Museum, Pine St., Doylestown, PA. 2-4 p.m.	8/25 215-345-0210
Extended Family Art Show, Delaware River Mill Society Prallsville Mills, Rte 29, Stockton, NJ	8/31, 9/1-3 609-397-3586

EVENT & LOCATION   2001   DATE, PHONE

Artsbridge Annual Members Exhibition, Artsbridge Gallery, Prallsville Mills, Rte. 29, Stockton, NJ	9/1-30 609-773-0881
Holcombe-Jimison Farmstead Museum: Celebration of Farming, Rte. 29, Lambertville, NJ. 10-5 pm.	9/8, 9 908-782-6653
Stover Mill Open House Stover Mill, River Road, Erwinna	9/1, 2 610-294-9420
Polish-American Festival Shrine of Our Lady of Czestochowa, Doylestown, PA	9/1-3, 8, 9 215-345-0600
Native Plant Sale, Bowman's Hill Wildflower Preserve, Rte 32, 2.5 miles south of New Hope, PA. 10-4	9/8, 9, 15, 16 215-862-2924
34th Annual Mill Street Run Bristol Borough Business Association, Bristol, PA. 9 a.m.	9/8 215-788-4288
Soclair Music Festival - A Grand Tour Soclair Brooks Farm, Lebanon, NJ. 4 p.m.,	9/9 908-236-6476
Scarecrow Competition & Display Peddler's Village, Lahaska, PA	9/10-10/28 215-794-4000
New Hope "Arty Awards" New Hope Eagle Hall, Sugan Rd. & 202, New Hope, PA	9/11 215-862-5030
Town & Country Players: "Communicating Doors" Rte. 263, Buckingham, PA	9/14, 15, 21-23 28, 29 215-348-7566

Scarecrow Festival	9/15, 16
Peddler's Village, Lahaska, PA	215-794-4000
Newtown Market Day	9/15
Newtown Historical Assn., Newtown, PA	215-968-4004
The Great Train Robbery	9/15, 16
Black River & Western Railroad, Flemington, NJ	908-782-6622
Exhibition: Compelled. Hunterdon Museum of Art	9/16-11/4
7 Lower Center St., Clinton, NJ	908-735-8415
Main Street Theatre: "Sleuth"	9/20-10/7
Quakertown, PA	215-536-3545
Watershed Festival, Bucks County Audubon	9/22
Society, 6324 Upper York Road, New Hope, PA	215-297-5880
72nd Annual Phillips' Mill Art Exhibition	9/22-10/28
Phillips' Mill, Rte. 32, New Hope, PA. Daily 1-5 p.m.	215-862-0582
Pearl S. Buck Golf Classic	9/24
Pearl S. Buck International, Perkasie, PA	215-249-0100
Oktoberfest 2001: Family Fun Weekend	9/28, 29, 30
Doylestown Township Central Park, New Britain Rd.	215-348-9915
Raritan Township Community Day	9/29
Lenape Park, Route 523, Raritan, NJ	908-284-8118
Artists of the Commonwealth	9/29-1/6
Michener Art Museum, 138 S. Pine St., Doylestown, PA	215-340-9800
Benefit Concert for Habitat for Humanity	9/29
Bucks County Choral Society, Central Bucks East,	215-598-6142
Holicong & Anderson Roads, Doylestown, PA	
Fall Art Festival, Doylestown Business	9/29, 30
Community Alliance, Doylestown, PA	215-340-9988
Filmfest	9/30
County Theater, Doylestown, PA	215-345-6789

2001

EVENT & LOCATION	**DATE, PHONE**
Arts Auction	TBA
New Hope Arts Commission, New Hope, PA	215-862-1699
Canal Walk 2001, Friends of the Delaware Canal	10/6, 13, 20, 27
South Main Street, New Hope, PA	215-862-2021
Walking Tour of Old Newtown	10/6/01
The Foundation of Architecture, 11 a.m.	215-569-3187
Flemington Crafts Festival	10/6, 7
Flemington Fairgrounds, Route 31, Flemington, NJ	908-284-8118
8th New Hope Outdoor Arts & Crafts Festival	10/6,7
New Hope, PA, 11-5	215-862-5030
Hunt's Mill Autumn Fest	10/7
Hunterdon Historical Museum, 56 Main St., Clinton, NJ	908-735-4101

Perkasie Annual Fall Festival Lenape Park, Perkasie, PA	10/7 215-257-5065
Season Concert Series, 7 pm Newtown Chamber Orchestra, Bucks County Community College, Swamp Road, Newtown, PA	10/7 215-598-0722
Folk Concert: Guy Davis Prallsville Mills, Stockton, NJ	10/13 609-397-3586
Musical Fireworks, New Hope Library Event at Lambertville-New Hope Rescue Squad, Lambertville, NJ	10/12 215-862-2330
Annual Savory Sampler Mercer Museum, Pine St., Doylestown, PA	10/12 215-345-0210
Fall State Craft Festival, PA Guild of Craftsmen Tyler State Park, Richboro, PA	10/12, 13, 14 215-579-5997
Historic Fallsington Day, fall celebration of the past. Historic Fallsington, 4 Yardley Ave., Fallsington, PA	10/13 215-295-6567
Bucks County Covered Bridge & Garden Tour Doylestown, PA	10/13 215-766-2211
Concordia Chamber Players Stephen Buck Theater, New Hope, PA, 3pm	10/14 or 10/21 215-297-5972
Doylestown Walking Tour, 11 a.m. Foundation for Architecture, meets at Michener Museum	10/14 215-569-3187
Autumn Open House Tour Lambertville Historical Society, Lambertville, NJ	10/17 609-397-0770
Main Street Theatre: "The Odd Couple" Quakertown, PA	10/18-11/4 215-536-3545
Famous Dances & Variations Riverside Symphonia, Lambertville, NJ	10/19, 20 215-862-3300
Town & Country Players: "Aesop's Fallibles" Rte. 263 Buckingham, PA 11am and 2 pm	10/19, 20, 16, 27 215-348-7566
Hunt's Mill Autumn Fest Hunterdon Historical Museum, 56 Main St., Clinton, NJ	10/19, 20, 26, 27 908-735-4101
24th Annual Historic Bristol Day Bristol, PA	10/20 215-781-9895
Bucks County Pumpkinfest Moravian Pottery & Tile Works, Swamp Rd., Doylestown, PA	10/20, 21 215-345-6644
Taking Liberties: Photographs by David Graham Michener Art Museum, Doylestown, PA	10/20-1/27 215-340-9800
Clinton Guild Pumpkin Fest Hunterdon Historical Museum, 56 Main St., Clinton, NJ	10/26 908-735-4101
Haunted Trails, Bucks County Audubon Society 6324 Upper York Road, New Hope, PA	10/26, 27 215-297-5880
Halloween Special Black River & Western Railroad, Flemington, NJ	10/27, 28 908-782-6622
Halloween Parade Newtown Business Assn., Newtown, PA	10/28 215-860-3410
Halloween Parade Milford, NJ	10/28 908-995-4854
Fall Festival and Closing Day, Holcombe-Jimison Farmstead Museum, Rt. 29, Lambertville, NJ 1-4 pm.	10/28 908-782-6653
Halloween Festivities in New Hope New Hope Chamber of Commerce, New Hope, PA	TBA 215-862-5030

2001

EVENT & LOCATION	DATE, PHONE
Bucks County Choral Society: All Night Vigil. National Shrine of Our Lady of Czestochowa, Doylestown, PA	11/2 215-598-6142
Apple Festival Peddler's Village, Lahaska, PA	11/3, 4 215-794-4000
Degrees of Figuration Hunterdon Historical Museum, 56 Main St., Clinton, NJ	11/11-1/6/02 908-735-4101
Exhibition: Frank Sabatino Hunterdon Historical Museum, 56 Main St., Clinton, NJ	11/11-1/6/02 908-735-4101
Pearl S. Buck Holiday Festival Pearl Buck International, Green Hills Farm, Perkasie, PA	11/13-12/30 215-249-0100
Pearl S. Buck Holiday Craft Show Pearl Buck International, Green Hills Farm, Perkasie, PA	11/13-12/02 215-249-0100
Handweavers of Bucks County: Fiber 2001 Show and Sale Memorial Bld., Washington Crossing Historic Park, Washington Crossing, PA	11/15-18 215-862-5965
Grand Illumination Opening Celebration, Peddler's Village, Lahaska, PA. 6-9pm	11/16 215-794-4000
Holidays at The Parry Mansion New Hope Historical Society, New Hope, PA	11/16-12/8 215-862-5652
Gingerbread House Competition and Display Peddler's Village, Lahaska, PA	11/16-1/6 215-794-4000
Folk Concert: Reilly & Maloney, Prallsville Mills, Stockton, NJ	11/3 609-397-3586
New Hope Autumn Antiques Show Eagle Fire House, New Hope, PA	11/17, 18 215-862-5828
Season Concert Series, 7 pm Newtown Chamber Orchestra, Church of God's Love, Newtown/Yardley Rd., Newtown, PA	11/18 215-598-0722
Santa Express Black River & Western Railroad, Flemington, NJ	11/23-25, 12/1, 2, 8, 9 908-782-6622
Annual Tree Lighting and Concert 131 Mill St., Bristol, PA	11/23 215-788-4288
Dickens' Days, Clinton Guild, Clinton, NJ	11/23, 24 908-735-8614
Christmas Candlelight Tour Parry Mansion, New Hope, Pa	11/25 215-862-5652
21 Annual Show - Bucks County Antique Dealers Assn. Delaware Valley College, Route 202, New Britain, PA	11/24, 25
Main Street Theatre: "The Gift of the Magi" Quakertown, PA	11/29-12/16 215-536-3545
Christmas Around The World, Riverside Symphonia and Bucks County Choral Society Riverside Symphonia, Lamberville, NJ	11/30-12/1 215-862-3300

2001

EVENT & LOCATION	DATE, PHONE
Street Caroling in Olde Towne Bristol Bristol Borough Business Assoc., Bristol, PA	TBA 215-788-9408
Children's Gallery Exhibition Michener Art Museum, 138 S. Pine St. Doylestown, PA	TBA 215-340-9800
A Colonial Christmas 1776 Washington Crossing Historic Park Washington Crossing, PA	TBA 215-493-4076
Winter Holiday Event Warwick Community Park, Warwick, PA	TBA 215-343-6100
A Historical Christmas in New Hope Santa Claus, Tree Lighting, Coryell's Ferry Militia. New Hope, Pennsylvania	TBA 215-862-5030
Community Lighting The Little Shul by the River, New Hope, PA	TBA 215-862-1912
Breakfast with Santa Newtown Business & Professional Assn., Newtown, PA	TBA 215-968-7550
Newtown Christmas Parade Newtown Business Assoc., Newtown, PA	12/1 215-860-3410
Christmas Open House Tour Newtown Historic Assoc., Newtown, PA	12/1 215-968-4004
Wildlife Art Exhibition, Bucks County Audubon Society Eagle Fire Hall, Sugan Rd., New Hope, PA	12/1, 2 215-297-5880
Country Christmas Weekend Peddler's Village, Lahaska, PA, 11-5pm	12/1, 2 215-794-4000
Hunterdon Holiday Parade Flemington Business Assn., Flemington, NJ	12/2 908-284-8118
Art Show benefiting Fox Chase Cancer Center Prallsville Mills, Rte. 29, Stockton, NJ	12/2 609-397-3586
Holiday Evening Tour - Fonthill Museum E. Court St. & Rte. 313, Doylestown, PA	12/5-7 215-348-9461
Clinton Guild Christmas Parade Clinton, NJ	12/7 908-735-8614
Bucks County Choral Society: Festival Of Christmas Location : TBA	12/7-9 215-598-6142
Holiday House Tour Bucks County Bed & Breakfast Association	12/8, 9, 15, 16 800-982-1235
Holiday Parade Newtown Business & Professional Assn. Newtown, PA	12/8 215-968-7550
Candlelight Holiday Open House - Fonthill Museum E. Court St., & Rte. 313, Doylestown, PA	12/9 215-348-9461

Durham Boat Drill, Washington Crossing Historic Park Washington Crossing, PA	12/9 215-493-4076
Annual Christmas Tree Lighting and Caroling, 6 pm Historic Fallsington, 4 Yardley Ave., Fallsington, PA	12/9 215-295-6567
Holiday Festivities for the Family - Fonthill Museum, Moravian Tile, E. Court St., & Rte. 313, Doylestown, PA	12/10 215-348-9461
Grand Tour Open House Fonthill Museum and Moravian Tile, E. Court St., & Rte. 313, Doylestown, PA	12/10 215-348-9461
Holiday Open House Michener Art Museum and Mercer Museum, Pine Street, Doylestown, PA	12/11 215-340-9800 215-345-0210
Candlelight Night in Clinton Clinton Guild, Clinton, NJ	12/13 908-735-8614
Christmas in Milford Milford, NJ	12/14 908-995-4854
Santa on Main Street Clinton Guild, Clinton, NJ	12/16 908-735-8614
Reenactment of Washington Crossing the Delaware Washington Crossing Historic Park Washington Crossing, PA	12/25 215-493-4076
First Night Bristol Bristol Borough Business Assoc., Bristol, PA	12/31 215-781-9895
First Night Flemington Flemington Borough, Flemington, NJ	12/31 908-968-7550
First Night Newtown Newtown, PA	12/31 215-968-7550

2002

EVENT & LOCATION	**DATE, PHONE**
New Hope Winter Antiques Show Eagle Fire House, New Hope, PA	1/19, 20 215-862-5828
2002 Annual Members Exhibition Hunterdon Museum of Art, 7 Lower Center St., Clinton, NJ	1/13-2/24 908-735-8415
William Vandever - Photography Hunterdon Museum of Art, 7 Lower Center St., Clinton, NJ	1/13-2/24 908-735-8415
Stylish Hats: 200 Years of Sartorial Sculpture Michener Art Museum, 138 S. Pine St., Doylestown, PA	1/19-4/14 215-340-9800
Concordia Chamber Players Stephen Buck Theater, New Hope, PA, 3pm	1/20 or 1/27 215-297-5972
Quilt Competition & Display Peddler's Village, Lahaska, PA	1/21-3/31 215-794-4000
Riverside Symphonia Chamber Players Riverside Symphonia, Lambertville, NJ	1/26 215-862-3300

2002

EVENT & LOCATION	DATE, PHONE
Bucks County Choral Society: Kids and The Choral Society Location : TBA	TBA 215-598-6142
Lambertville-New Hope Winter Festival Ice carving, tours, ice skating and more	2/1-3 215-862-2974
21st Annual Lambertville Historical Society Juried Exhibition, Coryell Gallery, The Porkyard, 8 Coryell St., Lambertville, NJ	2/4-4/18 609-397-0770
Roy C. Nuse: Figures and Farms Michener Art Museum, 138 S. Pine St., Doylestown, PA	2/9-5/5 215-340-9800
Phillips' Mill Winter Show Phillips' Mill Community Assn, Rte. 32, New Hope, PA.	2/15-17, 22, 23 215-862-0582
Season Concert Series, 7 pm Newtown Chamber Orchestra, Church of God's Love, Newtown/Yardley Rd., Newtown, PA	2/24 215-598-0722

2002

EVENT & LOCATION	DATE, PHONE
Ongoing Programs Hunterdon County Park System, Lebanon, NJ	Mar.-June 908-782-1158
Bucks Fever 2002, Central Bucks Chamber of Commerce Celebration of Bucks County's arts, festivals, history. Call for schedule of events.	Mar.-Oct. 215-348-3913
Guided tours of Bowman's Hill Wildflower Preserve, Washington Crossing Historic Park, 2 1/2 miles. south of New Hope, PA	Mar.-Nov. 215-862-2924
Bucks County Horse Park, Polo matches and other events. 8934 Easton Rd., Rt. 611, Revere, PA	Mar.-Dec. 610-847-8597
New Hope Spring Antiques Show Eagle Fire Hall, New Hope, PA	TBA 215-862-5828
Charter Day celebrating the birthday of Pennsylvania Pennsbury Manor, Morrisville, PA	TBA 215-946-0400
New Jersey Built and Unbuilt Hunterdon Museum of Art, 7 Lower Center St., Clinton, NJ	3/3-4/28 908-735-8415
Exhibition: Jim Toia Hunterdon Museum of Art, 7 Lower Center St., Clinton, NJ	3/3-4/28 908-735-8415

A Night at the Opera	3/8, 9
Riverside Symphonia, Lambertville, NJ	215-862-3300
125th Anniversary Concert - The Quakertown Band	3/10
112 N. Hellertown Ave., Quakertown, PA	
Annual Bucks Beautiful Garden Fair	3/16, 17
Delaware Valley College, Rte. 202, Doylestown, PA	215-348-3913
Bucks County Choral Society with Riverside Symphonia:	3/22-24
Elijah, location TBA	215-598-6142
Bunny Hoppening	3/27
Clinton Guild, Clinton, NJ	908-735-8614

2002

EVENT & LOCATION	**DATE, PHONE**
Annual Solebury School Art Festival, Solebury School	TBA
Phillips Mill Rd., New Hope, PA	215-862-5261
Annual Artsbridge Juried Exhibition	TBA
Prallsville Mills, Rte. 29, Stockton, NJ.	609-773-0881
Bucks County Designer House	TBA
Village Improvement Association, Doylestown, PA	215-345-2191
New Hope Art Tours	April-Oct.
Masterpiece Galleries, New Hope, Pennsylvania	215-862-4444
Community Sedar	TBA
The Little Shul by the River, New Hope, PA	215-862-1912
Concordia Chamber Players	4/7 or 4/14
Stephen Buck Theater, New Hope, PA, 3 pm	215-297-5972
Easter Bunny Express	4/17, 8, 13, 14
Black River & Western Railroad, Flemington, NJ	908-782-6622
Music of the Americas	4/20, 21
Riverside Symphonia, Lambertville, NJ	215-862-3300
Season Concert Series, 7 pm	4/21
Newtown Chamber Orchestra, Bucks County Community	215-598-0722
College, Swamp Rd., Newtown, PA	
Native Tree and Plant Sale, Bucks County	4/21, 22, 28, 29
Audubon Society, 6324 Upper York Road, New Hope, PA	215-297-5880
The Drawings of Ben Solowey	4/21-7/15
Michener Art Museum, 138 S. Pine St., Doylestown, PA	215-340-9800
Phillips' Mill Spring Show	4/26-28, 5/3, 4
Phillips' Mill Community Assoc., Rte. 32, New Hope, PA.	215-862-0582
Bucks County Invitational V	4/27-7/7
Michener Art Museum, 138 S. Pine St., Doylestown, PA	215-340-9800
Shad Festival	4/27, 28
Lambertville, NJ	609-397-0055
A-DAY	4/27, 28
Delaware Valley College, Rte. 202, Doylestown, PA	215-489-ADAY

2002

EVENT & LOCATION	DATE, PHONE
Annual Photographic Show Phillips' Mill, Rte. 32, New Hope, PA	TBA 215-348-9126
Guided Walking Tours of Lambertville 2nd and 4th weekend, 2pm Lambertville Historical Society, Lambertville, NJ	May-Oct. 609-397-0770
Bucks County Polo Club, Sunday Matches Bucks County Horse Park, Revere, PA	May-Oct. 610-847-8228
New Century Art Show New Hope Arts Commission, New Hope, PA	TBA 215-862-1699
Antique Show Prallsville Mills, Stockton, NJ	TBA 609-397-3586
Carversville Day, Historic Carversville Society Annual small town celebration, Carversville, PA	TBA 215-297-8054
Jazz Night Michener Art Museum, 138 S. Pine St., Doylestown, PA	TBA 215-340-9800
Annual House and Garden Tour New Hope Historical Society, New Hope, PA	TBA 215-862-5652
Spring Craft Celebration Tyler State Park, Rte 332, Richboro, PA	TBA 215-579-5997
Perkasie Old Towne Day and Historic Tour Perkasie, PA	TBA 215-453-8398
Musical Fireworks, New Hope Library Event at Lambertville-New Hope Rescue Squad, Lambertville, NJ	TBA 215-862-2330
Spring Open House, Rosade Bonsai Studio, 6912 Ely Rd., New Hope, PA. 10 am - 5 pm.	TBA 215-862-5925
Annual Antique Auto Show 131 Mill St., Bristol, PA	TBA 215-788-4288
Quakertown Alive! Upper Bucks Day of the Arts Throughout Quakertown, PA	TBA 215-536-2273
Memorial Day Encampment Washington Crossing Historic Park Washington Crossing, PA	Memorial Day 215-493-4076
Opening Day Celebration, Holcombe-Jimison Farmstead Museum, Rte. 29, Lambertville, NJ 1-4 pm	5/5 908-782-6653
Twilight party and reception at Historic Fallsington 4 Yardley Avenue, Fallsington, PA	5/4 215-295-6567
Strawberry, Flower & Garden Festival Peddler's Village, Lahaska, PA	5/4, 5 215-794-4000
Pansy Festival Clinton Guild, Clinton, NJ	5/4, 5 908-735-8614
Annual National Juried Print Exhibition Hunterdon Museum of Art, 7 Lower Center St., Clinton, NJ	5/5- 6/23 908-735-8415
Exhibition: Eileen Foti Hunterdon Museum of Art, 7 Lower Center St., Clinton, NJ	5/5- 6/23 908-735-8415

Beethoven's Eroica Riverside Symphonia, Lambertville, NJ	5/10,11 215-862-3300
Native Plant Sale, 10-4 daily. Bowman's Hill Wildflower Preserve, Rte 32, 2.5 miles S. of New Hope, PA	5/11,12 215-862-2924
Mercer Museum Folk Fest Pine St., Doylestown, PA	5/11, 12 215-345-0210
Bucks County Choral Society: "A Night at the Opera" Central Bucks East High School, Buckingham, PA	5/18 215-598-6142
The Great Train Robbery Black River & Western Railroad, Flemington, NJ	5/18, 19 908-782-9600
Spring Food Fun & Fitness Festival, Doylestown Business Community Alliance, Doylestown, PA	5/25 215-340-9988

2002

EVENT & LOCATION	DATE, PHONE
Children's Gallery Exhibition Michener Art Museum, 138 S. Pine St. Doylestown, PA	TBA 215-340-9800
Martha Washington Birthday Celebration, Washington Crossing Historic Park, Washington Crossing, PA	TBA 215-493-4076
Annual Croquet and Garden Party Riverside Symphonia, New Hope, PA	TBA 215-862-0948
Annual Spring Garden Tour New Hope Historical Society, New Hope, PA	TBA 215-862-5652
Red Mill Day Hunterdon Historical Museum, 56 Main St., Clinton, NJ	TBA 908-735-4101
British Car Day Hunterdon Historical Museum, 56 Main St., Clinton, NJ	TBA 908-735-4101
New Hope Summer Antiques Festival New Hope-Solebury High School, Bridge St., New Hope, PA	TBA 215-862-5828
Soclair Music Festival Soclair Brooks Farm, Lebanon, NJ	TBA 908-236-6476
Southampton Days Country Fair Tamanend Park, Southampton, PA	TBA 215-355-1714
Yardley Canal Festival Friends of the Delaware Canal, New Hope, PA	TBA 215-862-2021
Recycled Art Sale, Bucks County Audubon Society 6324 Upper York Road, New Hope, PA	TBA 215-297-5880
Annual Dinner Dance at Historic Fallsington Fallsington, PA	TBA 215-295-6567
Fine Art & Contemporary Crafts Show Peddler's Village, Lahaska, PA	6/1, 2 215-794-4000
Flag Day Happening Clinton Guild, Clinton, NJ	6/14 908-735-8614
Annual Meeting, Names added to Hunterdon County Farmers Honor Roll, Holcombe-Jimison Farmstead Museum, Rte. 29, Lambertville, NJ 1-4 pm.	6/30 908-782-6653

Sometimes entertainment comes from within. For the other times, check out the directory that follows. Photo: Martin E. Kennedy

Directory to Entertainment, Recreation & Museums
Please also refer to the Calendar of Events on pages 302-316.

AERIAL TOURS

SPORT AVIATION, INC., Van Sant Airport, 516 Cafferty Rd., PO Box 176, Erwinna, PA 18920. 610-847-8320. Sailplane flights, open cockpit biplane adventures, aerobatics, rentals, instructions, gift certificates. Soaring Society of America Business Member. Open every day 9 am until dusk. V, MC.

CARRIAGE RIDES

BUCKS COUNTY CARRIAGES, West End Farm, New Hope, PA 18938. 215-862-3582.

CHILDREN'S AMUSEMENTS

CAROUSEL VILLAGE AT INDIAN WALK, 591 Durham Rd., Wrightstown, PA 18940. 215-598-0707. Ride our antique carousel and C.P. Huntingdon train

CROSS CREEK FARM, Ringoes, NJ 08551. 908-806-3248. We specialize in children's parties.

HOT AIR BALLOONING

ALEXANDRIA BALLOON FLIGHTS, 93 Hickory Corner Rd., Milford, NJ 08848. 908-479-4878, members.aol.com/hotheir. Hot air balloon flights – depart daily from Sky Manor Airport. Flights from $160 per person – approx. 1 hour. Call Kevin Olsen, the region's most experienced balloonist at 888-HOTAIR7.

INTERNET

BUCKSNET, 215-757-3620. www.bucksnet. com. Bucksnet publishes the Bucks County

Bulletin Board & Events Calendar and hosts a wide variety of local businesses' web sites. 24 hours a day, 7 days a week.

MINIATURE GOLF COURSE

PINE CREEK MINIATURE GOLF, 394 Route 31, West Amwell, NJ 08551. 609-466-3803. 2 challenging 18-hole miniature golf courses over acres of countryside. Clubhouse. Lighted for night play. Open spring through fall and usually during winter. Call for hours. www.pinecreekgolf.com.

MUSEUMS

BYERS' CHOICE LTD., 4355 County Line Rd., Chalfont, PA 18914. 215-822-6700, Fax: 215-822-3847. www.byerschoice.com. New Visitors' Center and Gift Emporium transport you back to Victorian London. Heartwarming Caroler® and Kindle® villages. Free! Open weekends. Mon.-Sat. 10-5, Sun. noon to 5. V, MC.

FONTHILL, E. Court St., Doylestown, PA 18901. 215-348-9461. Mercer's home, stands as a grand castle with 44-rooms filled with decorative tiles and prints collected from around the world. Open all year except New Year's, Thanksgiving and Christmas. Guided tours only, reservations suggested. Mon.-Sat. 10-5 & Sun. noon-5. Last tour at 4 pm. Admission: $5 adults, $4.50 over age 62, $1.50 youth & free to children under 6. V, MC.

MARGARET R. GRUNDY MUSEUM, 610 Radcliffe St., Bristol, PA 19007. 215-788-9432. Victorian home of US Sen. Joseph R. Grundy. Mon.-Fri. 1 to 4. Sat. 1-3.

HISTORIC FALLSINGTON, 4 Yardley Ave., Fallsington, PA 19054. 215-295-6567. Pre-revolutionary village mirrors 300 years of American Architectural history. Open May thru October. Tours every hour, Mon.-Sat. 10-4, Sun. 1-4. Group tours by appointment.

HOLCOMBE-JIMISON FARMSTEAD MUSEUM, Route 29, Lambertville, NJ 08530. 908-995-2237 or 609-397-1810. A museum dedicated to collect, restore and preserve every variety of material illustrative of the history of Hunterdon County and New Jersey. Sundays 1-4 pm May-October. Tours can be arranged at other times.

HUNTERDON HISTORICAL MUSEUM, 56 Main St., Clinton, NJ 08809. 908-735-4101. April-October, Tues.-Sat. 10-4, Sun. 12-5. 10 acres of rural heritage featuring 1810 Red Mill, limestone quarry and more. Special events & family activities. Admission: adults $5.00, senior citizens $4.00, ages 6-16 $3.00, free under 6 years.

HUNTERDON MUSEUM OF ART, 7 Center St., Clinton, NJ 08809. 908-735-8415. Housed in a landmark stone grist mill, the museum mounts 12 exhibitions annually of cutting edge to traditional art, has an extensive educational program for all ages, and a museum shop. Tues.-Sun. 11-5.

JAMES A. MICHENER ART MUSEUM, 138 S. Pine St., Doylestown, PA 18901. 215-340-9800. www.michenerartmuseum.org. Exquisitely renovated historic site houses the finest collection of Pennsylvania Impressionist paintings in public or private hands including the spectacular 22-foot mural, A Wooded Watershed, by Daniel Garber. Important regional contemporary and figurative art and changing exhibitions, multi-media interactive exhibition, "Creative Bucks County: A Celebration of Art and Artists", the Nakashima Reading Room, beautiful outdoor sculpture gardens and a permanent exhibit on author James A. Michener. Blu's Café and Museum Shop. Group rates available. Tues.-Fri. 10-4:30, Sat. & Sun. 10-5, Wed. eve. until 9 pm. Major credit cards.

MARSHALL HOUSE, 60 Bridge St., Lambertville, NJ 08530. 609-397-0770. Childhood home of James W. Marshall, man whose discovery of gold in California in 1848 started the Gold Rush of '49. Museum depicting Lambertville life in early 19th century. Open 1-4 on the 2nd and 4th weekends of each month, May through October. Admission free. Write for information.

MERCER MUSEUM, Pine & Ashland Sts., Doylestown, PA 18901. 215-345-0210. www. mercermuseum.org. Open Mon.-Sat. 10-5, Sun. 12-5, Tues. evening 5-9. Adults $6.00, Senior citizens $5.50, Ages 6-17 $2.50, Under 6 free. Closed Thanksgiving, Christmas and New Years Day.

MORAVIAN POTTERY & TILE WORKS, 130 Swamp Road (Route 313), Doylestown, PA 18901. 215-345-6722. A working history museum with Mercer tiles being produced by original methods. Self guided tours, special programs, tiles for sale. Daily 10-4:45 except holidays.

PARRY MANSION MUSEUM, S. Main & Ferry Sts., PO Box 41, New Hope, PA 18938. 215-862-5652. Splendid small museum at the restored home of Benjamin Parry furnished to depict changing lifestyle from Colonial period to 1900. April 27 through Dec. 8. 1-5 pm, Fri.-Sun. Group tours by appt. any day. Admission: adults $5, senior & students $4, children under 12 $1.

THE PEARL S. BUCK HOUSE, a National Historic Landmark, 520 Dublin Rd., PO Box 181, Perkasie, PA 18944. 215-249-0100 or 800-220-2825. Discover the world of author and humanitarian Pearl S. Buck. House tour includes intercultural art and architecture; Nobel and Pulitzer Prizes. Guided tours available March through December: Tues.-Sat. at 10:30 am, 1:30 pm & 2:30 pm, Sundays 1:30 & 2:30 pm. Groups (15+) by appointment. AE, V, MC.

PENNSBURY MANOR, 400 Pennsbury Memorial Lane, Morrisville, PA 19067. 215-946-0400. 17thCentury country plantation of William Penn. April-Dec. Tues.-Sat. 9-5, Sun. 12-5.

PRALLSVILLE MILL, Delaware River Mill Society, Box 268, Stockton, NJ 08559. Mill complex dating to early 19th century. See calendar for special events.

SPRUANCE LIBRARY, Pine & Ashland Sts., Doylestown, PA 18901. 215-345-0210. Tues. 1-9, Wed., Thurs., Fri. and Sat. 10-5. Admission: adults $6.00, Over 60 years $5.50, Youth $2.50, Free under 6 years. Group rates available.

SUMMERSEAT, Morrisville Hist. Soc., Hill & Legion Aves., Morrisville, PA 19067. Georgian mansion used by Washington during Revolution. 1st Saturday of the month & by appt.

WASHINGTON CROSSING HISTORIC PARK, 1112 River Rd. Washington Crossing, PA 18977. 215-493-4076, www.fwchp.org. Site of General Washington's crossing of the Delaware on 12-25-1776. Museum shop featuring Williamsburg products & other 18th century reproduction items of interest. Park includes the Thompson-Neely house and Bowman's Tower. Tues.-Sat. 9-5, Sun.12-5.

MUSIC

JENNY'S BISTRO, Rte. 202 & Street Rd., Peddler's Village, Lahaska, PA 18931. 215-794-4020. Piano bar complements an evening of enjoyable intimate dining weekends from 8 pm - midnight. Major credit cards.

LAMBERTVILLE STATION RESTAURANT, 11 Bridge St., Lambertville, NJ 08530. 609-397-8300. Live Jazz & Blues in the downstairs pub every weekend with the area's finest talent. Blues: Fridays 9:30 pm - 1:00 am, Jazz: Saturdays 8 pm - 12 am. No cover charge.

RIVERSIDE SYMPHONIA, PO Box 650, Lambertville, NJ 08530. 609-397-7300 or 215-862-3300. www.riversidesymphonia.org. Professional orchestra and world-class soloists performing classical repertoire in the historically beautiful St. John The Evangelist Church, Lambertville, NJ. Masterworks, Chamber & Pops Subscription series. V, MC.

MUSIC/PRIVATE PARTIES

FRED MILLER'S SILVER DOLLAR PRODUC-TIONS: Musical & theatrical offerings including Broadway/Hollywood, Barbershop/Americana, Light & Grand Opera/Original Roast Material/ Singing Telegrams. 609-397-8700 or 215-230-8444. V, MC.

NATIONAL SHRINE

THE NATIONAL SHRINE OF OUR LADY OF CZESTOCHOWA, 654 Ferry Rd., PO Box 2049, Doylestown, PA 18901. 215-345-0600. www. polishshrine.com. View the Polish Madonna reproduction painting at our spiritual and pilgrim-age center. Tours upon request. Gift and book shop open daily 9-4:30 featuring Polish imports. Polish Festival held annually Labor Day weekend and weekend following. Call for mass schedule.

PARKS

BUCKS COUNTY DEPARTMENT OF PARKS, Core Creek Park, Box 358, RD 1, Langhorne, PA 19047. 215-757-0571. Active county park system. Call for information on special events and camping.

COMMONWEALTH OF PENNSYLVANIA, Bureau of State Parks, PO Box 1467, Harrisburg, PA 17120. 717-787-6640. Call or write for information.

HUNTERDON COUNTY PARK SYSTEM, Hwy. 31, RD 1, Lebanon, NJ 08833. 908-782-1158 or 782-PARK. Call or write for information.

N.J. DIVISION OF PARKS & FORESTRY, State Park Service, CN 404, Trenton, NJ 08625. 609-292-2797. Call or write for information.

RIVER RECREATION

BUCKS COUNTY RIVER COUNTRY, 2 Walters Lane, PO Box 6, Point Pleasant, PA 18950, 215-297-5000. www.rivercountry.net. World's River Tubing Capital! Canoeing, Rafting, Kayaking on the scenic Delaware River. 35 years of family fun for all ages. Open daily May-October 9-7. V, M.

THEATRE

PEDDLER'S VILLAGE MURDER MYSTERY DINNER. Peddler's Pub, Rte. 263, Lahaska, PA 18931. 215-794-4010. www.peddlersvillage. com. Dinner, dessert & death awaits. Interactive and fun dinner theatre where the audience guesses who-done-it. Fridays & Saturdays 8 pm. Schedule changes every four months. Major credit cards.

TRAIN EXCURSIONS

BLACK RIVER & WESTERN RAILROAD, Rt. 12 Stangl Road, Flemington, NJ 08822. 908-782-6622. www.brwrr.com. Scenic train rides through Hunterdon County aboard vintage coaches. Weekends and Holidays—April through December. Special events. Sat. & Sun. 11:30, 1:00, 2:30 & 4:00. Trains added Thurs. & Fri. in July & Aug. V, MC.

NEW HOPE & IVYLAND RAILROAD, 32 W. Bridge St., New Hope, PA 18938. 215-862-2332. www.newhoperailroad.com. Enjoy a real old-fashioned train ride through beautiful historic Bucks County countryside aboard one of our antique passenger cars. Also offering: song & story hour, brunch & dinner trains, birthday parties, group rates, charters, Santa trains, and more. Call for more information. Hours: seasonal. V, MC.

WILDFLOWER PRESERVE

BOWMAN'S HILL WILDFLOWER PRESERVE, River Rd., New Hope, PA. 18938. (2 1/2 miles south of New Hope). 215-862-2924. Walking trails through 100 acres of woods and meadows. Visitor Center and Gift Shop. Open daily 9-5, year round. FREE. Building Open 9-5. Grounds open 8:30 - sunset. V, MC, Disc.

WINERIES

BUCKINGHAM VALLEY VINEYARDS, Box 371, Rt. 413, Buckingham, PA 18912. 215-794-7188. You're welcome to visit, walk through the vineyards, tour the cool wine cellars, and sample the wines. There is no charge. Wines can be purchased by the bottle or case, at very reasonable prices. Tues.-Sat. 11-6, Sun. 12-4. V, MC.

SAND CASTLE WINERY, 755 River Rd. (Route 32), P.O. Box 177, Erwinna, PA 18920. 1-800-PA2-WINE, Fax: 610-294-9174. www.sandcastle winery.com. Please call for information regarding our summer concert series. Facilities available for receptions and private parties. Mon.-Fri. 9-6, Sat. 10-6, Sun. 11-6. Major credit cards.

UNIONVILLE VINEYARDS, 9 Rocktown Rd. Ringoes, NJ 08551. 908-788-0400. www. unionvillevineyards.com. Producer of award winning wines. The winery is open Thurs.-Sun. 11–4 for complimentary tasting and tours. Our wine shop features wine related items, gourmet foods, and gift baskets. Discounts on half and full case purchases. V, MC.

A listing of Theatre and Musical Organizations follows. Please call for current schedule.

Bristol Riverside Theatre - 215-785-0100
Bucks County Symphony - 215-348-7321
Bucks County Playhouse - 215-862-2041
Cold Brook Theatre - 908-832-0776
County Theatre - 215-345-6789
Hunterdon Symphony & Choral Union - 908-782-5160
Hunterdon Hills Playhouse - 908-730-8007
Langhorne Players - 215-860-0818
Lenape Chamber Ensemble - 215-294-9361

Main Street Theatre - 215-536-3545
New Hope Performing Arts Festival - 215-862-1699
Newtown Chamber Orchestra - 215-598-0722
Oldwick Community Players - 908-832-9544
Peddler's Village Dinner Theatre - 215-794-4000
Raritan River Music Festival - 908-213-1100
Riverside Symphonia - 215-862-3300
Silver Dollar Productions - 609-397-8700
Town and Country Players - 215-348-7566

Very Personal Healthcare for Pregnant Women

Logan Inn

The Toughest Clean Out Jobs in the World Done *Faster* than a Speeding Bullet

HUGHMAN POWER

Division of Hugh A. Marshall Contractors, Inc.
P.O. Box 182 • New Hope, PA 18938 • 215-862-2291

You Might be Tempted to
Kiss the Ground You Walk On

RUGS TO RICHES

Ready for Some Big Ideas to Increase Profitability?

We write ads that sell. We design ads that motivate. We place ads where they get response. We can help increase your bottom line. But don't take our word for it. Listen to what our clients have to say.

"We haven't sold as many Santas in this model in a long time. We know it has to be the ad." –Linda Foster, Pine Wreath & Candle Ltd.

"The ads are making a great impression with colleagues and buyers. I am selling more because of the recognition." –George Evans, G. Evans Ltd.

"We have feedback from patients, our numbers are doing exactly what we hoped they would do." –Dr. Jean Fitzgerald, Doylestown Women's Health Center

STRENK SANDOR ADVERTISING

Four Seasons Mall, 32 S. Main St., New Hope, PA 18938
215•862•5510   sandor@comcat.com

Shows of art, antiques and fine crafts are held periodically but all can be found every day year 'round in galleries and fine shops throughout the area. Photo: Martin E. Kennedy

Directory to Art, Antiques and Fine Crafts

The content of these listings is supplied by the establishments included.
Off-season hours may vary and an advance phone call is suggested.

ANTIQUES

ARTEFACT, The Village Barn, Rt. 263 & Edison Furlong Rd., Furlong PA 18925. 215-794-8790. Architectural Antiques featuring Fireplace Mantels, Beveled Windows, Garden Pieces, Stained Glass, French Doors, Newel Posts, Brass Chandeliers, Fluted Columns. Mon.-Fri. 12-5, Sat. 10-6. AE, V, MC.   p. 189

ASIANTIQUE, 401 W. Bridge St., New Hope, PA 18938. 215 862-8225. Asiantique specializes in Indonesian imports. We have fine teak wood furniture, architectural artifacts, unique collectibles, stone, sculptures and water fountains. Tues.-Sat. 10:30-6, Sun. 12-5, Mon. by appt. Major credit cards.   p. 44

BEST OF FRANCE ANTIQUES, 204 N. Union St., Lambertville, NJ 08530. 609-397-7817, 609-397-9881. Open every day 10 am-5 pm. French antiques, bronze and marble sculpture & lighting fixtures. Now representing La Cornue Kitchens. Appraisal, restoration and design services available.   pgs. 210-211

BEST OF FRANCE ANTIQUES, INC., at Chestnut Grove, 3686 Rt. 202 South, Buckingham, PA. 215-345-4253. Open Fri., Sat., Sun. 11-5. French antiques, incredible garden sculptures and fountains.Inside front cover and pgs.210-211

BROOKS ANTIQUES, 24 Bridge St., Frenchtown, NJ 08825. 908-996-7161. 19th Century painted country furniture, quilts, hooked rugs, folk art. Open: Wed.-Mon. 11-5 pm. Closed Tues..   p. 261

BURT SHEPP'S RIVERVIEW ANTIQUES, 1738 River Rd., Upper Black Eddy, PA 18972, 610-982-5122. www.riverview-antiques. A constantly changing selection of 18th , 19th & early 20th century furniture, early lighting, pottery, art work, silver, jewelry & collectibles. Sat. & Sun. 9-5, Wed., Thurs., Fri. 11-5. Closed Monday & Tuesday. V, MC, Disc.   p. 165

CHARMS FROM THE PAST, 129 W. Bridge St., New Hope, PA 18938. 215-862-9890. Hard to find French antique imports, both country and formal, artfully displayed in a charming historic building. Open: Thurs., Fri., Sat., Sun. 10-5.   p. 31

COCKAMAMIE'S, 9 W. Bridge St., New Hope, PA 18938. 215-862-5454. Specializing in Art Deco lighting, French Art Deco furniture, as well as a variety of Art Deco accessories. Celebrity autographs also available. Call for weekly schedule. All major credit cards.   p. 49

COLLECTIONS, P.O. Box 370, 152 Oldwick Rd., Oldwick, NJ 08858. 908-439-3736. A
continued

collection of shops featuring antiques and collectibles in a charming setting. Tues.-Sat. 11-4. V, MC. p. 271

CONSIGNMENT GALLERIES, 470 Town Center, New Britain, PA 18901. 215-348-5244. A 4,000 sq. ft. collection of only finer: antiques, furniture, china, sterling, jewelry, paintings, lamps, mirrors, glassware and collectibles. Mon.-Fri. 10-8, Sat. 10-5, Sun 12-5. V, MC, MAC. p. 185

ETTA MAE'S ANTIQUES CO., 506 H Dublin Pike (Route 313), Perkasie, PA 18944. 215-249-1925, FAX: 215-249-4640. An inspired assortment of antiques and collectibles in a beautiful country setting. You can find everything from antique coffee mills, advertising items and country furniture to estate jewelry, Native American art & artifacts and vintage bicycles. And, what you can't find, Etta Mae will gladly try and locate for you. Wed. 11-6, Fri.-Sun. 11-6, and by appointment. AE, V, MC. p. 167

FERRY HILL, 15 N. Main St., New Hope, PA 18938. 215-862-5335, www.ferryhill.com. Antiques and Decorative Arts. English and Continental porcelains, Staffordshire, Limoges, refinished trunks, jewelry, tapestries, paintings, screens, lighting – British Royalty items and a large selection of teapots, cups and saucers. Open every day. All major credit cards. p. 53

GARDNER'S ANTIQUES IMPORT CENTER, 6148 Lower York Rd., New Hope, PA 18938, 3 miles from Lambertville on Rt. 202 South. 215-794-8616 & 794-7759, www.gardnersantiques. com. Direct importer and wholesaler of French antiques, country French, Louis XV, Louis XVI, Art Nouveau, Art Deco and decorative accessories. Open daily 10:30-5:00 pm. AE, V, MC. Inside back cover.

G. EVANS LTD. ANTIQUES, #8 Bridge St., Lambertville, NJ 08530. 609-397-4411. A fine selection of antique European and Continental furniture, estate sterling, porcelains by Meissen, KPM, Coalport, Vienna, Ormolu mounted crystal by Baccarat, bronzes, enamels, fireplace equipment. An ever changing selection. Wed-Fri. 10-5, Sat. & Sun. 11-6. AE, V, MC. p. 219

HOBENSACK & KELLER, 57 W. Bridge St., PO Box 96, New Hope, PA 18938. 215-862-2406. Period and reproduction garden appointments for your discriminating taste, including urns, statues, fountains, fencing, benches. Also, oriental rugs and antiques. Mon.-Sat. 11-6, Sun. 1-5. Closed major holidays. p. 45

LACHMAN GALLERY, 39 N. Main St., New Hope, PA 18938. 215-862-6620, Fax: 215-862-6621. Specializing in the unusual . . . eclectic antiques, fine accent and conversational pieces you've boon looking for – certainly not your typical antique shop! Closed Mon. Open 11-5 with extended seasonal hours, and by appointment. AE, V, MC, Disc. p. 2

LEGACY ANTIQUES, INC., Rt. 202 & 179, New Hope, PA 18938. 215-862-6310, Fax: 215-862-9404. Direct importer of unique antique furniture and accessories from Europe. 5,000 sq. ft. of quality items from rustic, country, and formal. Antique restoration service available. Tues.-Sat. 10-6, Sun. 11-5, Closed Mon. All major credit cards. p. 51

LYONS ANTIQUES, 6220 Lower York Rd. (Rt. 202 & Aquetong Rd.) New Hope, PA 18938. 215-862-0160, Fax: 215-862-4757. The Rare . . . and the Unusual. 18th, 19th & 20th Century European hand carved Renaissance & Gothic style furniture & bronzes. Tues.-Sat. 10:30-5, Sun. 11-5. V, MC. p. 54

MILLER-TOPIA DESIGNERS, 35 N. Union St., Lambertville, NJ 08530. 609-397-9339. www. antiqueimporters.com. Antique importers, restoration specialists, wholesale prices, worldwide shipping, importing directly to you since 1968. Furniture, clocks, bronzes, lighting, mirrors, art. Mon.-Sun. 10-5. All major credit cards. p. 236

MONKEY HILL ANTIQUES, CRAFTS & GIFTS, 6465 Route 202, New Hope, PA 18938. 215-862-0118. www.monkeyhillantiques.com. Specializing in objects of history, design, imagination and surprise with an emphasis on painted furniture, primitives, folk art and pottery. Tues.-Sat. 10:30-6, Sun. 12-5. AE, V, MC. p. 21

MORTEN MONBERG, INTERNATIONAL ANTIQUES, 19 Bridge St., Stockton, NJ 08559. 609-397-7066, Fax: 609-397-7067. www. morten-monberg.com. A shop unique to the area, offering a variety of original antique colonial furniture from former Spanish colonies. Specializing in 150-200 year-old long tables in precious woods, & a full assortment of European antiques. Founder Morten Monberg has 25 years of experience in international antique trading. The main shop is located in Denmark where their on-site workshop makes the necessary restoration to every piece before it is shown in their shops. Open 7 days, 9-5, Sat. 9-7, and by appointment. AE, check. p. 6-7

OLD ENGLISH PINE, 202 N. Union St., Lambertville, NJ 08530. 609-397-4978. Over 5,000 sq. ft. warehouse showrooms. Imported antique pine furniture & 18th century English oak. Delivery available. (Established 1985). Tues.-Sun.10-6, closed Monday. AE, V, MC. p. 214

OXUS RIVER GALLERY, 25 Ferry St,. Lambertville, NJ 08530. 609-397-5690, Fax: 609-397-5695, www.oxusriver.com. Oriental & decorative rugs, Asian antiques ranging from antique Persian to contemporary natural dye productions. We source and design unique rugs for your home. Home visits are our pleasure. Thurs.-Mon. 11-6 & by appointment. Major credit cards. p. 221

THE PORKYARD, 8 Coryell St., Lambertville, NJ 08530. 609-397-2088. Our dealers carry fine 18th & 19th century formal and primitive country furniture and accessories in a unique setting. Wed.-Sun. 11-5 pm. p. 229

PRESTIGE ANTIQUES, Rt. 29, Lacework Bldg., Lambertville, NJ 08530, 609-397-2400. Direct importers of fine French & English furniture.
continued

Formal and country styles. Hundreds of pieces to choose from! 7 Days 10-5 pm.   p. 224

RIVER RUN ANTIQUES, 166 River Rd., (Rt. 32) Pt. Pleasant, PA 18950, 215-297-5303. Specializing in holiday items with emphasis on Halloween and Christmas. Also toys, games, child-related items and selective general line. Sat., Sun., Mon. 11-5.   p. 155

SALLY GOODMAN ANTIQUES, 21 W. Ferry St., New Hope, PA 18938. 215-862-5754. Discover the unexpected. Personally selected antique furniture, paintings, copper, brass, silver, framed and unframed engravings, Staffordshire, china, Quimper. Chance, appointment best! AE, V, MC.   p. 48

TRADING POST ANTIQUES, 532 Durham Rd., Wrightstown, PA 18940. 215-579-1020. A 15,000 square foot co-op showcasing 75+ dealers. Furniture, glassware, pottery, collectibles, mirror frames and fine art. Open 7 days 10-5. V, MC.   p 191

202 MARKET ANTIQUES, 5921 Route 202, Lahaska, PA 18931, 215-794-3405..www.market202.com. An ever-changing selection of a variety of merchandise from all centuries, decorative accessories & a full array of furniture. Major credit cards.   p. 119

WALKING MAN ANTIQUES, 18A Main St., Clinton, NJ 08809. 908-735-8636. www.walkingmanantiques.com. A select group of dealers offering a diverse collection of furniture, decorative accessories, folk art—and the unexpected. Open daily 10-5, Sunday 11-4. Closed Tues. AE, V, MC.   p. 268

ART EXHIBITIONS

ARTSBRIDGE ANNUAL EXHIBITION, P.O. Box 354, Lambertville, NJ 08530. 609-773-0881. www.artsbridgeonline.com. Annual national juried exhibition held each spring in April at Prallsville Mills on Route 29 in Stockton, NJ. A wide variety of media including paintings, photography, sculpture, and fine crafts.

PHILLIPS MILL ANNUAL ART EXHIBITION, Route 32, River Rd., Phillips Mill, 2 mi. north of New Hope, PA. In its 72nd year. A juried show of paintings, graphics & sculpture. All works for sale. September 22 through October 28, 2001. Open daily 1-5. Admission.

ART GALLERIES

BEYOND THE LOOKING GLASS FINE ART GALLERY, 33 Bridge St., Frenchtown, NJ 08825. 908-996-6464. Original paintings, drawings and etchings by Painter and Master Print-Maker Charles Klabunde, whose works are in major museums and private collections in the US & abroad. Sat. & Sun. 11-6, or by appt. Studio visits by appt. V, MC.   p. 257

BRION GALLERIES, 1293 Rt. 179 (3 mi. NE of downtown) Lambertville, NJ 08530. 609-397-7030, Fax: 609-397-7032, www.briongalleries.com. Seven galleries showing contemporary paintings, sculpture, photography & cartoons by over 20 living artists. Gift shop with crafts & antiques. Holiday antiques year-round. Wed. &

Thurs. 10-5, Fri. & Sat. 9-6, Sun 12-6. Closed Mon. & Tues. AE, V, MC.   p. 220

THE CORYELL GALLERY, At The Porkyard, 8 Coryell St., Lambertville, NJ 08530. 609-397-0804. Delaware Valley & Regional Artists, Special Exhibits, Fine Crafts. Wed.-Sun. 11-5. V, MC.   p. 229

GOLDEN DOOR GALLERY, 52 South Main St., New Hope, PA 18938. 215-862-5529. Fine art in the Bucks County tradition. Exhibiting the work of over forty 20th century artists, including originals by Ray Hendershot, Len Hillegass, James Ingraham, Peter Keating, Dorothy McNamara, Jean Franz Miller, Alexander Volkov, Alice Geddes Woodward, Dan & Pauline Campanelli. Tues.-Sat. 11-5, Sun. 1-5. AE, V, MC.   p. 49

GRATZ GALLERY & CONSERVATION STUDIO, 30 W. Bridge St., PO Box 118, New Hope, PA 18938. 215-862-4300. www.gratzgallery.com. 19th & 20th Century American and European oil paintings, Pennsylvania Impressionists & P.A.F.A. artists. Museum quality conservation services. Custom framing. Wed-Sat. 10-6, Sun. Noon-6, and by appointment. AE, V, MC.   p. 27

HARVEY GALLERIES, Penn's Purchase, Rt. 202, Lahaska, PA 18931, & 132 S. Main St., New Hope, PA 18938. Visit the outdoor fountain and sculpture garden in Lahaska. The largest selection of copper fountains, wall sculpture, caricatures, mobiles, abstract art and florals. Plus... sip coffee, and watch the sculpting taking place at the Lahaska studio. This summer sit in a full-sized working TIME MACHINE! Visit the Tin Man, the Scarecrow, and Alice in Wonderland...all in metal!! 215 794-5578. New Hope hours: Tues.-Fri. 11-5:30, Sat. & Sun. 10-5:30. Lahaska 106 daily. AE, V, MC.   p. 117

HOWARD MANN ART CENTER, 45 North Main St. (Rte. 29), at Coryell St., Lambertville, NJ 08530. 609-397-2300. Large showroom with almost 100 internationally known artists, including: Chagall, Picasso, Fazzino, Hessam, Boulanger, Tarkay, Miro, Dali, Ebgi, Erte, Wren. Wed-Sun 12-5. Closed Mon. & Tues. AE, V, MC.   p. 236

HREFNA JONSDOTTIR GALLERY, 24 Bridge St., Lambertville, NJ 08530. 609-397-3274. Original works by nationally recognized artists and current major and collected area artists: Suzanne Douglas, Ana Bayon, Jane Gilday and Kevin Broad. Extensive classic and contemporary frame selection. Conservation framing. Celebrating over 23 years of business. Mon.-Sat. 10-6, Sun. 11-5, Closed Tues. Major credit cards.   p. 237

LACHMAN GALLERY, 39 N. Main St. New Hope, PA 18938. 215-862-6620. "Voted Best Art Gallery 2000 in New Hope." Original paintings & prints by nationally acclaimed Bucks County artist, Al Lachman. Not your typical art gallery! Open 11-5, Thursday thru Monday, and by appt. (extended seasonal hours). Major credit cards.   p. 2

LAMBERTVILLE GALLERY OF FINE ART, 20 N. Union St., Lambertville, NJ 08530. 609-397-
continued

4121. Paintings to provide you with continuing pleasure. Area gallery for Guy A. Wiggins, Ted Goerschner, George Bramhall and Vladimir Teniaev. Exclusive gallery for Laurence A. Campbell. Thurs. thru Sun. 11-5 & by chance or appointment. V, MC.

LOUISA MELROSE GALLERY, 41 Bridge St., Frenchtown, NJ 08825. 908-996-1470. www.louisamelroseartcraft.com. The gallery features an exciting collection of art in all its forms. Find original paintings, one-of-a-kind jewelry, art, glass and more. Hours Winter: Wed.-Sun. 11-5. Summer: Tues.-Thurs. 11-5, Fri. & Sat. 12-6, and Sun. 12-5. Also in Buckingham Green at 4950P York Road, Buckingham, PA 18912. 215-794-7901, Hours: Mon.-Sat. 10-5. AE, MC, V.   p. 258

MADE TO ORDER, 44 Main St., Clinton, NJ 08809. 800-541-9810, 908-735-4244, Fax: 908-735-0235. www.madetoorder.net. Celebrate the wolf with wildlife photographer Dan Bacon. We offer thousands of beautiful photos of wolves, wildlife and nature. Tues.-Sat. 10:30-6, Thurs. until 7, Sun. 12-5. Closed Mon. for winter. AE, V, MC, Disc.   p. 269

MICHELYN GALLERIES, 416 Town Center, New Britain, PA 18901. 215-348-2011. Michelyn Galleries carries a wide selection of original art featuring contemporary artists as well as The New Hope School.   p. 184

NAGY GALLERY, 16 W. Bridge St., New Hope, PA 18938. 215-862-8242. Original works by Delaware Valley artists in oils, watercolors, giclee sculpture, blown glass and photography. New exhibits bi-monthly. Mon., Wed., Thurs. 12-6, Fri., Sat., & Sun. 12-7. V, MC, Disc.   p. 55

THE PICTURE GALLERY, 115 S. Main St., Unit D-2 New Hope, PA 18938. 215-862-5441. A unique collection of prints, lithographs, 3 dimensional art and copper plaques featuring local area scenes, Philadelphia skylines, sports, wildlife and floral designs. Custom framing also available. Open daily 11-7. Major credit cards.   p. 57

RIVERBANK ARTS, PO Box 402, 19 Bridge St., Stockton, NJ 08559. 609-397-9330, Fax: 215-297-0265. Featuring fine contemporary art & crafts. Over 100 area artists represented. Also specializing in a large selection of unframed works. Mon.-Wed. noon to 5, Thurs. & Sun. 10-6, Fri. & Sat. 11-7 and by appointment. AE, V, MC.   p. 251

RIVERRUN GALLERY, At The Laceworks, 287 S. Main St., Lambertville, NJ 08530. 609-397-3349. Contemporary fine art, all media, featuring regional artists. Changing exhibits. 10-5 daily, Sun. 12-5. Closed Tues. AE, V, MC.   p. 237

UPSTAIRS GALLERY, Shop 74, Peddler's Village, Rt. 263 & 202, Lahaska, PA 18931. 215-794-8486. A fine arts gallery featuring Bucks County artists. Original oils, watercolors, sculptures, graphics, porcelain, photography and jewelry. Staffed by artists. Mon.-Thurs. 10-6, Fri. & Sat. until 9, Sun. 11-6. V, MC.   p. 128

ART MUSEUMS

HUNTERDON MUSEUM OF ART, 7 Center St., Clinton, NJ 08809. 908-735-8415. Changing art and craft exhibits. Tues.-Sun. 11-5.

JAMES A. MICHENER ART MUSEUM, 138 S. Pine St., Doylestown, PA 18901. 215-340-9800. www.michenerartmuseum.org. Exquisitely renovated historic site houses the finest collection of Pennsylvania Impressionist paintings in public or private hands including the spectacular 22-foot mural, A Wooded Watershed, by Daniel Garber. Important regional contemporary and figurative art and changing exhibitions, multi-media interactive exhibition, "Creative Bucks County: A Celebration of Art and Artists", the Nakashima Reading Room, beautiful outdoor sculpture gardens and a permanent exhibit on author James A. Michener. Blu's Café and Museum Shop. Group rates available. Tues.-Fri. 10-4:30, Sat. & Sun. 10-5, Wed. eve. until 9 pm. All major credit cards.   p. 179

BONSAI

ROSADE BONSAI STUDIO, 6912 Ely Rd., 3 mi. N. of New Hope, PA 18938. 215-862-5925. Bonsai-plants, supplies, classes, workshops, boarding, grooming, special exhibitions. Visit one of America's outstanding Bonsai gardens. Fri.-Sun. 11-5, or by appt. V, MC.   p. 91

CRAFT GALLERIES

A MANO GALLERIES, 128 S. Main St., New Hope, PA 18938. 215-862-5122 & 36 N. Union St., Lambertville, NJ 08530. 609-397-0063. www.amanogalleries.com. TOP TEN GALLERY OF AMERICAN CRAFTS. Garden, home & office accessories, kaleidoscopes, jewelry, wearables, glass, clay, furniture in wood and iron. STICKS FURNITURE, UGONE LIGHTING, TABRA, THOMAS MANN, AND MANY MORE . . . 20 years in New Hope. Open Daily. Extended hours during holidays and fair weather. All major credit cards.   p. 24

ACCENTS & IMAGES, An American Craft Gallery, #59 Peddler's Village, Rt. 263, across from the Cock 'N Bull Restaurant, Lahaska, PA 18931. 215-794-7660. Area's leading selection of functional pottery, art glass, jewelry, wood, heirloom quality jewelry boxes, clocks, candles, fountains, kaleidoscopes, bird baths, wind chimes & garden sculptures, seasonal Christmas items including a large array of hand blown glass ornaments. Open daily. AE, V, MC.   p. 123

ART LEGENDS, Four Seasons Mall, 32 South Main St., New Hope, PA 18938, 215-862-6844, www.art-legends.com. Area's largest selection of contemporary Navajo rugs and pottery, Pueblo pottery, Pendleton blankets, and Navajo, Hopi and Zuni jewelry. Open every day. AE, V, MC.   p. 48

ARTISANS GALLERY, Shop #35, Peddler's Village, Lahaska, PA 18931. 215-794-3112, Fax: 215-794-5298. Celebrating our 20th year in Peddler's Village. Exciting collection by *continued* contemporary American craft artists/fine & funky jewelry, decorative & functional ceramics, kaleidoscopes, glass paperweights and vases, fountains, wearable art, wooden toys, games & boxes, mirrors & wallpieces, a great selection of painted wooden furniture by Sticks & Shoestring. Located on the Main Green. Open daily. Major credit cards. p. 103

CELT-IBERIA TRADERS, 9 S. Main St., Lambertville, NJ 08530. 609-773-0180, Fax: 609-773-0182. www.nolegsneeded.com/celt.html. A unique gallery featuring the finest artisans and crafts people of Ireland and Spain. Featuring Nicholas Mosse Pottery & Waterford crystal. Mon., Wed., Thurs., 11-6, Fri. 11-8, Sat. 11-10, adjusted seasonally. Major credit cards. p. 233

COUNTRY ACCENTS, 39 Peddler's Village, PO Box 653, Lahaska, PA 18931. 215-794-9390. Country folk art, home accessories, furniture, lamps and garden art. Mon.-Thurs. 10-6, Fri. & Sat. 10-9, Sun. 11-6. AE, V, MC, Disc. p. 128

CREATIVE HANDS, Peddler's Village, Box 79, Lahaska, PA 18931. 215-794-7012. Creative Hands focuses on world-wide, simply-designed, contemporary merchandise, expressing new ideas, uses, lifestyles, (emphasizing usefulness). Open daily 10-6, Fri. & Sat. 10-9, Sun. 11-6. AE, V, MC, Disc. p. 126

HEART OF THE HOME, 28 S. Main St., The Historic Flood House, New Hope, PA 18938. 215-862-1880. New Hope's largest selection of fine crafts for the home and garden. Over 400 artisans are featured in a 1795 building displayed in a home-like setting. Second floor galleries include bed and bath, baby gifts, toys, games and musical instruments. Open daily, extended summer and holiday hours. p. 97

TOPEO GALLERY, 35 N. Main St., New Hope, PA 18938. 215-862-2750, Fax: 215-862-2744. www.topeo.com. Fine American Crafts: Art Glass, gold and silver jewelry, bronze fountains, creative lighting. Voted one of the top ten galleries in USA. Open weekdays 10-6, Sat. 10-7, Sun. 10-6. All major credit cards. p. 3

TOPEO GALLERY SOUTH, 15 N. Main St., New Hope, Pennsylvania 18938. 215-862-4949. www.topeo.com. Fine American Crafts: Home Accessories, Art Pottery, Furniture, Lighting, Jewelry and Exotic Wood. Visit Topeo's new gallery. Open weekdays 10 – 6, Sat. 10 – 7, Sun. 10 – 6. All major credit cards. p. 3

THE ZEPHYR GALLERY, Shop #27 Peddler's Village, Lahaska, PA 18931. 215-794-8771. MarketFair, US Rt. 1 North, Princeton, NJ 08540. 609-419-1616. www.zephyrgallery.com. A creative adventure! The wildest in contemporary American crafts from hundreds of talented artisans. Fabulous furniture (Avner Zabari), unique jewelry, whimsical ceramic and metal sculpture and wonderful wearable art. Constantly changing. Outrageous! Open daily. All major credit cards. p. 124

FRAMING

RIVERRUN GALLERY, At The Laceworks, 287 S. Main St., Lambertville, NJ 08530. 609-397-3349. Fine custom framing at affordable prices as well as a large selection of gallery-made frames in standard sizes from $5.00. Daily 10-5, Sun. 12-5. Closed Tues. AE, V, MC. p. 237

SCULPTURE GALLERY

HARVEY GALLERIES, Penn's Purchase, Rt. 202, Lahaska, PA 18931 & 132 S. Main St., New Hope, PA 18938. Visit the outdoor fountain and sculpture garden in Lahaska. The largest selection of copper fountains, wall sculpture, caricatures, mobiles, abstract art and florals. Plus... sip coffee, and watch the sculpting taking place at the Lahaska studio. This summer sit in a full-sized working TIME MACHINE! Visit the Tin Man, the Scarecrow, and Alice in Wonderland . . . all in metal!! 215-794-5578. New Hope hours: Tues.-Fri. 11-5:30, Sat. & Sun. 10-5:30. Lahaska 10-6 daily. AE, V, MC p. 117

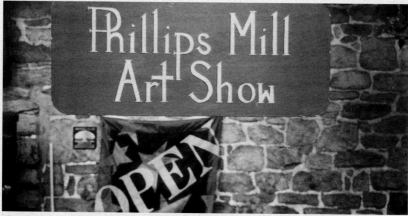

A seventy-two year old tradition continues each fall.

Discover Bucks County
Town & Country Living magazine

Bucks County Town & Country Living magazine is filled with over 150 pages of beautiful color photography, homes, gardens, bed n' breakfasts, crafts, art, history, dining and lots more. Published quarterly in the spring, summer, fall and winter, *Bucks County Town & Country Living* magazine has become one of the best regional magazines in the country.

Be sure to send for your copy today! We guarantee you'll love it and probably, like many others, want to begin a collection of your own.

Yes! I want to receive the next issue of *Bucks County Town & Country Living* magazine and be included as a subscriber for an additional three issues. A full year of *Bucks County Town & Country Living* magazine for only $11.95. Please send check or money order to:

Bucks County Town & Country Living
40 S. Main Street, Yardley, PA 19067
(215) 321-6040

Name _____

Address _____

City _____ State _____ Zip _____

Look below for lodging, both town and country, in homes as grand as this private estate.

Directory to Lodging

During the season reservations are always a good idea and in the off-season they are recommended. The content of these listings is supplied by the establishments.

AARON BURR HOUSE INN & CONFERENCE CENTER, 80 W. Bridge St., New Hope, PA 18938. 215-862-2520, Fax: 215-862-2570. www.new-hope-inn.com. Vintage village Victorian inn, ♦♦♦ AAA, ★★★ ✔MOBIL. All accommodations with private bath, oversized beds, AC and some with fireplaces and 2 person whirlpool tubs. Enjoy pool and tennis club privileges, welcoming refreshments, turndown service and more! Enjoy home baked breakfasts in your room, our flagstone patio or the dining room. Near NYC bus. Bike storage. We also lead workshops for aspiring innkeepers. Dinie and Carl, innkeepers since 1982. Single: $90, double: $90-255. Ideal for small conferences. Midweek, corporate and relocation rates available. AE, V, MC, checks.

BEST WESTERN-NEW HOPE INN, 6426 Lower York Rd. (Rt. 202), New Hope, PA 18938. 215-862-5221, 800-HOPE-202. www.bwnewhope.com. 152 Newly refurbished guest rooms in a country setting. 2 miles from Peddler's Village & 2 miles from the center of New Hope. Landscaped courtyard with outdoor heated pool, tennis court. Restaurant, lounge, meeting and banquet facilities. $89-149. Seasonal pkgs. Major credit cards. p.71

BLACK BASS HOTEL, Rte. 32, Lumberville, PA 18933. 215-297-5815. www.blackbasshotel.com. Established 1745, a step back in time in the European Country Inn tradition. Antique-appointed rooms, river views, continental breakfast, full service restaurant and bar. Next to the Delaware's only foot bridge. The nation's oldest continuously operating Pre-revolutionary inn. Rooms: $65 weekdays, $80 weekends+ tax. 1 Suite at $150 + tax, 1 at $175 + tax for 2 persons. Major credit cards. p. 142

BUCKS COUNTY BED & BREAKFAST ASSOCIATION OF PA, PO Box 154, New Hope, PA 18938. 215-862-7154. www.visitbucks.com. 44 select Bed & Breakfast Inns offering distinctive lodging in the historic Delaware River Valley. Relax at a riverside home, countryside farm, elegant estate or canalside barge stop. Romantic inn escapes, storybook weddings and corporate retreats. Web site lodging, restaurant & attraction information. On line guestroom availability and reservations.

CENTRE BRIDGE INN, 2998 N. River Rd., New Hope-Solebury, Pa 18938. 215-862-2048. www.centrebridgeinn.com. Est. 1705. Located in the village of Centre Bridge. Relax in the warmth and atmosphere of centuries gone by. Private baths and great views of the Delaware. Single & Double: $135. Corp. discount for weekly stays Sun. - Thurs. Suites: $175 and up. Major credit cards. p.139

CHESTNUT HILL ON THE DELAWARE, 63 Church St., Milford, NJ 08848. 908-995-9761, Fax: 908-995-0608. www.chestnuthillnj. com. Reflecting the gracious living of a more gentle era, Chestnut Hill awaits you with Victorian elegance. Relax on the spacious wrap-around veranda overlooking the peaceful Delaware River (and Bucks County). Selected as a romantic hideaway by *The Discerning Traveler*. River walk, gardens, 40 foot deck at river's edge. Breakfast and fresh flowers. $90-250. Reduced rates for corporate guests. "Country Cottage by the River" and the "Paradise Suite", both all-suite hideaways, are ideal for longer stays. NO SMOKING PLEASE. Honeymoon suite. Innkeepers: Linda & Rob Castagna. p. 263

CHIMNEY HILL FARM ESTATE & THE OL' BARN INN, 207 Goat Hill Road, Lambertville, NJ 08530. 609-397-1516 & 800-211-INNS. www.chimneyhillinn.com. On a country road nestled into the hillside above Lambertville resides the 1820 cozy fieldstone estate of Chimney Hill Inn; eight acres of gardens, romance and relaxation. Rated 4 lips in "Best Places to Kiss" & a featured

continued

Inn on the cover of *Country Inns and Country Roads Magazines*. Always written about, always recommended, a connoisseur's choice for Bed and Breakfast. Delicious homemade breakfast by candlelight, sherry and treats from the heart. 12 Luxury Rooms and Suites. Corporate/ meetings/relocation's welcome. AAA/ PAII/Mobil Approved. Rates: $125-325, Corp. rates available. AE, V, MC. p. 241

CORDIALS BED & BREAKFAST, 143 Old York Rd., New Hope, PA 18938. 215-862-3919, Fax: 215-862-3917. www.cordialsbb.com. Our 6 rooms include private baths, luxurious queen-size beds, air conditioning, cable TV, private balconies and decks. Continental breakfast complemented by fresh seasonal fruit. Less than a mile from downtown New Hope. Fresh flowers and snacks found in each room. Double: $85-130. All major credit cards. p. 79

EVERMAY ON THE DELAWARE, 889 River Road, PO Box 60, Erwinna, Bucks County, PA 18920. 610-294-9100, www. evermay.com. One of the finest small hotels in Bucks County. Featuring 18 air-conditioned rooms with private baths, furnished in Victorian antiques. Located on 25 acres of gardens, pastures and woodland between the Delaware River & Canal. A very private romantic retreat. $145-350. 2B Suite $350. V, MC, Cash, Personal Checks. p. 159

GOLDEN PHEASANT INN, 763 River Rd., (Rte. 32), Erwinna, PA 18920. 610-294-9595, 800-830-4474. www.goldenpheasant.com. Historic 1857 canalside inn overlooking the Delaware River. Six romantic guest rooms feature 4 poster king or queen canopy beds, antiques, fireplaces, Jacuzzi's, and river/canal views. Dinner: Wed.-Sun., Brunch 11-3, Weddings, Parties. Garden setting. Double: $95-225. Web site lodging availability and reservations. Major Credit cards. p. 157

GOLDEN PLOUGH INN OF PEDDLER'S VILLAGE, Rt. 202 and Street Rd., Peddler's Village, Lahaska, PA 18931. 215-794-4004. www.goldenploughinn.com. Luxurious inn features 66 individually appointed rooms and suites scattered throughout 18th-century style village. Pampering amenities such as individually controlled heat and A/C, cable TV, private bath, split of champagne and snack basket, in-room coffee/tea service, telephones, hearty continental breakfast. Optional whirlpools and gas-lit fireplaces. Seasonal and mid-week getaway packages. Send or call for brochure. All major credit cards. p. 122

THE GUESTHOUSE AT FRENCHTOWN, 85 Ridge Rd., Frenchtown, NJ 08825. 908-996-7474, Fax: 305-752-8253. www.frenchtown guesthouse.com.. Lodging with Bed & Breakfast ambiance in a 1780 Colonial Fieldstone home which is exclusively yours. Wide-planked wooden floors. Living room with fireplace and exquisite hand-carved wall-length mantel & bookcases carry you back to Revolutionary days. The dining room was originally the kitchen with an open hearth fireplace used for decades for preparing meals. Fully equipped kitchen with service for eight. Two bedrooms tastefully appointed with Queen beds. European continental breakfast.

Located on 70 secluded acres available for hiking, observing wildlife, sunset or the stars. Short or long term stays. Corporate amenities. Centrally located just 20 miles from Lambertville, Flemington, Clinton, NJ and New Hope, Lahaska, and Doylestown, PA. Double $185. AE, V, MC. p. 261

HONEY HOLLOW FARM BED & BREAKFAST, 2799 Creamery Rd., New Hope, PA 18938. 215-862-5336. www.honeyhollowfarm.com. "Best Hotel in New Hope", *National Geographic Traveler*. Nestled on 103 acres this restored colonial home affords enchanting views, fireplaces, romance. Step into this 300 year old private setting to be treated as honorary family and pampered with modern amenities. Double: $100-165. p. 73

HOTEL DU VILLAGE, 2535 N. River Rd., New Hope, PA 18938. 215-862-9911, Fax: 215-862-9788. www.hotelduvillage.com. Secluded estate on 10 acres with outdoor pool & tennis courts, only 5 minutes from New Hope. Stroll across the lawn to the inn's chef owned country French restaurant. Private baths, A/C, twin, double, queen or king-sized beds. Continental breakfast included. Double: $95 - 120, $170 - 2 room suite for 4 people. AE, Disc. p. 15

INN AT LAMBERTVILLE STATION, Bridge St. and The Delaware River, Lambertville, NJ 08530. 609-397-4400, outside NJ 1-800-524-1091, www.lambertvillestation.com. Nestled on the bank of the Delaware River, 45 antique filled rooms each with a view of the river, cable TV, and some with fireplaces. Continental breakfast and the New York Times along with many other special amenities. Sunday Night and Winter Weekend getaway packages available. Champagne Brunch served Sundays in our glass enclosed Riverside Ballroom overlooking the Delaware River. Riverside Ballroom available for weddings, banquets and conferences. Standard: $100-170, Deluxe: $110-190, Suites: $140-245. All major credit cards accepted. p. 223

THE INN AT PHILLIPS MILL, 2590 N. River Rd., New Hope, PA 18938. 215-862-2984. Stay at Phillips Mill – where the New Hope Impressionists started – in five cozy guestrooms in an 18th century stone barn. Candlelit dining by a fire in winter and on a flower-filled patio in summer. Small swimming pool and gift shop. $80-125 + tax, personal checks. p. 73

LAMBERTVILLE HOUSE, A National Historic Inn, 32 Bridge St., Lambertville, NJ 08530. 609-397-0200, 888-867-8859. www.lambertville house.com. 26 room National Historic Inn, jetted tubs, bathrobes, private baths, cordless phones, fireplaces, state of the art conference facilities and comfortable balconies. You will find your drink of choice at the New Left Bank Lounge. AAA ♦ ♦ ♦ ♦ $192-299. AE, V, MC. Disc. p. 231

LOGAN INN, 10 W. Ferry St., New Hope, PA 18938. 215-862-2300. www.loganinn.com. Exquisitely restored this year with loving care, this 18th century inn offers the traveler first-
continued

class comfort in the very center of this charming resort town. Sixteen beautifully appointed guest rooms have been decorated with discerning touches and are crowned with all the amenities expected of a luxury inn. Rates: $110-195 including continental breakfast. Two night minimum weekends. Complimentary parking. Major credit cards. p. 1

NEW HOPE INN, 36 W. Mechanic St., New Hope, PA 18938. 215-862-2078. A country inn offering many amenities including: heated outdoor pool, air conditioning, Cable TV, telephones, garden patios, free parking, bar and restaurant on premises. Our convenient in-town location is an easy walk from all of New Hope's attractions. Single/double: $105. Suites: $120-170. AE, V, MC. p. 71

THE NEW HOPE MOTEL, "THE MOTEL IN THE WOODS", 400 W. Bridge St. (Rte. 179), New Hope, PA 18938. 215-862-2800, Fax: 215-862-3962. AAA listed 28 rooms with decks, in 7 buildings on 5 acres with hundreds of century-old majestic trees. Heated outdoor pool, duck pond, Covered Bridge Lounge, rooms recently updated. Refrigerators, Cable TV, VCRs, AM/FM/CD Stereos, A/C, private phones with voicemail, private bathrooms, some with fireplaces. Rates: $59-119 all year. All major credit cards accepted. p. 71

PINEAPPLE HILL, 1324 River Rd., New Hope, PA 18938. 215-862-1790. www.pineapplehill.com. Rests on 6 acres, 4.5 miles from center of bustling town. Nine spacious rooms and suites, each with a private bath, TV, A/C, and fireplace. Balconies, canopy beds, and suites available. Full breakfast served daily at tables for two. Pool. Mobile and AAAuuu. Double occupancy: $116-249. Corporate rates from $81. Relocation & weekly rates available. V, MC, Disc., checks. p. 73

RAVENHEAD INN, 1170 Bristol Rd, Village of Hartsville, Warminster, PA 18974. Reservation number: 800-448-3619 or in PA: 215-328-9567, Fax: 215-328-9401. www.ravenheadinn.com. A B&B frequenters fantasy.four luxurious antique-filled rooms, private baths, in lovingly-restored 1849 manor house. Each room features cable TV/VCR, air conditioning & refrigerator. Sumptuous country breakfast. Close to Lambertville/New Hope antique shops, art galleries, Peddler's Village, Museums, Doylestown Historic District and Philadelphia. Double: $175-195. All major credit cards. p. 189

1740 HOUSE, River Road, Lumberville, PA 18933. 215-297-5661. www.1740house.com. The 1740 House is a country inn worthy of special note because of the stout determination of the hosts to give visitors a place to stay that is quiet, charming and memorable. Twenty-four air-conditioned, delightfully furnished bedrooms, each with bath and terrace, overlooking the Delaware River. In winter there is ice skating, a bit of skiing, a quiet winter walk along the old canal towpath. In summer, quite the other way, swimming, fishing and boating . . . and proprietors who know a thing or two about making you welcome. p. 145

SILVER MAPLE ORGANIC FARM AND BED & BREAKFAST, 483 Sergeantsville Rd. (Rt. 523), PO Box 156, Sergeantsville, NJ 08557-0156. 908-237-2192. www.silvermaplefarm.net. Escape to our authentic stone farmhouse, just 15 minutes from New Hope and Lambertville. Enjoy our swimming pool, hot tub, and tennis court on 20 beautiful acres. Country breakfast and snack. Fresh produce & flowers. Friendly farm animals. $89-139. Major credit cards. p. 254

TATTERSALL INN, Cafferty & River Roads, PO Box 569, Point Pleasant, PA 18950. 215-297-8233, 800-297-4988. www.tattersallinn.com. Escape to old Bucks and be pampered in this 250 year old stone manor house which features six antique furnished guestrooms, with private baths and A/C. Relax on broad porches and for cool evenings gather by the walk-in fireplace in the 1750 room for spiced cider and gingerbread. Breakfast in your room, on the veranda or in the dining room. Convenient to canal towpath for biking, jogging and walking. Antique shops, museums and fine dining nearby. Donna and Bob Trevorrow invite you to join them in their home. $95-145. ♦♦♦ AAA, ★★★Mobil Travel Guide approved and rated. V, MC, check. p. 155

WIDOW McCREA HOUSE, 53 Kingwood Ave., Frenchtown, NJ 08825. 908-996-4999, Fax: 908-806-4496. www.widowmccrea.com. Charming 1878 Victorian located in a splendid riverside village. Private cottage & spacious suite with working fireplaces and Jacuzzis. Three elegant guest rooms. Fine antiques throughout, queen-size feather beds, private baths, gourmet candlelit breakfast, complimentary bottle of wine, evening cordials. Please call for rates & availability. Major credit cards. p. 261

THE WOOLVERTON INN, 6 Woolverton Rd., Stockton, NJ 08559. 888-264-6648, www.woolvertoninn.com. "A blissfully lost in the hills refuge"- *NJ Countryside Magazine*. A 1792 stone manor on a grand estate by the Delaware River, surrounded by 400 acres of pastoral farmland and forest, yet only 5 minutes to Lambertville and New Hope. Full country breakfast served on our front porch in warm weather, by candle and firelight in winter. The inn offers many luxurious amenities such as whirlpool baths, private balconies and gardens, fireplaces and featherbeds, as well as gracious service and warm hospitality. Double: $105-265. ♦♦♦AAA, ★★★MOBIL. AE, V, MC. p. 249

YORK STREET HOUSE, 42 York St., Lambertville, NJ 08530. 609-397-3007 & 888-398-3199. www.yorkstreethouse.com. The elegant in-town-inn within walking distance of gourmet restaurants, antique shops & art galleries. 1909 Manor house featured in 1911 *House & Gardens* and 1991 *Country Living*. Mercer tile fireplaces, 1900 Waterford chandelier and leaded glass. Wicker rocking chairs on covered veranda overlook our gardens. Full gourmet candlelit breakfast. Five large guestrooms with private baths, TV, A/C, fireplaces, queen and king-sized beds. Luxury amenities. Parking. No smoking. Gift certificates. PAII. Laurie & Mark Weinstein, Innkeepers. AE, V, MC, Disc. p. 239

Serving Bucks County
for 137 Years
and Still Ticking

THE *First* NATIONAL BANK
AND TRUST COMPANY OF NEWTOWN

Founded in 1864

12 Offices in Central & Lower Bucks County

Doylestown	.....(215) 340-0500	**Richboro**	.......(215) 355-8211
Fairless Hills	....(215) 547-6410	**Solebury**	.......(215) 862-2600
Jamison	........(215) 343-9366	**Warminster**	......(215) 442-1544
Langhorne	......(215) 757-1577	**Washington**	
Levittown	.......(215) 946-8400	**Crossing**	........(215) 493-4088
Newtown	.......(215) 860-9100	**Wrightstown**	....(215) 598-7101
Trust Office	.....(215) 968-4872	**Yardley Road**	....(215) 968-3884

Five Star Bank

Visit us at our website: **www.fnbn.com**

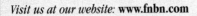

Member FDIC   MAC MONEY ACCESS CENTER®   LENDER   A Real Community Bank®

330

One of many river and canalside inns still in operation after more than 200 years.

Directory to Restaurants

During the season reservations are always a good idea and, for the restaurants where specified, are a must. Please note that off-season hours may vary. The content of these listings is supplied by the establishments. **If wine and spirits are served, the listing is followed by an asterisk.**

ANTON'S AT THE SWAN, Main & Swan Sts., Lambertville, NJ 08530. 609-397-1960. www. antonsattheswan.com. Distinctive American cuisine graciously presented in a sophisticated atmosphere rivaling any big city establishment. Menu changes monthly. Light fare in the adjacent Swan Bar, from potato and onion pizza to our famous NY Strip steaks at $14. Dinner: Tues. 6-9, Wed.-Sat 6-10, Sun. 4:30-8. Reservations suggested. AE, V, MC.* p. 241

ATRIO CAFE, 515 Bridge St., Stockton, NJ 08559. 609-397-0042. Eclectic food with a Brazilian flair. Prepared with local farm fresh ingredients. Tour the area and end your day by enjoying a dinner by candlelight in a comfortable and inviting setting. Dinner every day except. Mon., $16.95 aver. entrée. Reservations requested. BYOB. AE, V, MC. p. 251

BACI RISTORANTE, Routes 202 & 413, Buckingham, PA 18912. 215-794-7784. www. baciristorante.com. Fine Italian. Enjoy superb Italian cuisine in our charming stone walled restaurant circa 1709. Intimate, romantic dining by the fireplace, or seasonal balcony dining. Just minutes from New Hope and Doylestown. For lighter fare try our authentic "Heart of Oak" British pub downstairs with British dishes and 14 imported beers on tap. 00Lunch: 11:30-3, Dinner: 4-10. Reservations welcomed. AE, V, MC.* p. 137

BLACK BASS HOTEL, Rt. 32, Lumberville, PA 18933. 215-297-5770. Best river-view dining on the Delaware. Lunch, Dinner and the best Brunch in Bucks. Wedding and party accommodations available. American Continental. Lunch: $8.95-13.95, Dinner: $20.95-29.95, Brunch: $29.50 + tax, unlimited food and champagne.

Lunch: 11:30-3, Sun. Brunch: 11-2:30, Dinner: 5:30-9, Sat. until 10, Sun. 4:30-8:30. Live Piano Saturday. Reservations strongly advised. All major credit cards.* p. 142

THE BOAT HOUSE, 8, Coryell St.-at the Porkyard, Lambertville, NJ 08530. 609-397-2244. A small, sophisticated bar tucked down an alley and complemented by a fine restaurant, gallery and antique shops. Truly one of Lambertville's "hidden" treasures. Mon.-Sat. opens at 4. Sun. opens at 2. AE, V, MC.* p. 229

BUCKS BOUNTY RESTAURANT, 991 River Road (Rt.32), Erwinna, PA 18920. 610-294-8106. www.bucksbounty.com. Cuisine and atmosphere uniquely American and Bucks County. Creative dinner specials. Dining is casual, music is nostalgic. Outdoor seating in season. Takeout and catering available. Private dining room for up to 16 persons. Parking on site. Breakfast: $3.75-9.95, Lunch: $3.75-8.95, Dinner: $9.95-19.95. B: Sat. & Sun. 9-11 am, BR: Sat. & Sun.11-3:30, L: 11:30-4, D: 5-10 weekends, 5-8:30 weekdays. Reservations recommended. Closed Monday. Cozy pub now open and serving until 11 pm. Bank cards and personal checks. All major credit cards.* p. 161

THE CAFE, Corner of 519 & 604, Rosemont, NJ. 609-397-4097. *Gourmet Magazine* loved our butterscotch pudding. Fresh bright food in a genuine general store. The best of local produce. Less than 10 minutes from Lambertville/New Hope. Breakfast: $3.50-10, Lunch: $5.50-12, Dinner: $16.-25. Open weekdays 11-3, weekends 9-2. Dinner Wed.-Sun. Closed Monday. Reservations suggested for dinner. BYOB. V, MC. p. 254

CENTRE BRIDGE INN, 2998 N. River Rd., New Hope, PA 18938. 215-862-2048. www.centre-bridgeinn.com. Classic Casual. Features riverview dining on our brick terrace and romantic dining with an open fireplace and flickering candlelight. 10 Inn rooms. Lunch: $9-15, Dinner: $15-20. Dinner: 5-10. Reservations suggested. Major credit cards. AE, V, MC, Disc.*   p. 139

C'EST LA VIE, 20 S. Main St., New Hope, PA 18938. 215-862-1956. Delightful French bakery/cafe offering assorted breads, croissants, desserts and light lunch fare such as quiche. Cappuccino/espresso also served. Breakfast: $3 and up, Lunch: $5-8, Desserts: $2 and up. Tues.-Thurs. 7:30-5, Fri.-Sun. 7:30-6. Closed Mon. p. 66

CHURCH STREET BISTRO, 112 Church St., Lambertville, NJ 08530. 609-397-4383. Cozy and casual with rustic charm and a wood-burning stove. "New Bistro Cuisine" with traditional and contemporary menus that reflect the seasons bounty. Casual attire. Outdoor courtyard with chef's grill. Wed.-Mon. 5-10 Dinner, 12-3 Lunch, Sunday Brunch. Lunch: $5-14, Dinner: $16-24. All major credit cards accepted. Reservations suggested. *   p. 241

COCK 'N BULL, Rt. 263, off Rt. 202, Peddler's Village, Lahaska, PA 18931. 215-794-4010. www.peddlersvillage.com. A Bucks County tradition since 1962, serving traditional American fare plus some new contemporary dishes. Dine in a colonial-style setting with superb collection of antiques and folk art. Lunch: (no reservations taken) 11-3; Sunday Brunch: 9:30-2:30. Dinner: Mon.-Thurs. 5-9, Fri. 5-10, Sat. 4-10, Sun. 4-8. Reservations suggested for dinner. Special culinary events year round. Evening in the Colonial Kitchen, Monday evenings November thru March-Colonial menu choices plus hearth cooking demonstrations and visits by historical characters. King Henry's Feast, Thursday evenings-sumptuous buffet includes seafood and carved roasts. Murder Mystery every Friday and Saturday in Peddler's Pub. All major credit cards & Entertainment card accepted.*   p. 122

EVERMAY ON-THE-DELAWARE, 889 River Road, Erwinna, Bucks County, PA 18920. 610-294-9100. www.evermay.com.. Lodging with an award-winning prix fixe menu. Champagne & hors d'oeuvres plus six courses. An evening to remember. Very highly rated, Zagots and Fodors guides. Dinner: $68. One seating 7:30, Fri., Sat., & Sun. only. Reservations. V, MC.*   p. 159

FERNDALE, INN, 551 Churchill Rd. (Rt. 611), Ferndale, PA 18921. 610-847-2662. American/Continental. Chef-owned country inn serving fine and casual fare, featuring roast duck, fresh fish, pasta dishes and bar menu available nightly. Dinner: $17.25-21.95. Dinner: Mon., Wed., Thurs. 5-9, Fri. & Sat. 5-10, Sun. 4-8. Reservations appreciated. AE, V, MC.*   p. 166

THE FISH HOUSE, 2 Canal St. Lambertville, NJ 08530 609-397-6477, Fax: 609-397-6476. Seafood, American Chowder House. Spectacular choice of shellfish from around the world. Dining on the canal in the heart of Lambertville. Dinner: $15-25. Dinner: 5:30-10, Sunday Brunch: 11:30-3:30. Reservations requested dinner only. BYOB. All major credit cards.p. 232

FORGE AND ANVIL, 650 County Road 519, Barbertown, NJ 08825. 908-996-4271. www. forgeandanvilbeef.com. Traditional American. Unpretentious ambiance in a 175 year-old home, affording relaxed country dining with an emphasis on quality and selection. The extensive menu features choice steaks, lobster, veal, duck, chicken & pasta dishes. Families welcome. Lunch: $7-12, Dinner: $12-25. Lunch: 11 am–all day. Dinner: 5-9:30. AE, V, MC, Disc.*   p. 259

49 NORTH MAIN, 49 North Main St., Lambertville, NJ 08530. 609-397-5990, Fax: 609 397-8750. www.nolegsneeded.com/49north main.html. Casual New American. New American cuisine in a comfortable café atmosphere. Our "fresh approach" menu offers grilled fish, steak and specialty sandwiches. We also offer vegetarian dishes, homemade desserts, cappuccino & espresso. Non-Smoking. Lunch: $7-10, Dinner: $9-23. Lunch: Thurs.-Sat. 12-2:30. Dinner: Wed.-Sat. 5-9:30, Sun. 4-8. Reservations accepted but not required. AE, V, MC, Disc.   p. 240

THE FRENCHTOWN INN, 7 Bridge St., Frenchtown, NJ 08825. 908-996-3300. www. frenchtowninn.com. French Eclectic. A fine dining restaurant on the Delaware River with three romantic dining rooms and casual grill room serving French contemporary food with an extensive wine list. Rooms available for weddings, private parties and corporate meetings. Lunch: $6-15, Dinner: $6-27, Lunch: Tues.-Sat., 12-2, Sunday Brunch: 12-2:30 pm. Dinner: Tues.-Fri. 6-9, Sat. 5:30-9:30, Sunday: 5-8. Reservations suggested. AE, V, MC, Diners Club.*   p. 259

GOLDEN PHEASANT, 763 River Rd. (Rte. 32), Erwinna, PA 18920. 610-294-9595, 800-830-4474, www.goldenpheasant.com. Historic 1857 fieldstone inn nestled between Delaware River and Canal. Country French cuisine by Chef Michel served in canal-side greenhouse and tavern with fireplace. Dinner: Wed-Sun. Sunday Brunch: 11-3. Weddings. Parties. Lovely garden setting. Romantic lodging overlooking the river. Reservations. All major credit cards.*   p. 157

GOODNOE FAMILY RESTAURANT, 298 N. Sycamore St., Newtown, PA 18940. 215-968-3875, Fax: 215-968-5332. www.goodnoe.com. Goodnoe Family Restaurant is a Bucks County landmark. Come in and try our new menu. We are best known for our homemade ice cream and desserts and we still make a "real milkshake". Sun.-Thurs. 6 am-11 pm & Fri. & Sat. 6 am to midnight. Look for our ad across from the "Masthead".   p. 34

HAMILTON'S GRILL ROOM, 8 Coryell St., Lambertville, NJ 08530. 609-397-4343. Mediterranean Grill. Open grill, wood-burning oven, Southern French, Northern Italian, some Greek & Moroccan. Dinner: $16-30. Dinner: Mon.-Sat. 6-10, Sun. 5-9. Reservations suggested. BYOB. AE, V, MC.   p. 229

THE HARVEST MOON INN, 1039 Old York Rd., Ringoes, NJ 08551. 908-806-6020. www. harvestmooninn.com. Innovative American cuisine by award-winning chef/owner Stanley Novak. Formal and tavern dining in the historic 1811 Amwell Academy. Fireside dining in season. Private rooms up to 40. Garden weddings up to 200. Lunch: Tues.-Fri. 11:30-2:30. Dinner: Tues.-Thurs. 5-9:30. Fri. & Sat. 5-10. Sun. 1-8 in the tavern; 4-8 in dining room. Closed Mon. Reservations recommended. Major credit cards.*   p. 246

HAVANA, Restaurant, Bar, Catering, 105 South Main St., New Hope, PA 18938. 215-862-9897. Well known for outrageous and delicious world cuisine, outdoor patio bar, Mercer Tile Stone fireplace, great bands, incredible people watching. Lunch: $6.50-15, Dinner: $6.50-22. All major credit cards.*   p. 69

HORN & HARDART BAKERY & CAFÉ, 18 West State St., Suite 101, Doylestown Inn, Doylestown, PA 18901. 267-880-1901, Fax: 267-880-1902. Café Style. 1950's themed café with some past favorites of the original Horn & Hardarts along with Automat Blend coffee and daily specials. 7 am to 9 pm weekdays, 7 am to 11 pm weekends. AE, V, MC, Disc.   p. 178

HOTEL DU VILLAGE, 2535 N. River Rd., New Hope, PA 18938. 215-862-9911, Fax: 215-862-9788. Fine dining in the tradition of the chef owned regional restaurants of France. Romantic fireside dining in season. Drinks on our outside terrace. Dinner: Wed.-Sat., open at 5:30 pm, Sun. open at 3:00 pm, $17.95-22.95. Banquet facilities for up to 150. Corporate meetings and dinners. Reservations preferred. AE, Disc.*   p. 15

IL SOL D'ITALIA RESTAURANT, 255 N. Sycamore St., Newtown, Pa 18940. 215-968-5880, Fax: 215-579-8240. www.ilsolditalia.com. Contemporary southern Italian style & cuisine for casual or fine dining. Colorful outdoor dining. "Best of Bucks" four consecutive years. Live entertainment Wed., Fri., & Sat., Catering available. Lunch: $6-9, Dinner: $12-20. Lunch:Tues.-Fri., 11:30-3. Dinner: Tues.-Thurs. 4-11, Fri. & Sat. 4-12, Sun. -4-9. Reservations suggested. AE, V, MC.*   p .199

JEAN PIERRE'S, 101 S. State St., Newtown, PA 18940. 215-968-6201. www.letsmakeplans .com/jeanpierre. Elegant and refined dining in the country. Zagat rated "memorable, exquisite." Extensive wine list, knowledgeable service. Private meeting rooms. Call for hours and reservations. Major credit cards.*   p. 195

JENNY'S BISTRO, Rte. 202 and Street Rd., Peddler's Village, Lahaska, PA 18931. 215-794-4020. www.peddlersvillage.com. Fresh seasonal fare with a creative touch in a setting that combines Victorian elegance and country French. Signature dishes include Mushrooms Pennsylvania and Filet Chesterfield. Light fare and bar menu from 3 pm. Children's menu available. Piano bar on weekends after 8 pm. Lunch: Mon.-Sat. 11-3. Sunday Brunch: 10-3. Dinner: Tues.-Thurs. 4-9, Fri. 4-10, Sat. 5-10, Sun. 4:30-8. Reservations suggested. Major credit cards.*   p. 122

LA BONNE AUBERGE, Village II (off Mechanic St.), New Hope, PA 18938. 215-862 2462. www.bonneauberge.com. The only AAA♦♦♦♦ restaurant in Bucks County offering exquisite food in elegant surroundings with impeccably landscaped gardens. Entrees: $30-36. Light fare served in the cellar bar, Wed., Thurs., Fri., & Sun. Dinner only. Wed.-Sun. 5:30-9. Reservations suggested. AE, V, MC.*   p. 67

THE LAMBERTVILLE STATION RESTAURANT, Bridge St. and the Delaware River, Lambertville, NJ 08530. 609-397-8300. www.lambertville station.com. Dining with a view in our restored train station. New American cuisine. Live Jazz and Blues on weekends. No cover charge. Specializing in large parties, conferences, and weddings at our Restaurant and Riverside Ballroom. Open 7 days: Lunch: 11:30-3. Dinner: Sun.-Thurs. 4-9:30, Fri. & Sat. 4-11. Sunday Brunch: 11:30-3. Reservations suggested. AE, V, MC.*   p. 223

THE LANDING, 22 N. Main St., New Hope, PA 18938. 215-862-5711. www.landingrestaurant .com. Located on the Delaware, The Landing has been bringing great food to New Hope since 1976. The riverside terrace and bar in warm weather makes its al fresco dining the best in Bucks. Whether dining inside the non-smoking cozy dining room or out on the terrace, it's the picture-perfect place to dine. Serving delicious Regional American cuisine. Great wine list. The atmosphere is comfortable relaxed. Call for hours. On site parking. L: $7-12, D: $19-29. Sunday Brunch: a la carte. All major credit cards.*   p. 28

LOGAN INN, 10 West Ferry St., New Hope, PA 18938. 215-862-2300. www.loganinn.com. The ambiance of this exquisitely restored 18th century inn complements great classic American cuisine-succulent crab cakes, roast Long Island duckling, prime steaks. Dine any way that pleases you, elegant, casual, or while watching the world go by on an open terrace on Main Street. Wine and spirits. Serving Lunch: every day 11-3:30. Dinner: Sun.-Thurs. 4-10, Fri. & Sat. 4-11. Price range for Lunch: $5.25-11.95. Dinner: $12.95-25.95. Major credit cards.*   p. 1

LOS SARAPES, "Authentic Mexican Restaurant & Villa Tequila Bar." 17 Moyer Rd. & Rt. 202, Chalfont, PA 18914. 215-822-8858, 215-996-0699, Fax: 215-822-6149. www.lossarapes .com. Come and join us to enjoy the finest Mexican cuisine in Bucks/Montco. Visit our brand-new "VILLA TEQUILA BAR". Try from 60 different tequilas. Lunch: $8-10, Dinner: $13-24. Lunch: Tues.-Sat. 11-2, Dinner: Tues.-Thurs. & Sun. 5-9, Fri.& Sat. 5-10. Closed Mon.. Reservations needed for parties of 5 or more. AE, V, MC, Disc.*   p. 186

MARTINE'S, 7 East Ferry St., (corner of Ferry & Main), New Hope, PA 18938. 215-862-2966. Inspired cuisine. New Hope's best kept secret. Cozy English pub housed in Toll House circa 1752 with French dining room upstairs. Fireplace and outdoor dining in season. Open 7 days. Reservations suggested. Lunch: daily 11-4, Dinner: 5-10:30. Major credit cards.*   p. 67

MOONLIGHT, 36 W. Mechanic St., New Hope, Pa 18938. 215-862-3100, Fax: 215-862-3423. www. moonlightatnewhope.com. Upscale American. Don't miss this dining experience with it's white wrapped interiors. This restaurant is like walking into a dream. Lunch: $10-15, Dinner: $20-30. Lunch daily 12-2:30, Dinner daily 5:30-10. Reservations recommended. AE, V, MC, Disc.*   p. 69

ODETTE'S, S. River Rd., New Hope, PA 18938. 215-862-3000. Enjoy the scenic views & serenity of the Delaware River while dining. Private riverside rooms available. Piano bar. Seasonal cabaret shows. Lunch: Mon.-Sat. 11:30-3, Dinner: Mon.-Sat. 5-9:30, Sunday Brunch: 10:30-1:30, Sun. Dinner: 4-9. Lunch: $7-11, Dinner entrees: $17-29, Sunday Brunch: $18.95. Reservations suggested. AE, V, MC, Diners, Disc.*   p. 33

OTA-YA JAPANESE RESTAURANT, 21 Ferry St., Lambertville, NJ 08530. 609-397-9228. Exquisite Japanese cuisine featuring Teriyaki, Sukiyaki, Tempura, Sushi, Sashimi and vegetable dishes. New Hibachi Grill. Lunch: $6.95-13.95, Dinner: $14.75-24.95. Lunch: Tues.-Sat. 12-2:30, Dinner: 5-10 weekdays, 5-10:30 Fri. & Sat. Closed Monday. Reservations requested. AE, V, MC.   p. 240

OTA-YA JAPANESE RESTAURANT, Market at Newtown Place, 10 Cambridge Lane, Newtown, PA 18940. 215-860-6814. Exquisite Japanese cuisine featuring Teriyaki, Sukiyaki, Tempura, Sushi, Sashimi, and vegetable dishes. Lunch: $6.95-13.95, Dinner: $14.95-24.95. Lunch: Tues.-Fri. 12-2:30, Dinner: Tues.-Thurs. 5-9, Fri.-Sat. 5-10, Sun. 4-9. Closed Monday. Reservations requested. AE, V, MC.   p. 198

THE PINEVILLE TAVERN, Rt. 413, 1098 Durham Rd., Pineville, PA 18946. 215-598-7982. Enjoy casual fine dining with the real locals. One of the few remaining Bucks County Taverns that seems to get better every trip. 00Average Lunch: $6.00, average Dinner: $15.00. Mon.-Thurs. 11 am-11 pm, Fri. & Sat. 11 am-12 am, Sun. 12-9 pm. AE, V, MC.*   p. 191

THE RAVEN, 385 W. Bridge St. New Hope, PA 18938. 215-862-2081. Continental cuisine. Romantic country dining. Menu's change every 6 weeks. We are caring, comfortable and very civilized. Fireside dining in season. We welcome children 16 and older. Lunch/Brunch: noon-3, Dinner: 6-10. Lunch: $6.95-10.95. Dinner: $16.95-20.95, Sunday Brunch $6.50-10.50. Reservations for dinner only. V, MC. *   p. 40

THE RIVER'S EDGE, 50 S. Main St., New Hope, PA 18938. 215-862-5085. Salads, pasta, burgers, sandwiches, steaks, fish, homemade soups & desserts-in the center of town with a view of the Delaware. Same great menu all day. Mon.-Thurs. 11:30-9, Fri. & Sat. 11:30-10, Sun. 11:30-8. Reservations for 6 or more. AE, V, MC.*   p. 67

ROOSEVELT'S BLUE STAR & BLUE 52, 52 East Street, Doylestown, PA 18901. 215348-9000, 215-230-8429. www.rooseveltsbluestar .com. Progressive Creative American Cuisine. Lively and refreshing. Fresh ingredients. Tucked in Doylestown is a non-smoking restaurant with

a jazz bar across the alley. Live entertainment Fri. & Sat. nights. Lunch: $5-10, Dinner: $9-22.50. Lunch: Mon.-Sat. 11-4, Dinner: Mon.-Sat. 5-10, Sun. 4-9. Reservations for 6 or more. All major credit cards.*   p. 175

THE SERGEANTSVILLE INN, 601 Rosemont-Ringoes Rd., Sergeantsville, NJ 08557. 609-397-3700, Fax: 609-397-8836. Cozy 1734 inn with new American cuisine, knowledgeable and friendly service, and upscale atmosphere without the attitude. A perfect dining experience. Lunch: $5-14, Dinner: $14-21. Lunch: Tues.-Fri. 11:30-2:30, Sat. 11:30-2. Dinner: Tues. 5-9, Wed. & Thurs. 5-10, Fri. & Sat. 4:30-11, Sun. 12-9. Reservations recommended. All major credit cards.*   p. 255

SPOTTED HOG, Rt. 202 and Street Road, Peddler's Village, Lahaska, PA 18931. 215-794-4030. www.peddlersvillage.com. Casual dining in country setting. Friendly gathering place with tavern, featuring great selection of micro-brewed beers. Contemporary favorites from pizzas and calzones to grilled items and amazing desserts. Great breakfasts including health conscious alternatives. Children's menu. Breakfast: Mon.-Sat. 7-11, Sun. 7-noon. Lunch: Dinner, Snacks: Mon.-Thurs. 11:30-9, Fri. & Sat. 11:30 am-11 pm., Sun. 12:30-9.. Reservations not accepted. All major credit cards.*   p. 122

THE SUMMER KITCHEN, PO Box 325, Rt. 232 & Penn's Park Rd., Penn's Park, PA 18943. 215-598-9210. Contemporary International menu. In the heart of Bucks County owner chef Mario Korenstein presents an eclectic contemporary international menu in a charming country setting. Breakfast: $5-10, Lunch: $5-10, Dinner: $9-25. Breakfast: Sat. & Sun. 10-3, Lunch: Tues.-Sun. 11-4, Dinner: Wed., Thurs., Sun. 4-9, Fri. & Sat. 4-10, closed Monday. BYOB. AE, V, MC.   p. 193

SWAN HOTEL, 43 S. Main St., Lambertville, NJ 08530. 609-397-3552. Classic drinks. Unique bar menu. Outstanding collection of Delaware Valley Art. Tues.-Sat. 4 pm-2 am, Sun. 2 pm-11 pm. See listing for Anton's at the Swan.*   p. 240

THE TEA SHOPPE, 30 W. Bridge St., Suite 2, New Hope, PA. 18938. 215-862-0611. www.theteashoppe.net. Premium Teas. 30+ varieties of premium tea. Indoor/outdoor dining. Retail section includes: pre-packaged teas, tea accessories, teapots, gift baskets. AE, V, MC.   p. 54

WASHINGTON CROSSING INN, Rt. 532 & River Rd. (Rt. 32), Washington Crossing, PA 18977. 215-493-3634. www.washingtoncrossinginn .com. Continental cuisine. Historic country inn-adjacent to historic site of Gen. George Washington's crossing of the Delaware River in 1776. Fine casual dining, wedding receptions and banquets from 20 to 200-Martha's lounge cocktails and live music. Outdoor patio dining. Tues., Wed., Thurs. Lunch 11:30, Dinner:4:30; Fri & Sat., Lunch 11:30: Dinner: 5:00, Sunday Brunch: 10-2, Dinner: 2:00. Reservations recommended. Brunch: $7-12, Lunch: $7-12, Dinner: $15-25. AE, V, MC.*   p. 201

Directory to Local Websites

Included are sites of general interest about Bucks and Hunterdon Counties, followed by Area Guide Book advertiser sites. The general interest sites, together with the links found on those sites, offer a wealth of information on the area. For more information on advertisers in The Area Guide Book, visit their homepages at the addresses listed below.

Visit The Area Guide Book online at
www.areaguidebook.com
You'll find our directories with links to all of our advertisers, and more.

BUCKS COUNTY WEB SITES

Bucks County Community Web Links
www.tebweb.com

Bucks County Community Listings
www.livingplaces.com

Bucks County Conference and Visitors Bureau
www.bccvb.org

Bucks County Government Home Page
www.buckscounty.org

Central Bucks Chamber of Commerce
www.centralbuckschamber.org

Delaware Valley Outdoors
www.dvoutdoors.com

Lower Bucks County Online
www.lowerbucks.com

Lower Bucks County Chamber of Commerce
www.lbccc.org

New Hope Chamber of Commerce
www.newhopepa.com

Upper Bucks Chamber of Commerce
www.ubcc.org

HUNTERDON COUNTY WEB SITES

Clinton Town Site, Clinton Guild Business Assoc.
www.clintonnj.com

Flemington Business Association
www.fbanj.com

Frenchtown, NJ Online
www.frenchtown.com

Hunterdon County, New Jersey
www.co.hunterdon.nj.us

Hunterdon County Chamber of Commerce
www.hunterdon-chamber.org

Lambertville Area Chamber of Commerce
www.lambertville.org

New Jersey Division of Travel & Tourism
www.state.nj.us/travel/

New Jersey Online
www.hometownamerica.com/NJ/NJhome.html

AREA GUIDE BOOK ADVERTISERS

ARTS, ANTIQUES & FINE CRAFTS

A Mano Galleries, New Hope, PA
www.amanogalleries.com

Artefact, Furlong, PA
www.artefactantiques.com

Art Legends, New Hope, PA
www.artlegends.com

Brion Galleries, Lambertville, NJ
www.briongalleries.com

Burt Shepp's Riverview Antiques,
Upper Black Eddy, PA
www.RIVERVIEW-ANTIQUES.com

Celt-Iberia Traders, Lambertville, NJ 08530
www.nolegsneeded.com/celt.html

Ferry Hill, New Hope, PA
www.ferryhill.com

Gardner's Antiques, New Hope, Pa
www.gardnersantiques.com

Gratz Gallery, New Hope, PA 18938
www.gratzgallery.com

Harvey Galleries, New Hope & Lahaska, PA
www.harveygallery.com

Heart of the Home, New Hope, PA
www.heartofthehome.com

Lachman Gallery, New Hope, PA
www.lachmanstudios.com

Louisa Melrose, Frenchtown, NJ
www.louisamelroseartcraft.com

Lyons Antiques, New Hope, PA
www.lyonsantiques.com

MadeTo Order
www.madetoorder.net

Michelyn Galleries, Inc., New Britain, PA
www.michelyngalleries.com

Miller-Topia Designers, Lambertville, NJ
www.antiqueimporters.com

Monkey Hill, New Hope, PA
www.monkeyhillantiques.com

Morton Monberg International Antiques,
Stockton, NJ
www.morton-monberg.com

Nagy Gallery, New Hope, PA
www.nagygallery.com

Old English Pine, Lambertville, NJ
www.oldenglishpine.com

Oxus River Gallery, Lambertville, NJ
www.nolegsneeded.com/oxus

Riverbank Arts, Stockton, NJ
www.riverbankarts.com

Rosade Bonsai Studio, New Hope, PA
www.rosadebonsai.com

Topeo, New Hope, PA
www.topeo.com

202 Market, Lahaska, PA
www.market202.com

Walking Man Antiques, Clinton, NJ
www.walkingmanantiques.com

Zephyr Gallery, Lahaska, PA
www.zephyrgallery.com

ENTERTAINMENT, RECREATION, MUSEUMS

Alexandria Balloon Flights, Pittstown, NJ
http://members.aol.com/hotheir

Bowman's Hill Wildflower Preserve,
New Hope, PA
www.bhwp.org

Buckingham Valley Vineyards, Buckingham, PA
www.pawine.com

Bucks County River Country, Pt. Pleasant, PA
www.rivercountry.net

BucksNet, Langhorne, PA
www.bucksnet.com

Byers' Choice, Ltd., Chalfont, PA
www.byerschoice.com

James A. Michener Art Museum, Doylestown, PA
www.michenerartmuseum.org

Lakota Wolf Preserve, Columbia, NJ
www.lakotawolf.com

National Shrine of Our Lady of Czestochowa,
Doylestown, PA
www.polishshrine.com

New Hope Historical Society, Parry Mansion,
New Hope, PA
www.newhopehistoricalsociety.org

New Hope & Ivyland Railroad, New Hope, PA
www.newhoperailroad.com

Peddler's Village, Lahaska, PA
www.peddlersvillage.com

Pine Creek Miniature Golf, Ringoes, NJ
www.pinecreekgolf.com

Riverside Symphonia

riversidesymphonia.org

Sand Castle Winery, Erwinna, PA
www.sandcastlewinery.com

Sport Aviation, Inc., Erwinna, PA
www.digital-annex.com/SportAviation

Unionville Vineyards, Ringoes, NJ
www.unionvillevineyards.com

Washington Crossing Historic Park Museum
Shop, Washington Crossing, PA
www.fwchp.org

RESTAURANTS

Anton's at the Swan, Lambertville, NJ
www.antonsattheswan.com

Atrio Cafe, Stockton, NJ
www.bucksnet.com/atrio/

Black Bass Hotel, Lumberville, PA
www.blackbasshotel.com

Baci Ristorante, Buckingham, PA
www.baciristorante.com

Bucks Bounty Restaurant, Upper Black Eddy, PA
www.bucksbounty.com

Centre Bridge Inn, New Hop, PA
www.centrebridgeinn.com

Cock 'n Bull, Lahaska, PA
www.peddlersvillage.com

Ever May on-the-Delaware, Erwinna, PA
www.evermay.com

Forge and Anvil, Frenchtown, NJ
www.forgeandanvilbeef.com

49 North Main, Lambertville, NJ
www.nolegsneeded.com/49northmain.html

The Frenchtown Inn, Frenchtown, NJ
www.frenchtowninn.com

Golden Pheasant Inn, Erwinna, PA
www.goldenpheasant.com

Goodnoe Farm, Newtown, PA
www.goodnoe.com

Harvest Moon Inn
www.harvestmooninn.com

Horn & Hardart Bakery Café, Doylestown, PA
www.hornandhardart.com

Hotel du Village, New Hope, PA
www.hotelduvillage.com

Il Sol D' Italia Restaurant, Newtown, PA
www.ilsolditalia.com

The Inn at Lambertville Station,
Lambertville, NJ
www.lambertvillestation.com

Jean Pierre's Restaurant, Newtown, PA
www.jeanpierres.com

Jenny's Bistro, Lahaska, PA
www.peddlersvillage.com

La Bonne Auberge, New Hope, PA
www.bonneauberge.com

Lambertville House, Lambertville, NJ
www.lambertvillehouse.com

The Landing, New Hope, PA
www.landingrestaurant.com

Logan Inn, New Hope, PA
www.loganinn.com

Los Sarapes, Chalfont, PA
www.lossarapes.com

Moonlight, New Hope, PA
www.moonlightatnewhope.com

Odette's, New Hope, PA
www.odettes.com

The River's Edge, New Hope, PA
www.riversedgecomplex.com

Roosevelt's Blue Star, Doylestown, PA
www.rooseveltsbluestar.com

Sergeantsville Inn, Sergeantsville, NJ
www.sergeantsvilleinn.com

The Spotted Hog, Lahaska, PA
www.peddlersvillge.com

The Tea Shoppe, New Hope, PA
www.theteashoppe.net

Washington Crossing Inn,
Washington Crossing, PA
www.washingtoncrossinginn.com

LODGING

Aaron Burr House Inn, New Hope, PA
www.new-hope-inn.com

Best Western - New Hope Inn, New Hope, PA
www.bwnewhope.com

Black Bass Hotel, Lumberville, PA
www.blackbasshotel.com

Bucks County Bed & Breakfast Association of PA, New Hope, PA
www.visitbucks.com

Chestnut Hill on the Delaware, Milford, NJ
www.chestnuthillnj.com

Chimney Hill Farm Inn, Lambertville, NJ
www.chimneyhillinn.com

Cordials Bed & Breakfast, New Hope, PA
www.cordialsbb.com

Ever May on-the-Delaware, Erwinna, PA
www.evermay.com

Golden Pheasant Inn, Erwinna, PA
www.goldenpheasant.com

Golden Plough Inn, Lahaska, PA
www.goldenploughinn.com

The Guest House at Frenchtown, Frenchtown, NJ
www.frenchtownguesthouse.com

Honey Hollow Farm, New Hope, Pa 18938
www.honeyhollowfarm.com

Hotel Du Village, New Hope, PA
www.hotelduvillage.com

The Inn at Lambertville Station, Lambertville, NJ
www.lambertvillestation.com

Lambertville House, Lambertville, NJ
www.lambertvillehouse.com

Logan Inn, New Hope, PA
www.loganinn.com

New Hope Inn, New Hope, PA
www.newhopeinn.com

Pineapple Hill B & B Inn, New Hope, Pa
www.pineapplehill.com

Ravenhead Inn, Hartsville, PA
www.ravenheadinn.com

1740 House, Lumberville, PA
www.1740house.com

Silver Maple Organic Farm and Bed & Breakfast, Sergeantsville, NJ
www.silvermaplefarm.net.

Tattersall Inn, Pt. Pleasant, PA
www.tattersallinn.com

Widow McCrea House, Frenchtown, NJ
www.widowmccrea.com

Woolverton Inn, Stockton, NJ
www.woolvertoninn.com

York Street House, Lambertville, NJ
www.yorkstreethouse.com

SHOPPING

Alba Interiors, Frenchtown, NJ
www.albainteriors.com

The Baker, Milford, NJ
www.the-baker.com

Bien Dormir, Buckingham, PA
www.biendormirusa.com

Brass & Oak Gallery, Lahaska, PA
www.brassandoakgallery.com

Buckingham Valley Vineyards, Buckingham, PA
www.pawine.com

Bucks Country Gardens, Doylestown, PA 18901
www.buckscountrygardens.com

Bucks County Kitchens, Penns Park, Pa 18943
www.buckscountykitchens.com

Bucks County Town & Country Living Magazine, Yardley, PA
www.buckscountymagazine.com

Byers' Choice, Ltd., Chalfont, PA
www.byerschoice.com

Camel Walk, New Hope, PA
www.camelwalk.com

Chachka, Ewrinna, PA
www.chachkagourmet.com

Charles Tiles, Stockton, NJ
www.charlestiles.com

Clinton Book Shop, Clinton, NJ
www.clintonbookshop.com

Coda, Lambertville, NJ 08530
www.codahome.com

County Linen Center, Doylestown, PA
www.countylinen.com

Delaware Valley College, Doylestown, PA
www.devalcol.edu

Doylestown Bookshop, Doylestown, PA
www.doylestown-bookshop.baweb.com

Farley's Bookshop, New Hope, Pa
www.farleysbookshop.com

Flemington Business Assoc., Flemington, NJ
www.fbanj.com

Flying French Hens, Lambertville, NJ
www.flyingfrenchhens.com

The Golden Rhino, Lambertville, NJ
www.goldenrhino.com

Gothic Creations, New Hope, PA
www.gargoyles.org

Great Jones World, New Hope, Pa
www.greatjonesworld.com

Hairy Mary's, Upper Black Eddy, PA
www.hairymarysbuckscounty.com

Hankins & Associates, Doylestown, PA
www.i-kb.com

Heart Strings, Clinton, NJ
www.heartstringslifestyle.com

Hendrixson's Furniture Ltd, Furlong, PA
www.hendrixsonsfurniture.com

Holbert Motor Cars, Warrington, PA
www.holberts.com

Hydrangea, Lambertville, NJ
www.nolegsneeded.com/hydrangea

Kindred Quilts, Clinton, NJ
www.kindquilts.com

Knobs'N Knockers, Lahaska, PA
www.knobsnknockers.com

Lachman Gallery, New Hope, Pa
www.lachmanstudios.com

L'Avantage, The Day Spa, New Hope, PA
www.lavantage.bigstep.com

Liberty Village, Flemington, NJ
www.premiumoutlets.com/location/
liberty/libe.html

The Luggage Factory, Ringoes, NJ
www.luggagefactory.com

Made To Order
www.madetoorder.net

Max & Me Catering Co., Gardenville, PA
www.maxandme.com

Medieval Gallery, New Hope, PA
www.medievalgallery.com

Meow, Meow, New Hope, PA
www.meowmeow.com

Mercedes-Benz of Princeton, NJ
www.mbprinceton.com

Monroe Salt Works, Lahaska, Pa
www.moroesaltworks.com

Mt. Lake Pool & Patio, Doylestown, PA
www.mt-lake.com

New Hope Miniatures, New Hope, PA
www.newhopeminiatures.com

New Hope Photo, New Hope, PA
www.newhopephoto.com

Niece Lumber, Lambertville, NJ
www.niecelumber.com

Painted Lady, Lahaska, Pa
www.ePaintedLady.com

Peddler's Village, Lahaska, PA
www.peddlersvillage.com

Penn's Purchase, Lahaska, PA
www.pennspurchase.com

Pewter Cupboard, Doylestown, PA
www.pewtercupboard.com

Phillips' Fine Wines & Liquors, Stockton, NJ
www.phillipsfinewine.com

Phoenix Books, Lambertville, NJ
www.abcbooks.com/home/PHOENIXNJ

Piper Classics, Pipersville, PA
www.piperclassics.com

Rebel Hearts, New Hope, PA
www.rebelhearts.com

Renny Hortulus Farm Nursery, Wrightstown, PA
www.rennydesign.com

Rice's Sale & Country Market, New Hope, PA
www.ricesmarket.com

Rosade Bonsai Studio, Solebury, PA
www.rosadebonsai.com

Roxey Ballet Co., Lambertville, NJ
www.millballetschool.com

Sand Castle Winery, Erwinna, PA
www.sandcastlewinery.com

Scandinavian Touch, Lahaska, PA
www.scandinavian-touch.com

The Studio, Frenchtown, PA
www.greathomstyle.com

Superior Woodcraft, Inc., Doylestown, PA
www.superiorwoodcraft.com

Suzie Hot Sauce, New Hope, PA
www.suziehotsauce.com

Tail Waggers Botique, Washington Crossing, PA
www.myvetonline.com/wcahvet

Unionville Vineyards, Ringoes, NJ
www.unionvillevineyards.com

Verducci's, Flemington, NJ
www.verduccis.com

Worldwinds, New Hope, PA
www.worldwindinstruments.com

Ye Olde Yardley Florist, Yardley, Pa
www.yardleyflorist.com

SERVICES

Adam Shapiro, Weidel Realtors, New Hope, PA
www.buckscountyproperty.com

Bucks County Digital Imaging, Langhorne, PA
www.bucksdigital.com

Century 21 Unique Country Real Estate,
Ottsville, PA 18942
www.century21unique.com

Class-Harlan Real Estate, Doylestown, PA 18901
www.livingplaces.com/class-harlan

Coldwell Banker Hearthside Realtors,
Bucks County, PA
www.cbhearthside.com

Country Homes Real Estate,
New Hope, PA 18938
www.countryhomesrealest.com

E. J. Lelie Agency, Lambertville, NJ
www.ejlelie.com

Heritage Towers, Doylestown, PA 18901
www.heritagetowers.org

Kurfiss Real Estate, New Hope, PA
www.kurfiss.com

Lisa James Otto Country Properties,
New Hope, PA
www.lisajamesotto.com

Mitchell Williams Real Estate,
Erwinna, PA
www.mitchellwilliams.com

N. T. Callaway Real Estate, Princeton, NJ
www.ntcallaway.com

Robert G. Gavin, Inc., Upper Black Eddy, Pa
www.gavinrealtors.com

First National Bank & Trust Co., Newtown, PA
www.fnbn.com

Univest, Souderton, PA
www.univest-corp.com

Weidel Realtors, Pennington, NJ
www.weidel.com

Directory to Shopping & Services

The content of these listings is supplied by the establishments.
Off-season hours may vary and an advance phone call is suggested.

ADVERTISING

STRENK SANDOR ADVERTISING, Four Seasons Mall, 32 S. Main St., New Hope, PA 18938. 215-862-5510. A personal, service-oriented agency, designing promotional campaigns with proven results for over 18 years. Budget planning, copywriting, design, media selection, photography, printing. p. 320

AUTO DEALERS

HOLBERT MOTOR CARS, 1607 Easton Rd., Warrington, PA 18976. 215-343-1600 & 215-343-2890. Porsche, Audi, Volkswagen-Since 1955, from sales to routine maintenance and repair, understanding and caring for automobiles is a way of life for the Holbert family and our experienced, professional staff. AE, V, MC. p. 187

MERCEDES-BENZ OF PRINCETON, 2910 Route 1, Lawrenceville, NJ 08648. 609-771-8040. www.mbprinceton.com. Building relationships since 1982 with insight, integrity & passion. Parts & Service: Mon.-Fri. 7:45-6, Sat. for pick ups only 10-4. Showroom: Mon.-Thurs. 9-8, Fri. 9-6, Sat. 9-5. AE, V, MC, Disc. p. 39

BAKERY

THE BAKER, 60 Bridge St., Milford, NJ 08848. 908-995-4040. www.the-baker.com. Whole grain organic wheat bread & rolls available at our bakery & your local grocery store. Hours: 6-5 daily. p. 264

BANKING SERVICES

FIRST NATIONAL BANK & TRUST COMPANY, 215-860-9100. www.fnbn.com. Serving Bucks County since 1864, we have 12 offices in Central and Lower Bucks. At FNB we are committed to local ownership, operation and investment. We offer full service banking, trust and investment services. p. 330

UNION NATIONAL BANK, Logan Square, 6542D York Rd., Rt. 202, New Hope, PA 18938. 215-862-3750 and adjacent to Buckingham Green at Hunt Acres Center, York Rd., Rt. 202, Holicong, PA 18928. 215-794-5916, www.union national.com. Full service bank offering a variety of checking, savings and investment products as well as all types of loans. ATM available. M-W 9-4, Th 9-6, F 9-7, Sat 9-12. p. 37

BONSAI

ROSADE BONSAI STUDIO, 6912 Ely Rd., 3 miles No. of New Hope, PA 18938. 215-862-5925. Bonsai-plants, supplies. Visit one of America's outstanding Bonsai gardens. Plants, supplies, classes. Fri.-Sun. 11-5, or by appt. V, MC. p. 91

BOOKS

CANTERBURY TALES BOOK SHOPPE, #49 Peddler's Village, P.O. Box 472, Lahaska, PA 18931. 215-794-8719. Old time friendly service. Good selection of children and adult books and magazines. Film, newspapers, PA lottery. Mon.-Thurs. 10-6, Fri.-Sat. 10-9, Sun. 11-6. AE, V, MC, MAC. p. 129

CLINTON BOOK SHOP, 33 Main St. Clinton, NJ 08809, 908-735-8811, Fax: 908-735-0861. www.NJYP.com/clintonbookshop.htm. Fine NJ independent booksellers. Wonderful inventory of children and adult books. Accept phone orders, out-of-print searches & offer great service. Open daily. Major credit cards. p. 267

THE DOYLESTOWN BOOKSHOP, 16 S. Main St., Doylestown, PA 18901. 215-230-7610. One of Bucks biggest independent booksellers. Unusual books & best sellers, special orders, magazines galore, bargain book room, greeting cards, stationery, gifts, cafe. Sun.-Thurs. 9am-10 pm, Fri & Sat. 9-11. All major credit cards. p. 176

FARLEY'S BOOKSHOP, 44 S. Main St., New Hope, PA 18938. 215-862-2452, Fax: 215-862-5568. A classic, general bookstore with one of the East Coast's finest selections of books, greeting cards & audio products. Mon.-Thurs. 10-10, Fri. & Sat. 10-midnight, Sun. 10-8. AE, V, MC, Disc. p. 47

PHOENIX BOOKS, 49 N. Union St., Lambertville, NJ 08530, 609-397-4960. www.abcbooks .com/home/PHOENIXNJ. A large selection of books on all subjects. Used, rare, out of print. Jazz & classical records, CDs. Libraries & collections purchased. Mon.-Thurs. 11-5, Fri., Sat., Sun. 11-6. V, MC. p. 236

BUILDING SUPPLIES

C.A. NIECE LUMBER, Elm & North Union Streets, PO Box 68, Lambertville, NJ 08530. 609-397-1200. Full service building supply company. Mill work & kitchen/bath showrooms. Knowledgeable sales staff. ACE Hardware dealer. Mon.-Fri. 7-5:30, Sat. 7-4, Sun. 9-1. AE, V, MC, Disc. p. 243

CATERING

MAX & ME CATERING CO, PO Box 208, Gardenville, PA 18926. 215-766-3439. www. maxandme.com. All occasions. Off premise, full service catering; private and corporate. Fabulous food, beautifully presented. Chef: Max Hansen. Call for brochure. All major credit cards. p. 149

CAT LOVER'S EMPORIUM

MEOW, MEOW, Corner of Main & Bridge Sts., New Hope, PA. 215-862-0544. A true cat lover's paradise! With over 5000 different items you're sure to find that purr-fect gift for the cat or cat lover in your life. New dog department. Open 7 days. We ship worldwide. See our catalog at www.meowmeow.com. Major credit cards. p. 63

CHILDREN'S BOUTIQUE

THE CREATIVE CHILD, Store 6, Peddler's Village, Lahaska, PA 18931. 215-794-2500. Exceptional products fostering creative, imaginative and educational growth for infants to teens. Where imagination and joy are found in art. Mon.-Thurs. 10-6, Fri. & Sat. 10-9, Sun. 11-6. Major credit cards. p. 126

CHRISTMAS SHOPS

BYERS' CHOICE LTD., 4355 County Line Rd., Chalfont, PA 18914. 215-822-6700. www.byerschoice.com. Home of the Carolers® figurines, welcomes you to visit their museum, gift shop and see how the figurines are made. Mon.-Sat. 10-4, closed Sunday. V, MC. p. 10

PINE WREATH & CANDLE, LTD., PO Box 262, Peddler's Village, Shop #70 at the Grist Mill, Lahaska, PA 18931. 215-794-7060, Fax: 215-794-7077. A Christopher Radko Rising Star, Old World Christmas, Whitehurst, Snow Babies, Nativities, Lynn Haney, Snowbuddies, Pipkoe, Lang & Wise, David Frykman. Complete candle shop: Yankee, Colonial, Village, Williamsburg, Baldwin Brass and candle accessories. Mon.-Thurs. 10 to 6, Fri. & Sat. 10 to 9, Sun. 11 to 6. AE, V, MC, Disc. p. 107

CLEAN OUT SERVICE

HUGHMAN POWER, A division of Hugh A. Marshall Contractors, Inc., PO Box 182, New Hope, PA 18938. 215-862-2291. A licensed, insured, caring and responsible service company equipped to clean out properties, haul away debris and leave your place broom-swept clean. Owner, Hugh Marshall, will evaluate your needs and provide a free estimate. p. 16

CLOCKS

THE CLOCK TRADER, 6106 Lower York Rd., New Hope, PA 18938, Route 202, 3 miles south of New Hope, across from winery. 215-794-3163. Antique clocks our specialty, Howard Miller floor clocks, Black Forest cuckoo clocks. Watch and clock repair, sales, restorations, appraisals, house-calls. All work guaranteed. Ashley King proprietor. Tues.-Sun. 10-5. Closed Mon. AE, V, MC. p. 55

CLOTHING

CAMEL WALK, 352 W. Bridge St., New Hope, PA 18938. 215-862-9067. A unique boutique with contemporary fashions and accessories for men & women. Great gifts and always free parking. Enjoy a cappuccino while shopping. Open daily. Located in York Place across from The Raven. Major credit cards. p. 61

DRESSWELL'S, 10 Bridge St., Lambertville, NJ 08530. 609-397-2229. nolegsneeded.com/ dresswells. Casual clothing. Now featuring Thommy Bahama for men and women. The Dress-Down-Friday look. Mon.-Thurs. 10-6, Fri.-Sat. 10-9, Sun. 11-6. All major credit cards. p. 227

SAVIONI, 10 & 14 S. Main St., New Hope, PA 18938. 215-862-5010. Two fabulous shops of designer clothing for men and women - Valentino, Armani, Versace, Fendi, DKNY, Hugo Boss - to name a few. You won't be able to leave without a shopping bag. Mon.-Sat. 11-6, Sun. 11-7. p. 29

CLOTHING BOUTIQUE

THINGS WE LIKE, 20 Main St., Clinton, NJ 08809. 908-730-9888, Fax: 908-730-9888. Come lose yourself in the unique, diversified array of clothing, scarves, jewelry and gifts from all around the world. Open daily 10-5, Thurs. until 7, Sun. 12-4. AE, V, MC, Disc. p. 268

COLLECTIBLES

GLASS MASTERS OF THE VILLAGE, Shop #5 Peddler's Village (In the Courtyard by Jenny's), Lahaska, PA 18931. 215-794-3323. New owner presenting exciting new looks in collectible favorites-Fenton, Tutor Mint, Caithness Paper Weights, Old World (new & old), Robin's Nest. Mon.-Thurs. 10-6, Fri. & Sat. 10-9, Sun. 11-6. All major credit cards. p. 128

GREAT JONES WORLD, 40 W. Bridge St., New Hope, PA 18938. 215-862-6795. www. greatjonesworld.com. The greatest little toy store on the planet with the largest collection of Nighmare Before Christmas, Disneyana, Pez, Simpsons, metal lunchboxes, Billy Dolls and more. Call for hours. V, MC. p. 274

COUNTRY STORE

THE PATRIOT, Rt. 532, Washington Crossing, PA 18977. 215-493-5411. Old fashioned general store, gifts, souvenirs, reproductions. Light lunch Sat. & Sun. Ice cream & drinks everyday. Colonial service in this patriotic setting. Mon.-Sat. 10-5, Sun. 12:30-5. V, MC, Disc.   p. 203

DANCE

MILL BALLET SCHOOL, Official school of the Roxey Ballet Company. Non-profit ballet school and company. 243 North Union St. Lambertville, NJ 08530. School: 609-397-7244, Company: 609-397-7616, Fax: 609-397-6889. www.mill-balletschool.com. www.roxeyballet.com. World-class dance instruction. All ages-all levels. Children's classes/teens/professional. Roxey Ballet presents four full-length ballets annually. Mon.-Sat. 12-10. AE, V MC, Disc.   p. 237

DOG & CAT SPECIALTY BOUTIQUE

WELL BRED, 18 Main St., Clinton, NJ 08809. 908-730-7977, Fax: 908-730-8699. Distinctive accessories for canines, felines and humines. Gourmet pet bakery and one of a kind items for that special pet or pet lover. Pets on leash welcome! Open 7 days. Major credit cards. p. 269

DOLL HOUSES & MINATURES

MINIATURE CURIOSITIES, Shop 55, Peddler's Village, Lahaska, PA 18931. 215-794-9150. www.miniaturecuriosities.com. Bucks County's finest miniature shop specializing in fine hand crafted furniture & accessories. Let us help you make your miniature dreams come true. Mon.-Thurs.10-6, Fri. & Sat. 10-9, Sun. 11-6. Major credit cards.   p. 111

NEW HOPE MINIATURES, 127C S. Main St., New Hope, PA 18938. 215-862-5833, 800-296-4133, Fax: 215-862-3984. www.newhopeminiatures.com. Handcrafted miniature collectibles and accessories seldom found anywhere else, at guaranteed best prices, plus doll house kits by Real Good Toys. We ship world-wide. Member MIAA, C.I.M.T.A., N.A.M.E. Open seven days year round. Visit our new web site. AE, V, MC, Disc.   p. 54

DRUGS

BEAR APOTHECARY SHOPPE, 9 N. Union St., Lambertville, NJ 08530. 609-397-1351. Fine drugs & sundries. Most insurance plans accepted. Daily 8 am-7 pm, Sat. 8 am-5 pm, Sun. 8 am-1 pm V, MC.   p. 245

DRY CLEANING & LAUNDRY

STANLEY CLEANERS, (2 locations) 332 W. Bridge St., Clemens and Staples Shopping Center, New Hope, PA 18938. 215-862-2422 & corner of Church and Main Sts., Lambertville, NJ 08530. 609-397-0343. Established in 1951, family owned and operated. Complete dry cleaning, tailoring and laundry service. Lambertville: Mon.-Fri. 7-6, Sat. 7-4. New Hope: Mon.-Fri. 8-6, Sat. 8-4. AE, V, MC.   p. 81 & 245

EDUCATION

DELAWARE VALLEY COLLEGE, 700 East Butler Ave., Doylestown, PA 18901-2697. 215-345-1500, www.devalcol.edu. Delaware Valley College offers bachelor's degrees in more than 35 programs and a master of science degree in educational leadership.   p. 275

FARM MARKET

HOMESTEAD FARM MARKET, 262 N. Main St., Lambertville, NJ 08530. 609-397-8285. Locally grown produce, gourmet salad dressings, vinegars, jams & jellies, flowers, plants, garden supplies. Lots of fresh baked goodies. Enjoy a homemade muffin & fresh coffee. A seasonal Christmas shop. 8 am- 7 pm every day, Easter- Christmas. V, MC,   p. 243

NONE SUCH FARM MARKET, Rt. 263, Buckingham, PA 18912 (1/4 mi. south of Rt. 413). 215-794-5201. Our own & local farm grown produce, fresh baked goods, PA maple & honey, jams & jellies, dairy, frozen meats. On the farm: group tours, pick-your-own, pumpkins, festivals. Open year round, Mon.-Fri. 8-6:30, Sat. & Sun. 8-6. V, MC.   p. 135

FLEA MARKET

RICE'S SALE & MARKET, 6326 Greenhill Rd., New Hope, PA 18938. 215-297-5993. 30 Acre outdoor flea market. Hundreds of vendors. All types of merchandise, new, used, antique, produce. Amish meats. Open Tuesdays all year round 7-1 and Saturdays during the months of March thru December. ATM on property.   p. 96

FLORIST

POSSUMS', 30 Bridge St., Suite 3, New Hope, PA 18938. 215-862-2660. Serving all your floral needs, weddings & special events unusual gifts and home accessories.Closed Mon. & Tues. Open Wed.-Sat. 11-6, Sun. 12-5. AE, MC, V, Disc. MAC.   p. 61

YE OLDE YARDLEY FLORIST, 175 S. Main St., Yardley, PA 19067. 215-493-5656, 800-377-8374. www.yardleyflorist.com. Flowers from around the world, designs and decorative items for all occasions. Specialists in preserving bridal bouquets. Silks, dried, in-home or office consultations. M-Th & Sat 9:30-6, Fri 9:30-7, Sun 10-2. All major credit cards.   p. 207

FUNERAL HOME

VAN HORN McDONAUGH FUNERAL HOME, 21 York St. Lambertville, NJ 08530. 609-397-0105, Fax: 609-397-9394. The Lambertville - New Hope area's original funeral home. Experienced professional service in a gracious setting. Advance planning and financing available. p. 245

FURNITURE & ACCESSORIES

BRASS & OAK GALLERY, 6 Penn's Purchase, Lahaska, PA 18931. 215-794-7254. www.brassandoakgallery.com. Furnishings and accessories for home and officeiron beds, roll-top, flat top and computer desks, files, bookcases, oak tables/chairs, entertainment centers, bedroom furniture.   p. 104

CANE FARM FURNITURE, Rt. 519, Rosemont, NJ 08556. 609-397-0606. Authentic reproductions of Early American, Colonial & Shaker

continued

341

furniture. 17th & 18th Century American construction details, upholstered furniture, military & aviation prints, ephemera. Fri. & Sat. 10-5, Sun. 1-5.   p. 281

HENDRIXSON'S FURNITURE, 3539 Old York Rd., Furlong, PA 18925. 215-794-7325, Fax: 215-794-0983. www.hendrixsonsfurniture.com. Tues-Sat 10-5, Sun 1-5, Closed Mondays. V, MC.   p. 99

PIPER CLASSICS INC., Rt. 611, Pipersville, PA, 6 1/2 miles north of Doylestown, 215-766-0331. www.piperclassics.com. Classic handcrafted country furniture in pine, cherry & tiger maple, plus gifts and collectibles for the entire home. Also, leather and fabric upholstery, lighting, curtains, linens, Byers' Choice, Boyds. Lang Center. Open at 10 am Mon.-Sat. Closed Sundays. AE, V, MC.   p. 151

FURRIER

G. KUDRA FURS OF BUCKS COUNTY, Fifth Generation Furriers. 1135 Taylorsville Rd., Washington Crossing, PA 18977. 215-321-8378. Manufacturer of fine fur & leather garments all with impeccable craftsmanship. Cold fur storage. Expert cleaning & glazing, repair & restyling, conversions, remolding. AE, V, MC.   p. 202

GARGOYLES

GOTHIC CREATIONS, INC., 15 N. Main St., New Hope, PA 18938. 215-862-2799. A unique shop devoted to gargoyles, grave images, greenmen, tapestries, architectural elements, angles and much more! Over 500 different creations to choose from! Open daily. Extended summer & holdiay hours. V, MC.   p. 57

GIFTS

CHACHKA AT RIVER ROAD FARMS, Rt. 32, Erwinna, PA 18920. 610-294-9763. www. chachkagourmet.com. A stylish culinary shop. Famous Bucks County gift baskets, homemade jams and unusual food accents. We ship anywhere in the U.S. and worldwide. Bus groups welcome. 10-5 everyday but Tues. AE, V, MC, Disc.   p. 163

GLEN TO GLEN - Bucks County's Celtic Store. 31 South State Street, Newtown, PA 18940, 215-504-0626, Fax: 215-504-1289. Your source for Waterford and Galway Crystal, Belleek China, Mullingar Pewter, fine wool and linen products, food items, Guinness merchandise, music, videos, pottery, jewelry. Heraldry and genealogical assistance. Irish Dance and Finnians collections. Open 7 days. Major credit cards.   p. 195

JENNETT'S JACARANDA TREE, 26 N. Main St., New Hope, PA 18938. 215-862-2338. Handcrafted items, antique reproductions, stained glass, hand blown crystal oil-candles, sand sculptures, wind chimes, Delft, Riccio thimbles, dolls, Irish linen towels and more. Closed Tues. & Wed. AE, V, MC, Disc.   p. 59

PEWTER CUPBOARD, 1776 Easton Rd., (Rt. 611, South of Doylestown) Doylestown, PA 18901. 215-345-1759, Fax: 215-364-3355. www.pewtercupboard.com. A specialty gift shop for discriminating buyers featuring the finest quality pewter from all major suppliers. Engraving, bridal registry & attendant gifts. Mon.-Sat. 10-5, Fri. 10-7, extended holiday hours. Major credit cards and MAC.   p. 176

THE PINK DAISY, Yardleyville Square, 90 W. Afton Ave., Yardley, PA 19067. 215-321-2248. Elegant gifts and American craft gallery. Specializing in fine china, crystal and flatware. Bridal registry...free gift wrap and UPS available. Mon.-Fri. 10-5:30, Sat. 10-5. AE, V, MC, Disc.   p. 206

REBEL HEARTS, 81 S. Main St., New Hope, PA 18938. 215-862-6040. www.rebelhearts .com. A whimsical collection of unique and handmade gifts, jewelry and home accessories specializing in the motifs of hearts and stars. Sun. thru Fri. 11-6, Sat. 11-9, with extended hours during the summer months. AE, V, MC, Disc.   p. 63

SCANDINAVIAN TOUCH, New Expanded Location: 5743 Rt. 202, Lahaska, PA 18931. 215-794-8138. Wrought iron candle holders and chandeliers, table linens, books, wood and ceramic collectibles, decorative accessories, Swedish crystal, and clogs for the whole family. Open every day. AE, V. MC.   p. 115

TIN MAN ALLEY, 12 West Mechanic St., New Hope, PA 18938, 215-862-1110. A unique gift store/art gallery featuring retro toys, pop art, Kitsch collectibles, pedal cars and cool home décor. Thurs. thru Mon., 11-7. Closed Tues. and Wed., extended summer hours. Major credit cards. AE, V, MC.   p. 65

GOURMET FOODS

THE STUDIO, 12 Bridge St., Frenchtown, NJ 08825, 980-996-7424, Fax: 908-996-7434. www.greathomestyle.com. Your source for international design, contemporary gifts, decorative accessories, personal care and gourmet foods. Wed.-Mon. 10-6. Closed Tues. AE, V, MC.   p. 261

SUZIE HOT SAUCE, 19A W. Bridge St., New Hope, PA 18938. 800-60-SAUCE, 215-862-1334. www.suziehotsauce.com. Everything hot & spicy: sauces, salsas, snacks and much more. Stop in and sample, visit our website or call toll free. Sun.-Fri. 11-6, Sat. 11-7. Closed Wed. AE, V, MC, Disc.   p. 66

VERDUCCI'S SPECIALTY MARKET, 176 Highway 202, Ringoes, NJ 08551. 908-788-7750. Prepared foods by our in-house chefs; meats, game, poultry selected by our master butcher; seafood from around the globe; award-winning international baked goods; gourmet catering with custom menus, specialty groceries. Mon.-Fri. 9-7, Sat. & Sun. 8-6. All major credit cards.   p. 286

HAIR SALON

AVALON HAIR DESIGN, 152 W. State St., Doylestown, PA 18901. 215-345-0722. An upscale salon without the attitude for a style to fit your lifestyle. Our bimonthly classes keep our internationally trained stylists up to date. Kevin O'Neill, owner. Tues.-Sat. by appt.   p.178

HARDWARE

KNOBS 'N KNOCKERS, Street Road, Shop 22 Peddler's Village, Lahaska, PA 18931. 215-794-8045, Fax: 215-794-0435. www.knobsnknockers.com. Specialty hardware for your doors, cabinets, bath, hearth, kitchen, garden, home and office. Knobs 'n Knockers, defining lifestyles for over 20 years. Mon.-Thurs. 10-6, Fri. & Sat. 10-9, Sun. 11-6. AE, V, MC.   p. 125

HEALTH CARE SERVICES

DOYLESTOWN WOMEN'S HEALTH CENTER, 708 Shady Retreat Rd., Suite 7, Doylestown, PA 18901. 215-340-2229. Personal health care for pregnant women and all the women in your family. Our independent team of OB-GYN specialists are there to provide you with a positive approach to your health care needs.   p. 177

PLANNED PARENTHOOD, 301 South Main St., Doylestown, PA 18901, 215-348-0555; 721 New Rodgers Rd., Bristol, PA 19007, 215-785-4591; 1532 Park Ave., Quakertown, PA 18951, 215-536-2684; 3103 Hulmeville Rd., Bensalem, PA 19020, 215-638-0629. We offer Bucks County residents high quality family planning services at an affordable cost & testing & treatment for sexually transmitted diseases for men & women.

HOME & GARDEN

ALBA INTERIORS, 15 Trenton Ave., Frenchtown, NJ 08825. 908-996-5320. www. albainteriors .com. Alba Interiors offers European antiques, modern, contemporary home furnishings mixed with their own custom designs and a full range of interior design services. Open 11-6 Wed. thru Sun. AE, V, MC.   p. 258

BIEN DORMIR, 4950 York Rd., P.O. Box 48, Buckingham, PA 18912. 215-794-9721, 215-794-9726. www.biendormirusa.com. Luxury European Bedding Store featuring Palais Royal, Bellino, and other fine linen lines; bath & tabletop. Le Jacquard Francaise also available. Mon. -Fri. 10-5, Sat. 10-4. Major credit cards.   p. 137

BUCKS COUNTRY GARDENS, 1057 N. Easton Road (Rt. 611) Doylestown, PA 18901, 215-766-7800. www.buckscountrygardens.com. Area's leading garden center and landscape design/build firm. "We make your world beautiful", nursery, greenhouse, garden shop, patio furniture, gift and Christmas. Open 7 days, Jan.-Mar. 9-5, April-June 8-8, July-Dec. 8-6. Major credit cards.   p. 173

CASA CASALE, PO Box 344, Lahaska, PA 18931. 215-794-1474. 100% Italian imports including Vietri and Ceramica Varm Ceramics, copper cookware, Venetian masks, L'erbario bath products, imported foods, cooking accessories, artwork, music and seasonal gifts. Sun. 11-6, Mon.-Thurs. 10-6, Fri. & Sat 10-9. AE, V, MC, Disc.   p. 105

CHARLES TILES, INC., 760 County Route 523 (Sergeantsville Rd.), Stockton, NJ 08559. 609-397-0330. www.charlestiles.com. Exquisite showroom, custom designs, and the largest quality selections of decorative, hand-painted, quarry, terra cotta, and custom tiles, marble, granite and limestone. Knowledgeable, personal service to the trade as well as to the public. Mon.-Fri. 10-4:30, Sat. 9-2. V, MC.   p. 285

CODA, 32 Bridge St. (at the Lambertville House), Lambertville, NJ 08530. 609-397-3770. An exciting mixture of gift items and accessories for you and your home. Open Mon.-Thurs. 10:30-5, Fri. & Sat. 10:30-8, Sun. 10:30-5. Major credit cards.   p. 234

COOKERY WARE SHOP, #66, Peddler's Village, PO Box 106, Lahaska, PA 18931. 215-794-8477. Area's most extensive collection of quality cookware and accessories, in our expanded shop. Mon.-Thurs. 10-6, Fri. & Sat. 10-9, Sun. 11-6. AE, V, MC, Disc.   p. 112

COUNTY LINEN CENTER, 22-28 S. Main St., Doylestown, PA 18901. 215-348-5689, Fax: 215-230-9608. www.countylinen.com. WE DO IT ALL! At everyday low prices. Linens, carpets, custom and ready-made bedding, window treatments, home furnishings, lamps & accessories. Personal service. Mon.-Thurs. 9:30-5:30, Fri. 9:30-9:30, Sat. 9:30-5:30. AE, V, MC, Disc.   p. 181

DISTINCTIVE DINETTES, 245 Rt. 202/31 South, Flemington, NJ 08822. 908-806-3086. Areas largest display of kitchen, dinette and dining room furniture. From country to contemporary. Lowest prices guaranteed! Mon., Wed., Fri., Sat., 10-5. Thurs. 10-7:30, Sun. 12-4. Closed Tuesday. V, MC, Disc.   p. 295

FERRY HILL, 15 N. Main St., New Hope, PA 18938. 215-862-5335. www.ferryhill.com. Antiques and Decorative Arts. English and Continental porcelains, Staffordshire, Limoges, refinished trunks, jewelry, tapestries, paintings, screens, lighting-British Royalty items and a large selection of teapots, cups and saucers. Open every day. All major credit cards.   p. 53

FLYING FRENCH HENS, 28 A Bridge St., Lambertville, NJ 08530. 609-397-6300. www.flyingfrenchhens.com. Discover the countryside style of France in handpainted fine furniture, Provencal pottery, table linens, dinnerware, specialty foods and Belgian chocolates. Open everyday 11-6. AE, V, MC, Disc.   p. 235

HEART STRINGS, 10 Main St., Clinton, NJ 08809. 908-735-4020, Fax: 908-735-6564. www.heartstringslifestyle.com. We offer design consultation and a shop filled to the brim with home furnishings and accessories, gifts, jewelry, linenes, and clothing for women, babies and children. Open 7 days.   p.267

HAIRY MARY'S, 1937 River Rd., Upper Black Eddy, PA 18972. 610-982-0450, Fax: 610-982-5616. www.hairymarysbuckscounty.com. Treasures for your home and garden. Antiques, collectibles, garden items, pottery, herbs, plants and cut flowers. Full landscape, flower design service. Daily 10-5. All major credit cards.   p. 165

HYDRANGEA, 99 S. Main St., Lambertville, NJ 08530. 609-773-0377, Fax: 609-773-0279. www.nolegsneeded.com/hydrangea. Antiques, furniture, accessories (pillows, lamps, table wear, etc.) for the home. Garden ornaments, pots,
continued

containers and fresh flowers, interior design. Open everyday 11-6. Major credit cards. p. 229

INTERIORS FOR GRACIOUS LIVING & HOME, 370 West Bridge St., New Hope, PA 18938. 215-862-3304. A beautifully romantic home furnishings store. Nationally known for custom draperies, upholstery, bedding and exquisite accessories and gifts. Open 7 days, Mon.-Sat. 9:30-5:30, Sun. 12-5. Major credit cards. p. 20

MONROE SALT WORKS, Shop #62, Peddler's Village, Lahaska, PA 18931. 215-794-3685. www.monroesaltworks.com. Beautiful salt glazed pottery made in Maine. Oven, microwave and dishwasher safe. Toys, candles, jewelry and other unusual gift items. Mon.-Thurs. 10-6, Fri. & Sat. 10-9, Sun. 11-6. AE, V, MC, Disc. p. 127

MT. LAKE POOL & PATIO SHOPS, Doylestown Shopping Center, Doylestown, PA 18901. 215-348-8990. 707 N. Easton Rd., Willow Grove, PA 19090. 215-657-2300. www.mt-lake.com. Area's largest pool & patio shop featuring Woodard, Winston, Tropitone, Lyon-Shaw, Lloyd Flanders. Complete pool service and restoration. Sun. 12-4, Mon., Tues., Thurs., Sat. 9-5, Wed. & Fri. 9-8. All major credit cards. p. 180

PAINTED LADY, Shop 43, Street Rd. & Peddler's Lane, Peddler's Village, PA 18931. 215-794-9969. www.epaintedlady.com. A must-see shop with something for everyone. Renovators will appreciate our granite sinks, country French bowl sinks, hand painted indoor & outdoor furniture and accessories. Interior decorators welcome. Mon., Tues, Wed, Thurs., Sun. 10-6, Fri. & Sat. 10-9. Anytime by appt. Major credit cards. p. 106

THE STUDIO, 12 Bridge St., Frenchtown, NJ 08825, 980-996-7424, Fax: 908-996-7434. www.greathomestyle.com. Your source for international design, contemporary gifts, decorative accessories, personal care and gourmet foods. Wed.-Mon. 10-6. Closed Tues. AE, V, MC. p. 261

TESORO, 27 Bridge St., Lambertville, NJ 08530. 609-397-7225. Get in touch with the detailed feminine side of your decorating self with chairs upholstered and embellished with tassels, cords, and pillows; serene pastoral paintings; antique finish garden ornament, and more dreamy décor. Open daily 11-6. AE, V, MC. p. 235

INSURANCE

PIDCOCK AGENCY, 315 W. Bridge St., New Hope, PA 18938. 215-862-2001. Independent agents representing Traveler's, Great American, Ohio Casualty, Harleysville, Old Guard and Chubb. Full lines for personal and commercial needs. Mon.-Fri. 8-4:30. p. 79

JEWELRY

B. ADORNED, 1 South Main St., Lambertville, NJ 08530. 609-397-2770. Handcrafted, custom made jewelry specializing in fine gem stones, appraisals and repairs. Wed. thru Mon. 11-5. Closed Tues. Major credit cards. p. 233

DIANA VINCENT JEWELRY DESIGNS, 1116 Taylorsville Rd., Washington Crossing, PA 18977, 215-493-0969. International award-winning jewelry designer. Tues.-Fri. 10-6, Sat. 10-5. AE, V, MC. p. 209

MADE TO ORDER, 44 Main St., Clinton, NJ 08809. 800-541-9810. 908-735-4244, Fax: 908-735-0235. www.madetoorder.net. 23 years - designers & makers of jewelry - gold, platinum, silver. Swarovski Crystal, Peggy Karr Art Glass, Wolf and Wildlife Art Gallery. Tues.-Sat. 10-6, Sun. 12-5, Thurs. until 7. Closed Mondays for winter. AE, V, MC, Disc. p. 269

SCHATZIES TREASURES, Fine Jewelry. Four Seasons Mall, 32 S. Main Street, New Hope, PA 18938. 215-862-9694. A fine jeweler in New Hope-for excellence in craftsmanship and attentive, personal service. Custom designs, remounting, repairs, wedding rings. Mon.-Sat. 10:30-6, Sun. 11-6. AE, V, MC, MAC. p. 32

KITCHEN & APPLIANCES

BUCKS COUNTY KITCHENS, INC. Rt. 232 & Penns Park Rd., Penns Park, PA 18943. 215-598-3505. www.BucksCountyKitchens.com. The place to go for award-winning designers, furniture-quality cabinetry, fair & reasonable pricing & labor you can count on! Tues. thru Fri. 10-5, Sat. 12-4. Closed Sun. & Mon. p. 193

HANKINS & ASSOCIATES, INC., 2571 Furlong Road, Furlong, PA 18925. 215-794-5930, Fax: 215-794-5931. www.I-KB.com. Creative design solutions, featuring fine custom cabinetry for every room of your home. Counters, appliances, professional installation. Member: NKBA, SEN, CBCC. Mon., Tues., Thurs. 8 am-6 pm., Wed. 8 am-8 pm. Evenings & Sat. by appt. p. 277

HENDRICKS APPLIANCES, 21 Bridge St., Stockton, NJ 08559, 609-397-0421. Family owned for three generations. Fine appliances including Sub-Zero, Asko, Jenn-Air, and most major brands. We stand behind our products with authorized service. Mon.-Thurs. 8:30-5, Fri. 8:30-8, Sat. 8:30-3. V, MC. p. 250

Mac DONALD KITCHEN & BATH DESIGNS, INC., 71 N. Main St. Lambertville, NJ 08530, 609-397-8500. Cabinetry for any room in your home. Appliances and fixtures too. Complement anything from a gourmet kitchen to a butler's pantry. Mon.-Fri. 9-5, Sat. 9-1. p. 215

SUPERIOR WOODCRAFT, INC., 160 N. Hamilton St., Doylestown, PA 18901 (6 blocks from the courthouse), 215-348-9943. Fine handcrafted cabinetry made in Doylestown. Kitchens, libraries, home offices, bathrooms, wall units and more. Visit our showroom and design studio. Free consultation. Visit our website www.superiorwoodcraft.com. p. 11

LEATHER

BEARPAW LEATHER, 36 Main St., Clinton, NJ 08809 and 38 Main St., Chester, NJ 07930. 908-735-7351 & 908-879-8897. A wide selection of footwear, handbags, belts, jewelry, coats, wallets, briefcases and much more. Dansko, Naot, Ariat, Frye & Brighton. Clinton open daily 10-5, Thurs. 10-7, Sun. 12-4. Chester open daily 10:30-5, Thurs. 10:30-7, Sun. 12-5. Major credit cards. p. 269

STERLING LEATHER, Peddler's Village, Lahaska, PA 18931, 215-794-7101 & 97 S. Main St., New Hope, PA 18938. 215-862-9669. Over fifteen hundred men's and women's jackets in stock, western boots, hats, Minnetonka moccasins, handbags, leather accessories, leather clothes. Mon.-Thurs. 10-6, Fri. & Sat. 10-9, Sun. 11-6. All major credit cards. p. 131

LUGGAGE

THE LUGGAGE FACTORY, 76 Highway 202 (3 miles south of the Flemington circle) Ringoes, NJ 08077. 908-788-4810, Fax: 908-788-2832. www.luggagefactory.com. The Luggage Factory—quality, service & value since 1980. Featuring Tumi, Hartmann, Andiamo, Samsonite, Travelpro, Delsey, Atlantic, Ricardo and Jansport. Luggage. Leathergoods, Business Cases. Open daily 9-8, Sun. 10-6. Call for winter hours. Major credit cards. p. 288

MARBLE & GRANITE

HUNTERDON MARBLE WORKS, 257 Rts. 202/31, Flemington, NJ 08822. 908-788-3600, Fax: 908-788-0544. Large imported selection of marble, granite, limestone and slate. Our outstanding reputation is based on our superior fabrication and installation. Mon.-Fri. 9-5, Sat. 9-3, Closed Sun. Major credit cards. p. 295

MEDIEVAL GALLERY

MEDIEVAL GALLERY, 82 South Main St., 2nd floor, New Hope, PA 18938. 215-862-4800. www.medievalgallery.com. Bringing you back to an era of chivalry & romance, from the medieval knights to the Samurai warrior. We offer period-inspired clothing, arms & armor, art & antiques, Celtic jewelry & collectables. Mon.-Fri. 11-9, Fri. & Sat. 10 am-midnight, Sun. 10-8. AE, V, MC, Disc. p. 45

MUSIC & MUSICAL INSTRUMENTS

WORLDWINDS MUSICAL INSTRUMENTS, 18 W. Mechanic St., New Hope, PA 18938. 215-862-5766. www.worldwindsinstruments.com. Eclectic selection of handcrafted instruments imported from native cultures worldwide; featuring drums, flutes, whistles, didgeridoos, gongs, chimes and percussion instruments. Mon.-Sat. 11-7, Sun. 12-6. Major credit cards, AE V, MC, Disc. p. 59

NATURAL FOODS

EARTH FOODS, Buckingham Green, Rt. 202, Buckingham, PA 18912, 215-794-5311. Natural groceries, vitamins, herbs, homeopathic remedies, aromatherapy, books, body care. Mon.-Fri. 10-6, Sat. 10-5. All major credit cards. p. 134

PLUMSTEADVILLE NATURAL FOODS, 5764 N. Easton Rd. (Route 611) PO Box 477, Plumsteadville, PA 18949. 215-766-8666. Natural groceries, fresh organic produce, bulk items, vitamins, supplements, herbal and homeopathic remedies. Personal care, books & aromatherapy. Trained herbalist on staff. Mon.-Fri. 9:30-6:30, Sat. 9:30-5, Closed Sun. V, MC. p. 151

NURSERY

PAXSON HILL FARM, 3265 Comfort Rd., New Hope, PA 18938. 215-297-1010. Unique garden center in a farm setting with unusual annuals and perennials, cutting garden, pond fish, water gardening supplies, and farm animals. AE, V, MC. p. 93

RENNY'S HORTULUS FARM NURSERY, 60 Thompson Mill Rd. Wrightstown, PA 18940. 215-598-0550. www.rennydesign.com. Specializing in unusual and hard-to-find perennials, tropical standards and topiaries. Extraordinary collection of begonias, hostas and specialty plants. Summer hours: 7 days a week 8-5. Winter hours: Mon.-Sat. 8-4:30. Major credit cards. p. 192

ORIENTAL RUGS

LACHMAN GALLERY, 39 N. Main St., New Hope, PA 18938. 215-862-6620. Authentic beautifully handmade Persian & oriental rugs woven from fine silk and wool in the old world tradition. Open 11-5, Thurs. thru Mon., and by appt. AE, V, MC, Disc. p. 2

OXUS RIVER GALLERY, 25 Ferry St., (at S. Union St.), Lambertville, NJ 08530, 609-397-5690, Fax: 609-397-5695. For the collector and enthusiast, Oxus River Gallery is a charming locale to find Oriental and decorative carpets, Tibetan & Himalayan antiques & unique upholstery. Thurs.-Mon. 11-6. Open late most Fridays. Also by appt. All major credit cards. p. 221

RUGS TO RICHES, Cinema Plaza, 240 Hwy. 202-31 North, Flemington, NJ 08822. 908-782-8010, Fax: 908-782-1991. Specialize in fine hand-made and machine woven area rugs. Expert installation of superior quality broadloom. Mon.-Sat. 10-5, Sun. 12-5. AE, V, MC, Disc. p. 287

PARTY RENTALS

BRILLMAN'S RENTAL BARN, Rts. 202 & 32, (next to toll bridge) New Hope, PA 18938. 215-862-5591. Everything you need to make your event extra special: tents, tables, chairs, dance floors, linens, crystal, silver, bars, gazebos, grills, staging & carnival equipment. Mon.-Sat. Call for reservations. V, MC. p. 83

PET BOUTIQUE

TAIL WAGGERS BOUTIQUE, 1240 Route 532, Washington Crossing, PA 18977. 215-493-8284, Fax: 215-493-9889. www.myvetonline.com/wcahvet. Washington Crossing Animal Hospital. A full service small animal hospital serving the community's beloved pets 215-493-5986. A shop for pampered pets, pet food, supplies and unique gifts. Mon. 8:30-7, Tues.-Fri. 8:30-6, Sat. 8:30 -12. V, MC. p. 204

PEWTER

PEWTER PLUS, Shop #3, The Courtyard (near Jenny's) Peddler's Village, Lahaska, PA 18931. 215-794-2244. Classic and creative pewter. Original folkart collections from Williraye, American Chestnut, Lang Graphics and Lizzie High. Mon.-Thurs. 10-6, Fri. & Sat. 10-9, Sun. 11-6. AE, V, MC, Disc. p. 129

PHOTO SUPPLIES & FILM

NEW HOPE PHOTO, York Place, 358 W. Bridge St. (next to Mobil station) 215-862-9333. www.newhopephoto.com. Film, single use cameras, video tape, batteries, cameras and accessories. Hundreds of beautiful picture frames and photo albums. Kodak Image Maker Copy Print Station for reprints and enlargements from your photos in just 5 minutes. Mon.-Thurs. 9:30-6, Fri. till 8, Sat. 9:30-5.   p. 81

PRINTING AND PREPRESS

BUCKS COUNTY DIGITAL IMAGING, 832 Town Center Drive, Langhorne, PA 19047. 215-757-3600, Fax: 215-757-3838. www.bucksdigital.com. If you need color flyers, handouts, posters, we're your digital color experts! We supply on-demand digital color printing, large-format color printing, laminating, and mounting as well as page layout, scanning and prepress. We're proud to handle all the prepress for *The Area Guide Book.* Mon-Fri 8am-9pm. AE, V, MC.   p. 273

PUBLISHING

BUCKS COUNTY TOWN & COUNTRY LIVING MAGAZINE, 40 S. Main St., Yardley, PA 19067. 215-321-6040, Fax: 215-321-6044. www.bucks countymagazine.com. *Bucks County Town & Country Living* is the magazine for people who appreciate the history, small towns, homes, furniture, gardens, crafts, antiques, food and art of Bucks County.   p. 326

ENANDEM GRAPHICS, INC., P.O. Box 43, Lambertville, NJ 08530. 215-862-5094. Publishers of *The Area Guide Book.*

QUILTS

KINDRED QUILTS, 14 Main St., Clinton, NJ 08809. 908-730-8896, Fax: 908-730-8895. www.kindquilts.com. Quality cotton fabrics abound along with hand-dyed wools, primitive stitcheries, classes and supplies. Mon. thru Sat. 10-5, Sun. 12-4. V, MC, Disc.   p. 268

REAL ESTATE

ADAM SHAPIRO-WEIDEL REALTORS, NEW HOPE, 403 Old York Rd., New Hope, PA 18938. 215-862-9441, direct 800-246-0702. www.BucksCountyProperty.com. Stone houses, country, river and horse properties, farms and historic locations in Upper Bucks County. p. 81

CENTURY 21 UNIQUE COUNTRY REAL ESTATE, 7790 Easton Rd., PO Box 41, Ottsville, PA 18942. 610-847-2002, Fax: 610-847-2847. www.centruy21unique.com. Serving Bucks County for over 20 years. Our unique Bucks County properties include historical farmhouses, vacation retreats & new construction.   p. 169

CLASS-HARLAN REAL ESTATE, JoAnn Maroney, 15 W. State St., Doylestown, Pa 18901. 215-348-8111 ext. 18, Fax: 215-348-1721. www.livingplaces.com/class-harlan. Buying or selling real estate in Central Bucks? I know the Central Bucks County market! Sixteen years of full time experience! Call me!   p. 181

COLDWELL BANKER HEARTHSIDE REALTORS OFFICES, 5895 Lower York Rd., PO Box 299, Lahaska, PA 18931. 1-800-442-8257, Fax: 215-794-8589. www.cbhearthside.com. Serving all of Bucks County with offices in Buckingham, Doylestown, Dublin, Lahaska, Levittown, New Hope, Newtown, Richboro, Yardley and Washington Crossing. Complimentary relocation packages available.   p. 113

COUNTRY HOMES REAL ESTATE, 5144 York Rd., Holicong; Mailing address: PO Box 664, New Hope, PA 18938, 215-794-5700, 800-647-0533, Fax: 215-794-7610. Country Homes agents can offer their expertise on PA and NJ properties with enthusiasm and dedication. Our clients know that they can always reach a person not just a machine.   p. 132

E. J. LELIE AGENCY, Eugene C. Lelie, Broker of Record. 69 Bridge St., Lambertville, NJ 08530. 609-397-1700, Fax: 609-397-1702. www.ejlelie.com. Personalized with every real estate service. Serving the surrounding area for two generations. In the heart of historic Lambertville. Mon.-Sat. 9-5, Sun. 12-5.   p. 243

KURFISS REAL ESTATE, 6038 Lower York Rd, New Hope, PA 18938, 215-794-3227; 188 N. Main St., Doylestown, PA 18901, 215-348-5400; 1099 General Knox Rd., Washington Crossing, PA 18977, 215-493-9260; 3244 Rt. 212, PO Box 84, Springtown, PA 18081, 610346-6912. www. kurfiss.com. Kurfiss Real Estate offers distinctive homes in every price range. Charming traditional and country homes, farms, estates and new construction. Let us help you find your dream home. 60 experienced agents licensed in PA and NJ offer buyer and seller representation. Exclusive affiliates of Christies' Great Estates.   p. 17

LISA JAMES OTTO COUNTRY PROPERTIES, 1 South Sugan Rd., New Hope, PA 18938. 215-862-2626. www.lisajamesotto.com. Lisa James Otto Country Properties is a boutique real estate firm specializing in country homes, farms, estates and finely constructed new homes in PA. and NJ. Lisa James Otto Country Properties -A boutique real estate firm near the river's edge. Daily 8:30-6:00.   p. 23

MITCHELL WILLIAMS REAL ESTATE, PO Box 222, 905 River Rd., Erwinna, PA 18920. 800-222-1176, 610-294-1018. www.mitchellwilliams.com. Sophisticated Country Living, Serving Delaware River Valley, Hunterdon & Bucks County. Members several multiple listing services. Offering buyer & seller representation. Open 7 days. 9-5.   p. 159

N. T. CALLAWAY REAL ESTATE, 739 Sergeantsville Road, P. O. Box 157, Sergeantsville, NJ 08557. 609-397-1974. www.ntcallaway.com. N.T. Callaway Real Estate offers residential and commercial brokerage and is an exclusive affiliate of Sotheby's International Realty with two offices, one in Princeton and one in Sergeantsville. The company serves New Jersey and Pennsylvania. Mon.-Fri. 9-6, Sat. 9-5, Sun. 10-5.   p. 25

PIDCOCK REAL ESTATE & INSURANCE, 315 W. Bridge St., New Hope, PA 18938. 215-862-2001, Fax: 215-862-2424. Farms, business brokerage income properties, commercial buildings, since 1939. p. 79

ROBERT G. GAVIN, INC. REALTORS, PO Box 220, 1620 River Road, (at the Milford, NJ Bridge), Upper Black Eddy, PA 18972. 610-982-5050, Fax: 610-982-5804; and 189 S. Main St. (lower level), Doylestown, PA 18901. 215-348-3100, Fax: 215-348-1950. Specializing in in-town and country homes, private secluded retreats, farms, estates, land & buyer brokerage. Referrals welcome. p. 164

WEICHERT REALTORS, Bobbie Paul, GRI, C.S.P. Relocation Specialist, 149 S. Main St., Doylestown, PA 18901. 215-345-7171 Ext. 125, Fax: 215-345-9523. bobbiepaulemail@msn.com. Professional, personal service specializing in Bucks County from condos to estate properties. p. 175

WEIDEL REALTORS, 238 W. Delaware Ave., Pennington, NJ 08534. 800-934-3351, Fax: 609-737-3807, www.weidel.com. Weidel Realtors is a full-service real estate organization offering mortgage services, homeowners and title insurance, national relocation services and a real estate pre-licensing school. p. 352

RETIREMENT COMMUNITY

EVERGREEN TERRACE, 777 Ferry Road, Doylestown, PA 18901. 215-340-5256. Evergreen Terrace is a 42-bed nursing facility for long-term, sub-acute and rehabilitative care. We offer attractively furnished private rooms with full private baths. 24 hrs. a day, 7 days a week. p. 183

HERITAGE TOWERS, 200 Veterans Lane, Doylestown, PA 18901. Toll free 800-781-4301, 215-345-4300, Fax: 215-345-4927. Enjoy care-free living in a full service community located in picturesque Doylestown with independent residential, assisted living and skilled nursing. p. 171

SHOPPING COMPLEXES

LIBERTY VILAGE PREMIUM OUTLETS, One Church St., Flemington, NJ 08822. 908-782-8550, Fax: 908-782-2994. www.premiumoutlets.com/location/liberty/libe/html. Located in downtown, historic Flemington featuring over 80 designer apparel and brand name outlet stores in a charming colonial American village setting. Polo Ralph Lauren Factory Store, Ralph Lauren Home Collection, Brooks Brothers, Calvin Klein, Donna Karan, Cole Haan, Tommy Hilfiger, Nautica, Timberland & many more. Visit the Management Office above Nautica for gift certificates, strollers & wheelchairs. ATM on site. Open 7 days. Apr 1-Jan 1: Sun-Wed 10-6, Thurs-Sat 10-9; Jan 2-Mar 31 every day 10-6. Major Credit Cards. p. 293

PEDDLER'S VILLAGE, Rtes. 202 & 263, PO Box 218, Lahaska, PA 18931. 215-794-4000. www.peddlersvillage.com. One of Bucks County's most picturesque destinations. Enjoy 75 quality specialty shops and restaurants, country inn lodging, edutainment center including operating antique carousel, and nationally recognized seasonal events situated among spectacular gardens and winding brick walkways. Old fashioned hospitality, warm, personal service. Stroller rentals. Mon.-Thur. 10 6, Fri.-Sat. 10-9, Sun. 11-6. Call for extended holiday hours. Closed Thanksgiving, Christmas & New Year's Day. All major credit cards. p. 122

PENN'S PURCHASE FACTORY OUTLET STORES, 5861 York Rd., P.O. Box 81, Route 202, Lahaska, PA 18931. 215-794-0300. Forty of the best names in women's and men's Fashions, home accessories and jewelry at 20-50% off everyday retail prices. Located in a charming country village setting. Open seven days a week. Hours: Mon.-Fri. 10-8, Sat. 9-8, Sun. 9-6. Visit Adidas, Nautica, G. H. Bass and Osh Kosh B'Gosh. Call for brochure and events calendar. p. 98

SKIN CARE

LA BELLA VITA, Holistic Skincare Studio, 23 W. Ferry St., New Hope, Pa 18938. 215-862-7008. Enjoy the very best in skincare and massage services in an environment of comfort, privacy and professionalism. Integrating a holistic health perspective with the latest techniques and products for a truly unique experience. By appointment only, Tues-Sat. Evenings Tues and Thurs. Major credit cards accepted. p. 79

SPA

L'AVANTAGE, THE DAY SPA, 441 N. York Rd., New Hope, PA 18938. 215-862-3456. A day of total care for the body with the most advanced techniques in physical well-being. Full day, half day and a la carte services available. Send for our brochure. Limousine service available. Spa hours: Mon.-Sat. 9-5. AE, V, MC. p. 77

STORAGE FACILITIES

MAGILL STORAGE, 6814 Lower York Rd., New Hope, PA 18938. 215-862-6933. Self storage facility with standard and climate controlled units. Fully fenced, gated and alarmed. Access 7 days a week, Mon.-Sun. 7am–7pm. V, MC. p. 83

TILE

BELLA TILE, 5782 Easton Rd. Plumsteadville, PA 18947. 215-766-1660. Quality ceramic and porcelain tile that will stand the test of time; and children and pets! We also carry carpet, hardwood and laminates. Mon.-Fri. 9-6, Sat. 9-3. AE, V, MC, Disc. p. 151

TOURIST INFORMATION

BUCKS COUNTY CONFERENCE & VISITORS BUREAU, PO Box 912, 152 Swamp Rd., Doylestown, PA 18901. 800-836-BUCK, 215-345-4552. www.bccvb.org.

CENTRAL BUCKS CHAMBER OF COMMERCE, 379 N. Main St., Doylestown, PA 18901, 215-348-3913. Sponsors of "Bucks Fever" and "Bucks Beautiful", among many other activities.

THE CLINTON GUILD, PO Box 5082, Clinton, NJ 08809. 908-735-8614. www.clintonnj.com.

continued

The village of Clinton, the most photographed spot in New Jersey. Home of the Hunterdon Historical Museum, Hunterdon Museum of Art, fine shops featuring artists and craftsmen, sights, services and activities. Call for schedule of events. p. 267

FLEMINGTON BUSINESS ASSOCIATION, PO Box 564, Flemington, NJ 08822. 908-284-8118. www.fbanj.com. Discover Historic Flemington, the heart of Hunterdon Co. Call for free visitor's brochure. Visit our website for information on special events, shopping, dining and lodging. p. 291

FRENCHTOWN TOURIST INFORMATION, www.frenchtown.com. Discover New Jersey's "left bank" with unique galleries, shops and highly acclaimed restaurants. A tree lined multi-purpose trail hugs the Delaware River offering walking, biking, picnicking and much more.

LIBERTY VILAGE PREMIUM OUTLETS, One Church St., Flemington, NJ 08822. 908-782-8550. New Jersey Tourist Information Center in the management office above Nautica. p. 293

NEW HOPE BOROUGH VISITORS CENTER, 1 W. Mechanic St., (corner S. Main and Mechanic Sts.) PO Box 633, New Hope, PA 18938. 215-862-5880 or 215-862-5030 for personal assistance. www.newhopepa.com. Call or write for information on shopping, dining, lodging, activities and events for the whole family. p. 000

TOYS

GOOD TOYS, 12 Main St. Clinton, NJ 08809. 908-735-2058, Fax: 908-735-2058. The name says it all. Open daily. V, MC. p. 267

WELCOMING SERVICE

LAURIE SCHWAB "NEW NEIGHBORS", 7 Columbine Ct., Flemington, NJ 08822. 908-782-2571. Complimentary service welcoming newcomers to the area and providing local community/civic information. New Neighbors is a personalized advertising and public relations service for local businesses and professionals. New Neighbors-"Your Community Connection". p. 290

WINE SHOPS

PHILLIPS' FINE WINES & LIQUORS, Box O, 17 Bridge St., Stockton, NJ 08559. 609-397-0587, 888-343-1012. www.phillipsfinewine.com. Fine wines & liquors from around the world and over 101 domestic and imported beers. 10% full case discount. 9-9 Mon.-Thurs., 9-10 Fri. & Sat., 12-6 Sun. AE, V, MC. p. 249

WELSH'S WINES, 8 S. Union St., Lambertville, NJ 08530. 609-397-8243. Worldwide selection of wines. V, MC. p. 232

WINERIES

BUCKINGHAM VALLEY VINEYARDS, Box 371, Rt. 413, Buckingham, PA 18912. 215-794-7188. You're welcome to visit, walk through the vineyards, tour the cool wine cellars, and sample the wines. There is no charge. Wines can be purchased by the bottle or case, at very reasonable prices. Tues.-Sat. 11-6, Sun. 12-4. V, MC. p. 135

SAND CASTLE WINERY, 755 River Rd. (Route 32), PO Box 177, Erwinna, PA 18920. 1-800-PA2-WINE, Fax: 610-294-9174. www.sandcastlewinery.com. Please call for information regarding our summer concert series. Facilities available for receptions and private parties. Mon.-Fri. 9-6, Sat. 10-6, Sun. 11-6. All major credit cards. p. 157

UNIONVILLE VINEYARDS, 9 Rocktown Rd. Ringoes, NJ. 08551. 908-788-0400. www.unionvillevineyards.com. Producer of award-winning wines. The winery is open Thursday through Sunday 11-4 for complimentary tasting and tours. Our wine shop features wine related items, gourmet foods, and gift baskets. Discounts on half and full case purchases. V, MC. p. 247

Always the best of friends.

Index
to Towns & Maps

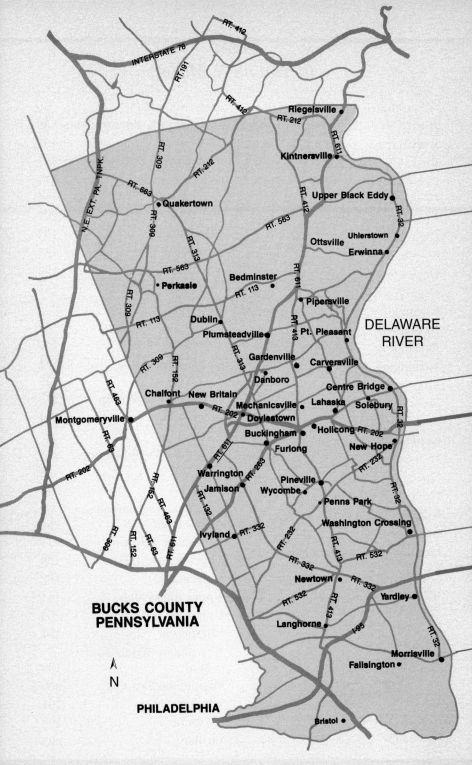

RT. 412

INTERSTATE 78

RT. 191

RT. 412

RT. 412

Riegelsville

RT. 212

RT. 212

RT. 611

Kintnersville

RT. 309

RT. 412

Upper Black Eddy

N.E. EXT. PA. TNPK.

RT. 663

RT. 563

RT. 32

RT. 309

Quakertown

Ottsville

Uhlerstown

Erwinna

RT. 313

RT. 563

RT. 611

Bedminster

Perkasie

RT. 113

Pipersville

RT. 309

RT. 113

Dublin

Plumsteadville

RT. 413

Pt. Pleasant

DELAWARE
RIVER

RT. 313

Gardenville

Carversville

RT. 309

RT. 152

Danboro

Centre Bridge

Chalfont

New Britain

Mechanicsville

Lahaska

Solebury

RT. 463

RT. 202

Doylestown

Holicong

RT. 202

RT. 32

Montgomeryville

Buckingham

RT. 611

Furlong

New Hope

RT. 202

RT. 69

RT. 263

RT. 232

Warrington

Pineville

RT. 202

Jamison

Wycombe

RT. 32

RT. 152

RT. 463

RT. 132

Penns Park

RT. 611

Washington Crossing

RT. 309

RT. 152

Ivyland

RT. 332

RT. 292

RT. 413

RT. 532

RT. 69

Newtown

RT. 332

RT. 332

Yardley

BUCKS COUNTY
PENNSYLVANIA

RT. 532

RT. 413

Langhorne

I-95

RT. 32

N

Morrisville

Fallsington

PHILADELPHIA

Bristol

350

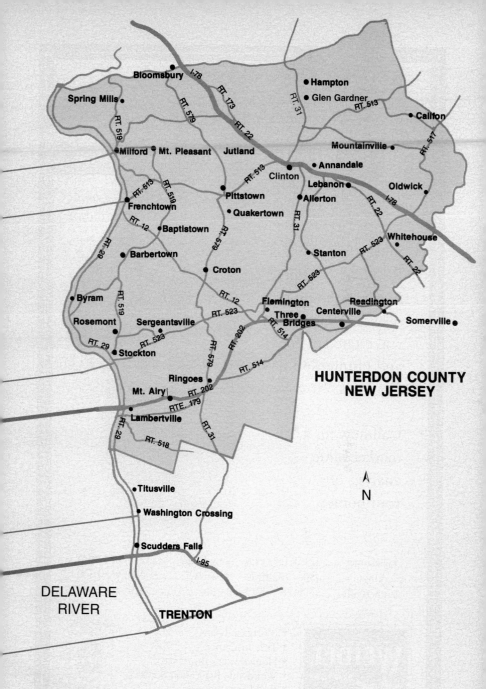

HUNTERDON COUNTY NEW JERSEY

Bloomsbury

Spring Mills

Hampton
Glen Gardner

Califon

Milford • Mt. Pleasant   Jutland

Mountainville

Frenchtown

Pittstown   Clinton

Annandale

Lebanon

Oldwick

Baptistown

Quakertown

Allerton

Barbertown

Croton

Whitehouse

Byram

Stanton

Rosemont   Sergeantsville

Flemington
Three
Bridges

Readington
Centerville

Somerville

Stockton

Ringoes

Mt. Airy

Lambertville

N

Titusville

Washington Crossing

Scudders Falls

DELAWARE
RIVER

TRENTON